PIVOT POINT

PIVOT POINT FUNDAMENTALS: COSMETOLOGY
SCIENCE

1st Edition
4th Printing, October 2021
Printed in China

Pivot Point International, Inc.
Global Headquarters
8725 West Higgins Road, Suite 700
Chicago, IL 60631 USA

847-866-0500
pivot-point.com

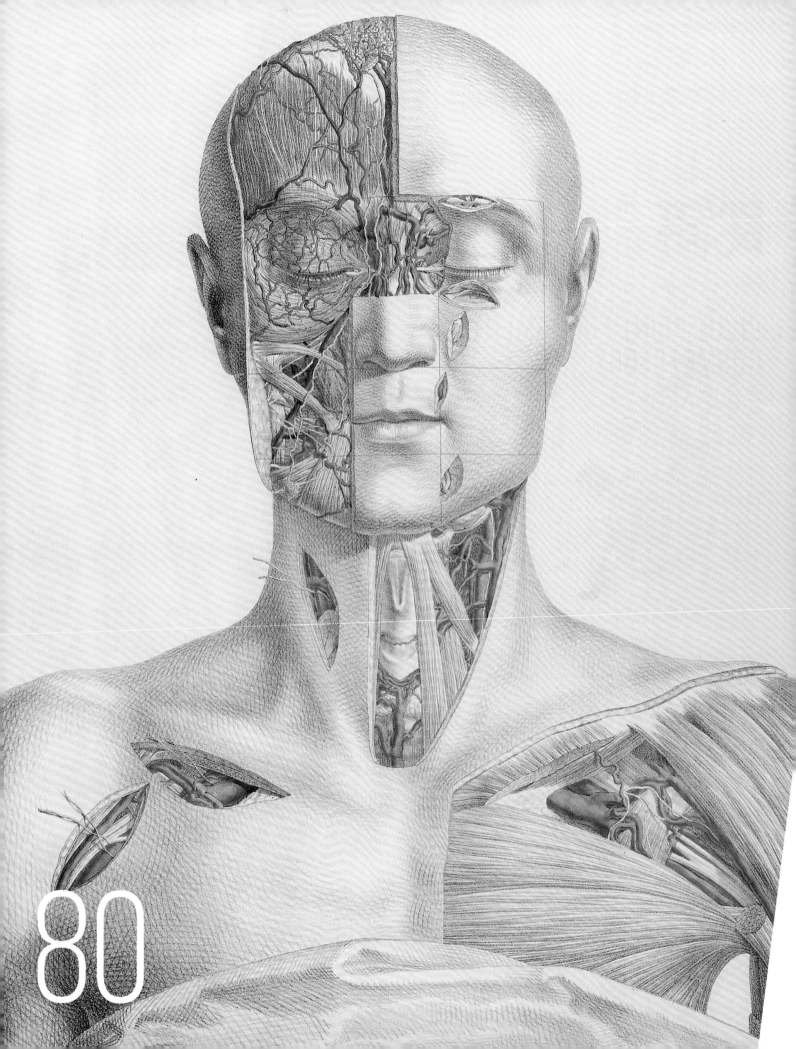

CONTENTS

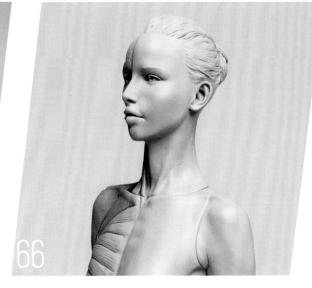

Microbiology 2
Infection Control 16
First Aid 38
Building Blocks of the Human Body 46
The Skeletal System 55
The Muscular System 66

The Circulatory System 80
The Nervous System 93
Principles of Electricity 104
Electricity in Cosmetology 119
Matter 135
pH 148

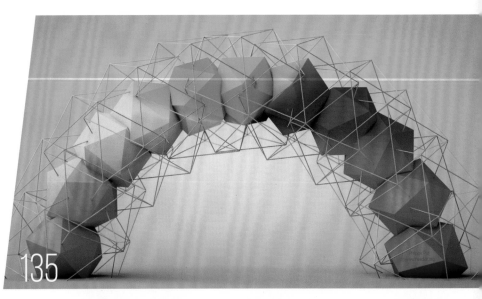

Hair Care Product Knowledge 157
Hair Theory 175
Hair Care 187
Shampoo and Scalp Massage Theory 202
Shampoo and Condition Guest Experience 215
Shampoo and Condition Workshop 229
Scalp Massage Workshop 241

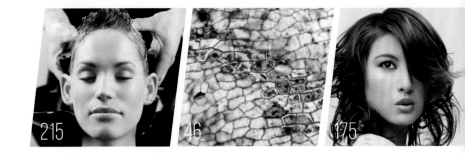

What do you think is the most cost-effective intervention for the worldwide control of disease?

102ᶜ.1

ICROBIOLOGY

might seem like a big word to describe the study of small organisms. Yet that's exactly what microbiology is, the study (ology) of small (micro) living (bio) organisms called microbes, such as bacteria.

INSPIRE //

Because infectious bacteria and viruses are easily transmitted from person to person, it is important that a salon professional, coming in contact with many people on a daily basis, understands particular aspects of microbiology.

ACHIEVE //

Following this lesson on *Microbiology*, you'll be able to:

>> Define the types and classifications of bacteria and viruses

>> Identify the growth and reproduction patterns of bacteria and viruses

>> Explain the difference between bacteria and viruses

>> Give examples of external parasites that would prevent offering salon services

>> Describe the reason behind using universal precautions in the salon

>> Classify the two basic ways the body fights infections

FOCUS //

MICROBIOLOGY

Bacteria

Viruses

External Parasites

Infection

Immunity

102^c.1 | MICROBIOLOGY

A basic knowledge of microbiology is important to you as a salon professional so that you can prevent the spread of disease through proper disinfection within the salon.

It is your responsibility to protect your clients' health and your own. Take the steps necessary to ensure that potentially infectious organisms aren't transmitted in the salon via the use of contaminated (dirty) tools and implements.

BACTERIA

Bacteria, sometimes called germs or microbes, are one-celled micro-organisms. The study of bacteria is referred to as **bacteriology**. While there are thousands of different kinds of bacteria, they can generally be classified into two types:

1. **Nonpathogenic: Non-disease-producing bacteria**

2. **Pathogenic: Disease-producing bacteria**

NONPATHOGENIC BACTERIA

Nonpathogenic bacteria are harmless and can be very beneficial.

>> Some bacteria have medical applications.

>> Other bacteria, like some found in certain dairy products (such as yogurt), have health-enhancing properties.

>> Still other bacteria cause the decay of refuse or vegetation and thereby improve the fertility of soil.

>> **Approximately 70% of all bacteria are nonpathogenic and many live on the surface of the skin.**

PATHOGENIC BACTERIA

Pathogenic bacteria live everywhere in your environment and even exist inside your body.

>> Several different types of pathogenic bacteria are harmful because they cause infection and disease, and some produce **toxins** (poisons).

>> Infectious bacteria can be easily spread in the salon by using unsanitary implements or via dirty hands and fingernails.

When a disease spreads from one person to another via contact, it is referred to as **contagious** or **communicable**.

Examples:
Common cold
Hepatitis
Measles

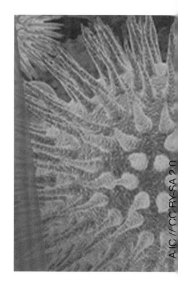

Bacteria are single cells with one of three basic shapes. Remember that you won't be identifying them with a microscope in the salon; you'll need to prevent their growth and spread. Classified below by shape and kind are the more common pathogenic bacteria that you might encounter.

1. **Cocci** (**KOK**-si) are spherical (round-shaped) bacterial cells, which appear singularly or in groups.

To remember, think C = circle and Cocci. There are three groups of Cocci:

a. **Staphylococci** (staf-i-lo-**KOK**-si) (referred to as staph)

» Pus-forming bacterial cells

» Form as grape-like bunches or in clusters

» Present in abscesses, pustules and boils

» Some types won't cause infection but others could be fatal

b. **Streptococci** (strep-to-**KOK**-si)

» Pus-forming bacterial cells

» Form in long chains and can cause septicemia (sometimes called blood poisoning), strep throat, rheumatic fever and other serious infections

c. **Diplococci** (dip-lo-**KOK**-si)

» Bacterial cells that grow in pairs

» Cause of certain infections, including pneumonia

To remember, Diplo means double.

2. **Bacilli** (ba-**SIL**-i)

» Most common form of bacterial cells

» Bacilli are bar- or rod-shaped cells that can produce a variety of diseases including tetanus, bacterial influenza, typhoid fever, tuberculosis and diphtheria

To remember, think B = bar and Bacilli.

Bacilli

3. **Spirilla** (speye-**RIL**-a)

» Spiraled, coiled, corkscrew-shaped bacterial cells

» Cause highly contagious diseases such as syphilis, a sexually transmitted disease (STD); cholera; and Lyme disease

To remember, think S = spiral and Spirilla.

Spirilla

Bacteria can cause infections by invading the body through a break in the skin or through any of the body's natural openings (nose, mouth, eyes, ears and genitals). An infection occurs when an insufficient number of antibodies are produced by the body's defense (immune) system to "fight" harmful bacteria.

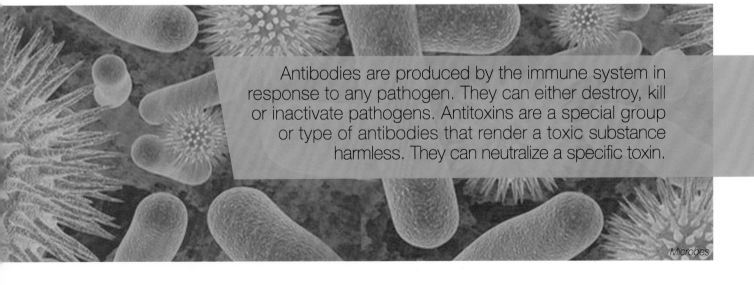

Antibodies are produced by the immune system in response to any pathogen. They can either destroy, kill or inactivate pathogens. Antitoxins are a special group or type of antibodies that render a toxic substance harmless. They can neutralize a specific toxin.

Microbes

GROWTH OF BACTERIA

Bacteria go through a growth cycle that consists of two stages: an active stage and an inactive stage.

Active Stage:

>> Bacteria reproduce and grow rapidly.

>> Reproduction usually takes place in dark, damp or dirty areas where a food source is available.

>> As the bacteria absorb food, each cell grows in size and divides, creating two new cells—similar to the budding process in plants.

Inactive Stage:

>> Bacteria are not always active; when conditions are unfavorable, the cells die or become inactive.

>> Some bacteria, such as anthrax and tetanus, also have a normal inactive or dormant stage. When the environment makes the bacteria's survival difficult, some bacteria enter this inactive stage by creating spherical spores.

>> Bacteria that form spores can only be destroyed by sterilization or the use of a product labeled as sporicidal (able to kill spores). Spore bacteria do not pose a threat to the salon environment.

>> Other bacteria can survive for a long time in extreme heat or cold. When conditions again become favorable for the bacteria's growth, the bacteria return to the active stage.

MOVEMENT OF BACTERIA

Because of their tiny size, bacteria can travel easily from place to place through air or water, from you to your client and vice versa.

>> Cocci, for example, utilize air or dust movement.

>> Bacilli and spirilla have the ability to move by themselves by using hair-like projections called **flagella** (flah-**JEL**-ah) or **cilia** (**SIL**-ee-a), which extend from the sides of the cell.

>> A wave-like motion from flagella and a rowing-like motion from cilia can easily propel the cell through a liquid.

Model of a Virus

DISCOVER**MORE**

Under favorable conditions, bacteria can reproduce as many as 16,000,000 offspring in 12 hours.

....

Bacterial reproduction, called binary fission, is being studied in laboratories around the world to uncover the genetics of harmful bacteria. By knowing how they grow and divide, scientists can begin targeting how to interfere with the growth cycle.

VIRUSES

When the word virus comes up, you probably think of the common cold or flu. The truth is there are many diseases caused by viruses, including respiratory and gastrointestinal infections, chicken pox, mumps, measles, smallpox, yellow fever, rabies and hepatitis.

Virus	Sub-microscopic particle (much smaller than bacteria) that causes familiar diseases like the common cold, which is caused by a filterable virus.
	» Requires living hosts—such as people, plants or animals—to multiply; otherwise, it can't survive.
	» When a virus enters your body, it invades some of your cells and takes over, redirecting them to produce the virus.
	» Viruses are not treatable with antibiotics, while bacterial infections can generally be treated with appropriate antibiotics.
	» Vaccinations can be a preventative measure for certain viruses.

EXAMPLE VIRUSES

Hepatitis B Virus (HBV)	Bloodborne pathogen that causes a highly infectious disease that infects the liver.
	» HBV is a vaccine-preventable disease.
	» Inoculation is often recommended for personal service workers, such as nurses, doctors, teachers and salon professionals, since they work closely with the public.
	» Check with your local health agency or doctor to determine if you are a candidate for this inoculation.
Human Immunodeficiency Virus (HIV)	Virus that can lead to Acquired Immunodeficiency Syndrome (AIDS).
	» HIV interferes with the body's natural immune system and causes it to break down.
	» Scientists have gained a great deal of knowledge about HIV and how it is spread and how to prevent it.
	» HIV is spread when body fluids from an infected individual are absorbed into the bloodstream of an uninfected individual. The fluids from the infected person must contain sufficient amounts of the virus.
	» Fluids known to contain sufficient amounts of HIV are blood, semen, vaginal fluids and breast milk. Body fluids must enter the uninfected person for that person to be infected.
	» Infectious fluids can enter through sexual intercourse, sharing needles or syringes, childbirth, cuts or sores (that are exposed to the infectious materials) and other instances where the body fluid of one individual enters the body of another.
	Adapted from "AIDS: The War Within," Museum of Science and Industry, Chicago, IL
Human Papillomavirus (HPV)	Common viral infection that can lead to health problems such as genital warts, plantar warts, cervical changes and cervical cancer.
	» HPV is often invisible and difficult to kill.
	» Presents yet another reason why consistent and appropriate infection control procedures within the salon environment are so important.

EXTERNAL PARASITES

External parasites (**PAR**-ah-sights) are organisms that live on or obtain their nutrients from another organism called a host.

>> External parasites generally cause harm to the host.

>> Parasitic fungi are molds and yeasts that produce such contagious diseases as ringworm (tinea capitis), honeycomb ringworm (favus) and nail fungus, and noncontagious conditions such as dandruff or seborrheic dermatitis (stubborn dandruff).

Tinea Capitis
(Ringworm of the Scalp)

>> Parasitic mites are insects that cause contagious diseases, such as itch mites (scabies) and head lice (pediculosis capitis).

>> Professionals prevent the spread of contagions (fungi, bacteria, and mites) through proper disinfection procedures.

A mosquito is an example of an external parasite that lives on the blood of a host.

DISCOVER**MORE**

Biofilm is a type of slime that is created when a bacterial colony and water are present. The sticky nature of the colony adds to its growth and difficulty to remove. It is because of this type of colonization that infection control procedures in the salon are critical.

Dental plaque is an example of biofilm in the human body, or the slime buildup around a drain in a foot bath might be a suspicious area in the salon.

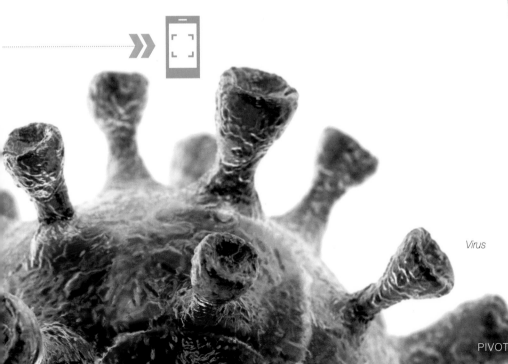

Virus

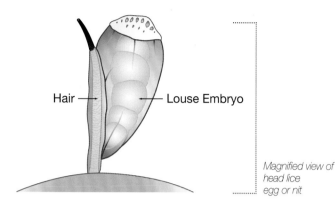

Hair — | — Louse Embryo

Magnified view of head lice egg or nit

Head lice are transmitted directly from one person to another, or by contact with articles that have come in contact with an infested person (such as combs and brushes, etc.).

>> The presence of head lice is usually accompanied by head scratching, redness and/or small bite marks on the scalp.

>> Close inspection of the hair and scalp with a fine-tooth comb, a strong light and a magnifying glass will sometimes reveal the tiny, tan to grayish adult lice.

>> It's more likely to see their eggs, called nits, which are whitish, oval specks attached to the hairstrands about ¼" (.6 cm) from the skin.

>> Head lice infestation is very easy to control, if detected, by using a pediculicide (lice-killing) shampoo.

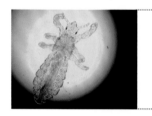

Magnified view of adult louse

Parasitic fungi are molds and yeasts that produce contagious diseases such as ringworm (tinea), ringworm of the scalp (tinea capitis), honeycomb ringworm (favus) and noncontagious conditions such as dandruff or seborrheic dermatitis (stubborn dandruff).

Tinea Capitis (Ringworm of the Scalp)

Professionals prevent the spread of contagions (mites and fungi) through proper disinfection procedures.

INFECTION

An **infection** occurs when disease-causing (pathogenic) bacteria or viruses enter the body and multiply to the point of interfering with the body's normal state. There are six signs of infection: pain, swelling, redness, local fever (heat), throbbing and discharge.

Direct Transmission (direct contact)	Spread of infectious disease when an infected person touches or exchanges body fluids with someone else
Indirect Transmission	Infectious disease that can spread through the air or contact with a contaminated object
Contagious Infection Communicable Disease	Transmitted from one person to another, usually through touch or through the air
Micro-Organisms	Spread to a new person frequently >> Cause no infection unless they actually enter the body
Bloodborne Pathogens	Disease-causing bacteria or viruses that are carried through the blood or body fluids >> Can be spread in the salon through haircutting, waxing, tweezing, nipping or anytime the skin is broken

Common means of spreading infection in a salon include:

>> Open sores

>> Unclean hands and implements

>> Coughing or sneezing

>> Common use of drinking cups and towels

>> Use of same implements on infected areas and noninfected areas

Contamination – The action of making an object or substance unclean or impure.

Cross-contamination – The unintentional transfer of harmful bacteria from one person, object or surface to another with harmful effects.

Decontamination – The removal of dirt, oil and/or pathogens from an object.

Infections can be controlled by:

» Personal hygiene

» Public awareness

» Practicing infection control procedures in the salon

Check your area regulating agency for specific guidelines on dealing with contagious disease.

» If you have a contagious disease, it is important that you practice infection control procedures in order to not spread the infection.

» Refer a client with a contagious disease to a physician.

There are two basic classes of infection:

1. **A local infection** is located in a small, confined area. This is often indicated by a pus-filled boil, pimple or inflamed area.

To remember, think local = little.

2. **A general (or systemic) infection** occurs when the circulatory system carries bacteria and their toxins to all parts of the body.

To remember, think general = giant.

It is possible for a person to carry disease-producing bacteria or viruses with no recognizable symptoms of the disease. Such a person is called an **asymptomatic carrier**. For this reason, the same infection control procedures should be used with all clients. This practice is called **universal precautions**. An example of a universal precaution is disinfecting salon equipment and implements.

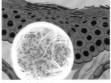
Local Infection

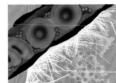
A General or Systemic Infection

SALON**CONNECTION**
Everyone's Job

In our salon it is everyone's job to pitch in to make sure we appear spotless, shiny and spectacular. That means you can't just walk by something lying on the floor or not stop to wipe up spilled water. It means that we all play a role in keeping the workstations, reception area, restrooms and yes, even the front sidewalk, clean and inviting. It is everyone's job.

IMMUNITY

Immunity is the ability of the body to destroy infectious agents that enter the body. To remember, think immunity gives you ammunition to fight disease. The body has remarkable defense mechanisms that fight infections in two basic ways:

1. **Active immunity** results when exposure to a disease organism triggers the immune system to produce antibodies to that disease.

>> Exposure to the disease organism can occur through infection with the actual disease (resulting in natural immunity), or introduction of a killed or weakened form of the disease organism through vaccination (vaccine-induced immunity), such as polio or flu.

>> With either natural immunity or vaccination, if an immune person comes into contact with that disease in the future, their immune system will recognize it and immediately produce the antibodies needed to fight it.

>> Active immunity takes time (usually several weeks) to develop.

>> Active immunity is long-lasting, and sometimes life-long.

2. **Passive immunity** is provided when a person is given antibodies to a disease rather than producing them through his or her own immune system.

>> A newborn baby acquires passive immunity from its mother through the placenta.

>> A person can also get passive immunity through antibody-containing blood products such as immune globulin, which may be given when immediate protection from a specific disease is needed (such as rabies).

>> The major advantage to passive immunity is that protection is immediate.

>> Passive immunity lasts only for a few weeks or months.

Adapted from cdc.gov.

Remember, because infectious bacteria and viruses are easily transmitted from person to person, it is important that a professional cosmetologist, coming in contact with many people on a daily basis, understands particular aspects of microbiology.

LESSONS LEARNED

The types and classifications of bacteria and viruses include:

Nonpathogenic bacteria, which are harmless and can be beneficial

Pathogenic bacteria, which can cause infection, disease and produce toxins, include the following types:

Cocci	Diplococci
Staphylococci	Bacilli
Streptococci	Spirilla

Viruses, which are sub-microscopic particles that cause disease, include:

Common cold	Yellow fever
Respiratory and gastrointestinal infections	Rabies
Chicken pox	Hepatitis
Mumps	HIV
Measles	HPV
Smallpox	Polio

The growth and reproduction patterns of bacteria and viruses include active and inactive stages.

Examples of external parasites that would prevent offering salon services include:

Ringworm	Itch mites
Honeycomb ringworm	Head lice
Nail fungus	

The relationship of bacteria and viruses to the spread of infection is the reason behind universal precautions.

The two basic ways the body fights infections include active and passive immunity.

102ᶜ.2 //
INFECTION CONTROL

≫≫

Have you ever walked into someone's home or a place of business and wanted to leave because it was messy or dirty?

INSPIRE //

A clean, healthy salon environment is inviting and safe for you and your clients.

ACHIEVE //

Following this lesson on *Infection Control*, you'll be able to:

>> State the difference between cleaning, disinfection and sterilization

>> Explain the disinfection method for tools and multi-use supplies that have been in contact with blood or body fluids and those that haven't

>> Identify infection control procedures used in the salon

FOCUS //

INFECTION CONTROL

Cleaning

Disinfection

Efficacy

Sterilization

Infection Control Procedures

102ᶜ.2 | INFECTION CONTROL

Infection control is the term used to describe efforts to prevent the spread of communicable diseases. In terms of your future in the salon, it means that you will be taking steps to prevent the exposure of infectious materials on the supplies, tools and equipment you use. In the past infection control practices were referred to as sanitations or the act of using the practices as "sanitizing." "Sanitation" and "sanitizing" are currently being seen as nonprofessional terms used in the marketplace with the term "cleaning" used by infection control professionals. Infection control practices can be divided into three main categories.

3 INFECTION CONTROL CATEGORIES	DESCRIPTION
CLEANING	Standards apply to removing dirt and debris to aid in preventing the growth of microbes
DISINFECTION	Standards require products to destroy or kill certain microbes on nonporous surfaces
STERILIZATION	Standards state that <u>all</u> microbes must be killed or destroyed

Salon/Spa and Barber Shop Tools:
Thoroughly preclean. Completely immerse brushes, combs, scissors, clipper blades, razors, tweezers, manicure and other tools for 10 minutes (or as required by your area's regulatory agency).

Wipe dry before use. Fresh solution should be prepared daily or more often when the solution becomes diluted or soiled.

*Virucidal: For Complete Instructions for Hepatitis B Virus (HBV) and Human Immunodeficiency Virus (HIV-1) DISINFECTION Refer To Enclosed Hang Tag .

Statement of Practical Treatment: In case of contact, immediately flush eyes or skin with plenty of water for at least 15 minutes. For eye contacts, call a physician. If swallowed, drink egg whites, gelatin solution or if these are not available, drink large quantities of water. Avoid alcohol. Call a physician immediately.

You will notice that methods vary from cleaning products to disinfectant products. Disinfecting methods do not work instantly, but require some time to destroy microbes. Times for immersion (soaking) in a disinfectant, storage practices and application methods will vary for each product.

The only way you can be sure that a product will do what you want it to do—whether you are cleaning, disinfecting or sterilizing—is to read the label and follow the directions.

Preventing the growth of microbes (cleaning), killing certain microbes (disinfecting) and killing <u>all</u> microbes (sterilizing) are three different functions.

» CLEANING

Cleaning means the process of scrubbing to remove dirt and debris to aid in preventing the growth of microbes. Cleaning is the first level of infection control. It is important to note that cleaning methods clean and reduce microbes on the surface, but do not kill microbes.

Infection control practices for cleaning of the schoolroom or salon require shared responsibilities from everyone on the team in order to provide a healthy environment. In fact, proper cleaning practices remove most of the microbes from the surface. Remember these important points about cleaning practices:

» Do not kill microbes, but help in the prevention of the growth of microbes

» Reduce the amount of organic matter that contributes to future growth of microbes

» Require a mechanical or scrubbing process that causes microbes to loosen for removal

There are three methods for cleaning tools, which include washing with soap and water, using an ultrasonic unit or using a cleaning solvent (e.g., on metal bits for electric files).

Rules of infection control are developed by regulating agencies, such as the Occupational Safety and Health Administration (OSHA), the Environmental Protection Agency (EPA) and licensing boards to protect the consumer. These rules require salons and cosmetology schools to keep the working areas, styling tools and all equipment in an appropriate condition.

» To do so, salons employ infection control methods to meet the required guidelines.

» Review the Cleaning Guidelines and Ventilation Guidelines charts to gain knowledge in the steps taken to prevent the growth of microbes.

Sanitizers are chemical products used to reduce microbes on nonporous surfaces. An **antiseptic** is a sanitizer product that can be applied to the skin to reduce microbes. Antiseptics are sometimes referred to as waterless sanitizers.

» Antiseptics can't replace hand washing and can't be used to clean tools or equipment.

» Antiseptics are appropriate for use only after proper hand washing or cleansing has occurred.

Sweep or vacuum all hair clippings after each service to prevent slipping.

CLEANING GUIDELINES

An overview of various cleaning practices for a healthy environment.

Wash your hands with soap and warm water before beginning each client service.

Wear clean, freshly laundered clothing.

Avoid touching your face, mouth or eyes while performing services.

Never place tools, combs, rollers or bobby pins, etc., in your mouth or pockets.

Dispense all semi-fluids and powders with a shaker, dispenser pump, spray-type container, spatula or disposable applicator.

Launder all client gowns and headbands properly before reusing.

Use a new or laundered cape on each client. Never allow the protective cape to touch the client's neck.

Use disposable towels or freshly laundered, thoroughly dried towels on each client.

Store soiled towels in a covered receptacle until laundered.

Clean and remove hair and debris from all tools before disinfecting.

Sweep or vacuum all hair clippings from the floor after each service.

Discard emery boards, cosmetic sponges and orangewood sticks after each use or give to the client (based on your area regulatory agency requirements), unless the manufacturer has specified that the product used can be disinfected. The guiding principle here is discard or disinfect.

Clean shampoo bowls before and after each use.

Empty waste receptacles daily.

Provide well-lit work areas.

Provide hot and cold running water.

Provide disposable drinking cups. Clean sinks and water fountains regularly.

Provide clean restrooms that are well-stocked with toilet tissue and disposable towels.

Never use restroom areas for storage of chemicals.

Never allow pets or animals in service area except for service animals as identified in the Americans With Disabilities Act.

Never use the salon for cooking or living quarters.

Keep salon free from insects and rodents.

Allow smoking only in designated areas.

VENTILATION GUIDELINES
An overview of various ventilation practices for a healthy environment

Maintain an average room temperature of about 70° Fahrenheit (21° Celsius).

Supply air mechanically through vents and air returns, using blower fans to circulate the fresh air and/or by opening windows and doors.

Vent air sufficiently so that the air does not have a stale, musty odor or contain the odor of sprays, bleaches or various other chemical solutions.

Change air conditioner filters as needed. Air conditioners permit changes in the quality and quantity of air as they cool, dehumidify (remove moisture) and cleanse pollutants from the air.

Change forced-air furnace filters as needed. Exhaust fans help circulate the air but do not clean it. Forced-air furnaces heat the air and cleanse it to a degree.

Provide local exhaust ventilation for areas in which chemicals are mixed or artificial nails are applied. Always keep all bottles capped when not in use.

Ensure the fan in the unit is powerful enough to draw or blow the chemical vapor or dust away when using localized exhaust systems in chemical mixing, manicure, color, relaxing or perm areas, etc., in an attempt to improve the safety of the salon professional and client.

» DISINFECTION

Disinfection is the second level of infection control. Disinfection standards require products to destroy or kill certain microbes on nonporous surfaces. These standards apply to all tools and multi-use supplies used by the salon professional.

Disinfectants are chemical products used to destroy or kill most bacteria (except bacterial spores), fungi and viruses on nonporous surfaces.

» **Bactericidals (kill harmful bacteria), tuberculocidals (kill tuberculosis), fungicidals (destroy fungi), virucidals (kill viruses) and pseudomonacidals (kill pseudomonas) are all categories of disinfectant products designed to kill specific organisms.**

» Disinfection products are toxic. The disinfecting chemicals are very strong and work well to disinfect tools and multi-use supplies, but could be harmful to your skin.

» Follow manufacturer's directions regarding the use of disinfectants.

The **Occupational Safety and Health Administration (OSHA)** is the regulating agency under the U.S. Department of Labor that enforces safety and health standards in the workplace. OSHA standards require that employees be informed of the dangers of the materials used in the workplace and the exposure they might have to toxic substances. Safety Data Sheets (SDS) and labeling of products are two important regulations that this group has put in place to assist in safe operations.

The **Canadian Centre for Occupational Health and Safety (CCOHS)** is the Canadian equivalent of OSHA.

>> **Safety Data Sheets (SDS)** are designed to provide the key information on a specific product regarding 16 key categories, which include:

1. Product identification

2. Hazard identification

3. Composition information

4. First-aid measures

5. Fire-fighting measures

6. Accidental release measures

7. Handling and storage

8. Exposure controls and personal protection

9. Physical and chemical properties

10. Stability and reactivity

11. Toxicology information

12. Ecological information

13. Disposal consideration

14. Transport information

15. Regulatory information

16. Revision date

>> OSHA also enforces the labeling of products to include:

- Ingredients
- Associated hazards
- Combustion levels
- Storage requirements

Labeling of products and distribution of Safety Data Sheets (SDS) are the responsibility of the manufacturer, however, if you store items in the dispensary, such as a spray bottle that contains water, that bottle needs to be labeled clearly to allow appropriate use.

Remember that for your protection and safety, it is your right as an employee to know what is contained in a product being used! OSHA standards are important to the industry and help ensure general safety, especially with regard to mixing, storing, labeling and disposing of chemicals.

» EFFICACY

Important to the area of infection control is the term **efficacy**, which means "ability to produce results" or "effectiveness." The U.S. **Environmental Protection Agency** (**EPA**) approves the efficacy of products used for infection control. This means that a manufacturer submits a product to this agency for verification of effectiveness against certain organisms such as bacteria, fungi, viruses and/or pseudomonas. The manufacturer lists this efficacy (effectiveness against) on the label of the product.

Once the EPA determination has been made, an **EPA registration number** is given to the product along with approval of the efficacy claims on the label, stating what the product will destroy or be effective against. This registered number also ensures the product is both safe and effective.

» In relation to disinfectant products, efficacy labels on all disinfectants inform the user about what the product is "effective in fighting against."

  ■ An example might be a disinfectant that states "effective against Human Hepatitis B Virus (HBV) and Human Immunodeficiency Virus (HIV)."

Your area regulatory agency will require you to use a product that is an approved EPA-registered disinfectant with certain efficacy labels. A different disinfectant is required for incidents that include blood exposure. In the case of an incident involving exposure to blood or body fluids, an approved EPA-registered hospital disinfectant would be required.

» **EPA-registered disinfectant** refers to chemical products assigned by the EPA as being effective on nonporous surfaces to control the spread of disease. An approved EPA-registered disinfectant has an efficacy demonstrated against both *Salmonella choleraesuis* and *Staphylococcus aureus*. An approved EPA-registered disinfectant is assigned to the EPA's general category and is also called a broad-spectrum disinfectant.

EPA-registered hospital disinfectant refers to chemical products assigned by the EPA as being effective to work in a hospital setting. Approved EPA-registered hospital disinfectants are used on nonporous surfaces and control the spread of disease with an efficacy demonstrated against *Salmonella choleraesuis* and *Staphylococcus aureus*, just like the approved EPA-registered disinfectant, but the difference is that the approved EPA-hospital registered disinfectant is also effective against *Pseudomonas aeruginosa*. Most regulatory agencies require an approved EPA-registered hospital disinfectant for incidents involving exposure to blood and body fluids. Check with your area regulatory agency for required usage. Some salons choose to use an approved EPA-registered hospital disinfectant for all disinfection, although it is only required for exposure to blood and body fluids and generally is more expensive.

ALERT!

Bloodborne pathogens are infectious micro-organisms in human blood that can cause disease in humans. These pathogens include, but are not limited to, Hepatitis B (HBV), Hepatitis C (HCV) and Human Immunodeficiency Virus (HIV). Needlesticks and other sharps-related injuries may expose workers to bloodborne pathogens.

The OSHA (Occupational Safety and Health Administration) Bloodborne Pathogens Standard requires the use of an approved EPA-registered hospital disinfectant when tools and multi-use supplies come into contact with blood or body fluids.

Be guided by your area's regulatory agency as to what efficacy standard you need to use. The most important thing for you to know is that the efficacy label will tell you what the disinfectant is effective against. One standard may guide you for disinfection of all tools and multi-use supplies that have NOT come in contact with blood or body fluids, and another standard may guide you for disinfection of all tools and multi-use supplies that HAVE come in contact with blood or body fluids.

TYPES OF DISINFECTANTS

Disinfectants are available in varied forms, including solution (concentrate or liquid), spray and wipes that have EPA approval for use in the salon industry. Avoid misleading promotions for additive, powder or tablet products that promise a shortcut disinfecting power. There are no approved shortcuts. You will want to find an approved EPA-registered disinfectant that is effective and quick-acting. When choosing one from your beauty supply vendor, consider the following:

» Is it nonirritating to the skin?

» Is it in compliance with your area's regulatory agency or health department?

» Is it economical and easy to purchase?

» Is it easy to use?

» Does it work quickly? Contact time listed on the label will provide this information. Contact time identifies the amount of time a disinfectant needs to be in direct contact with the surface or item to be disinfected and then to completely dry. Contact time needs to be followed for the disinfectant to be effective. Most disinfectants have a 10-minute contact time, while a disinfectant wipe might have a 2-minute contact time.

» Is immersion time required? Many approved EPA-registered disinfectants require that tools are cleaned and then immersed in a disinfectant solution. Often complete immersion will be required, which means the entire tool is covered by the liquid disinfectant, including the finger grips, for example, on a pair of shears.

» Is it noncorrosive (harmless to metal tools and nonporous supplies)?

» What type of container is recommended for storage and usage?

Look for an EPA-registered number along with an efficacy label stating that the product is an effective:

» Bactericidal

» Virucidal

» Fungicidal

» Pseudomonacidal

DISCOVER MORE

MRSA (methicillin-resistant *Staphylococcus aureus*, **pictured**) is a highly contagious bacterium that enters the skin through open wounds and can cause extremely serious staph infections. MRSA may initially appear as pimples or boils and is resistant to most antibiotics. MRSA can be particularly problematic because many people who are infected do not show any symptoms, meaning that they can unknowingly spread it to others. Proper disinfection procedures using the approved EPA-registered disinfectant are required to reduce exposure and protect consumers.

»» BRUSH OR COMB DISINFECTION PROCEDURE

1. Remove all hair from the brush or comb.

2. Wash the brush or comb thoroughly with soap and water to remove any dirt, grease or oil.

3. Rinse, and dry the brush or comb completely before immersing to avoid dilution.

4. Immerse the brush or comb completely in disinfectant solution. Follow guidelines for contact time from manufacturer.

5. Remove the brush or comb with forceps, tongs or gloved hands. Follow manufacturer's directions for rinsing and drying.

6. Store in a disinfected, dry, covered container or cabinet until needed.

Important to remember:

»» Always follow the manufacturer's directions and wear gloves and safety glasses when working with disinfectants.

»» Read the directions carefully and follow recommended safety precautions.

»» Always note and follow specific immersion times.

»» Preclean tools before immersing them in a disinfectant. Failure to preclean tools will prohibit proper disinfection.

Disinfectant Types

Quaternary Ammonium Compounds
 	
KWAT-ur-nayr-ee
uh-**MOH**-neeum
KAHM-poundz
 	
"Quats"
	» Refers to a group of disinfectants able to be used in the salon (most effective of this group is called multiple quats)
	» Multiple quats is a blend of quats working together to increase the effectiveness of the disinfectant product
	  ▪ Usually able to disinfect within 10 minutes
	  ▪ May contain additives to prohibit rusting of tools
	  ▪ Can cause contact dermatitis and nasal irritation
	  ▪ Tools are generally rinsed following immersion, dried and then stored in a disinfected, dry, covered container

Sodium Hypochlorite **5.25% Concentrate** **Bleach**	» Needs to have an EPA-registration number and contain at least 5% sodium hypochlorite, diluted to a 10% solution (9 parts water to 1 part bleach) » Bleach needs to contain chlorine bleach or it is not a disinfectant » Should not be stored longer than 3 months (if mixed with water it is only effective for 24 hours) » May damage floor finishes, carpets, clothing and other fibers when used in higher concentrations » Generally used on larger surfaces such as countertops » Not usable for metal tools, combs or brushes » Corrosive to eyes and skin and is a respiratory irritant » Rinsing is required if direct eye or skin contact occurs » Contact the center for poison control if swallowed
Tuberculocidal Disinfectants	» Chemical product proven to kill tuberculosis in addition to the organisms destroyed through the use of hospital disinfectants

Should I Discard or Disinfect?

Single-use or disposable refers to porous items like neck strips, cotton balls, bobby pins, emery boards, paper towels, gloves, sponges, gauze, pumice stones and wooden sticks. These porous items are appropriately called single-use because they are discarded after each use. Because their structure makes it impossible to remove all visible residue and/or because they are so porous they would fall apart, they are discarded.

Multi-use or reusable refers to nonporous items such as shears, combs, metal pushers, rollers used for wet hairstyling, and color bowls that can be disinfected. If nonporous items have been cleaned, and then disinfected with an approved, EPA-registered disinfectant, they can be used again. If the nonporous items have been exposed to blood or body fluids, they need to be cleaned, and then disinfected with an approved EPA-registered hospital disinfectant.

Tools or supplies that come in contact with the client during a service must be discarded or disinfected.

DISINFECTION GUIDELINES

The disinfection guidelines shown below provide an overview of the primary infection control procedures used for disinfection in the salon environment.

Disinfection Guidelines
An overview of disinfection practices for a healthy environment

Disinfect metal tools and nonporous supplies after each use before using them on another client.

>> Many regulating agencies are very specific in their rules pertaining to precleaning metal tools thoroughly with soap and water before immersing in any disinfectant solution. Precleaning tools eliminates any minute particles that could cling and cause infection; failure to preclean prohibits the disinfectant from being effective.

>> Use an approved EPA-registered disinfectant on metal tools and nonporous supplies; check with your area regulatory agency.

>> Use an approved EPA-registered hospital disinfectant solution to ensure safety in the case of exposure to blood or body fluids.

>> Never pick up and use a dropped item such as a tool, cape or towel—even though the floor may have been cleaned; always continue the service with new supply or a clean, disinfected tool.

Follow complete immersion and contact time listed on disinfectant products.

>> For large surfaces, such as a workstation:

  ▪ Clean the surface.

  ▪ Apply liquid or spray disinfectant and allow the surface to stay wet for the recommended contact time (usually 10 minutes).

  ▪ Complete immersion means the disinfectant covers all surfaces of the item(s) being disinfected for the entire recommended time.

>> Generally two wipes are used when disinfecting tools and nonporous supplies; use a new wipe for each different surface:

  ▪ Use the first wipe to completely clean the surface of all dirt and debris, then discard the wipe.

  ▪ Use a second wipe to thoroughly wet the surface; repeat as needed to ensure the surface remains visibly wet for two minutes at room temperature; discard the second wipe.

  ▪ Store the disinfected tool or nonporous supply in a disinfected, dry, covered container.

  ▪ This tool or supply is considered to be decontaminated or free from dirt, oil and/or microbes.

Disinfect unplugged electrical appliances using an approved EPA-registered disinfectant.

>> There are wipes or sprays available for use in cleaning and disinfecting electrical items since they have moving parts that should not be placed in liquid.

>> Disinfect clipper guards by immersing in a disinfectant solution.

>> Follow manufacturer's directions.

Launder towels/linens in a timely manner; accumulated towels/linens could present a safety hazard (due to chemicals that may be present).

>> Be sure towels/linens are thoroughly dry before storing to avoid mildew or bacterial growth.

>> Store soiled towels/linens in covered containers away from the fresh supply.

>> Laws for how to deal with blood-stained items such as towels, linens, capes, gowns or headbands can be found on your area regulatory agency website or the OSHA website.

DISINFECTION PRECAUTIONS

Since the use of chemical disinfecting agents can be dangerous, they need to be used cautiously to prevent mistakes and accidents. When using these chemical agents, work in a well-ventilated area, keep a first-aid kit on hand and always remember to take the precautions shown here.

Disinfection Precautions and Disposal of Related Items

Ensure proper storage and labeling of disinfectants.

>> Tightly cover and label all containers.

>> Store in a cool, dry area (air, light and heat can weaken their effectiveness).

>> Purchase chemicals in small quantities.

>> Keep disinfectants out of reach of children.

>> Label and properly store prepared commercial disinfectant products, such as household bleach, to clean shampoo bowls, sinks, floors, working surfaces and bathroom fixtures.

Ensure proper use of disinfectants.

>> Remove items from disinfectant solution by using tongs, gloves or a draining basket.

>> Avoid inhaling or spilling chemical solutions.

>> Avoid contact with skin or eyes.

>> Wipe up all spills immediately.

>> Wear single-use, nonlatex gloves and safety glasses when handling all chemicals.

>> Wash hands with soap and water after handling all chemicals.

Follow the manufacturer's directions to mix, use and dispose of disinfectants.

>> Wear gloves, a protective apron and safety glasses when mixing disinfectants.

>> Dilute concentrates according to manufacturer's directions.

▪ If a disinfectant is a concentrate and requires mixing with water, the label will clearly state this information.

▪ Always add disinfectant to water when diluting a concentrate. This prevents foaming, which could cause an incorrect ratio for mixing.

>> Change disinfectant solution as directed by the manufacturer's directions.

>> Dilute excess chemicals with water and then rinse down the sink or follow manufacturer's directions.

>> Rinse empty chemical containers and place in a covered bin.

Follow the manufacturer's directions to dispose of sharp objects and aerosol cans.

>> Dispose of sharp objects (razor blades, insulin needles, etc.) in a sealable, puncture-proof, sharps container—strong enough to protect you, the client and others from accidental puncture wounds that could happen during the disposal process.

>> Do not pierce or burn aerosol cans.

Be sure to keep a Safety Data Sheet (SDS) on file for all chemicals you are using.

>> Refer to SDS for proper handling if spills occur.

>> Refer to SDS for procedures if contact with eyes and skin occurs.

>> Consider maintaining a Cleaning and Disinfection record book that stores information related to usage, maintenance and requirements. Be guided by your regulatory agency.

STERILIZATION

Sterilization is the third and most effective level of infection control. Sterilization procedures kill or destroy all microbes. You will be guided by your area's regulating agency for standards regarding cosmetology services and sterilization procedures.

>> Usually sterilization does not apply to cosmetology services because you are not puncturing or invading the skin when performing these services. However, some area regulatory agencies allow facials as cosmetology services, which could include the use of lancets. Lancets are disposable items that must be disposed of in a puncture-proof container.

>> Sterilization methods are costly, time-consuming and require a high degree of quality control to ensure results.

The amount of blood or body fluids that might be present during an offered service is a prime factor when regulators decide if sterilization procedures are required. Sterilization procedures are normally required for electrolysis and some esthetics services.

>> For example, needles used by electrologists and lancets used by estheticians to invade (puncture) the skin require sterilization, or they are designed to be disposable.

Sterilization standards require the use of a liquid sterilant and/or moist or dry heat, calibrated to various temperatures, to produce a surface free from all living organisms, even bacterial spores.

>> Specific calibrations and timeframes are normally required for sterilization procedures.

>> Periodic checks by manufacturer representatives or approved technicians are assigned to ensure that procedures and equipment are being used in the proper way.

>> Often an autoclave, a piece of equipment that uses steam at high pressure to sterilize objects, is used.

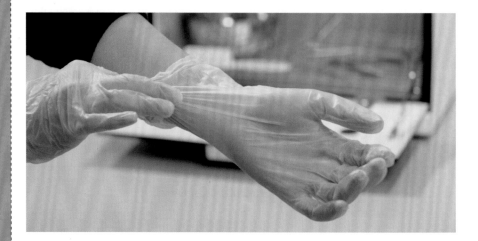

Sterilization procedures kill or destroy all microbes.

In summary...

METHODS	ITEMS	PROCEDURE
STERILIZATION Kills All Microbes	>> Tools that are used to puncture or invade the skin	>> Use a liquid sterilant and/or moist or dry heat, calibrated to various temperatures to produce a microbe-free result on nonporous substances
DISINFECTION Kills Certain Microbes	>> Tools and multi-use supplies that have come in contact with blood or body fluids	>> Use an approved EPA-registered hospital disinfectant; mix and immerse according to manufacturer's directions or as required by your regulatory agency
	>> Tools and multi-use supplies that have NOT come in contact with blood or body fluids	>> Use an approved EPA-registered disinfectant; mix and immerse according to manufacturer's directions
CLEANING Removes Dirt and Debris	>> Countertops, sinks, floors, toilets	>> Use an approved EPA-registered cleaning product. Label will state "appropriate for floors, countertops, sinks, toilets, towels and/or linens"
	>> Towels, linens	>> Use laundry detergent unless a disinfectant detergent is required by your regulatory agency
	>> Your hands before each service	>> Use soap and warm water
	>> Your hands and client's hands and/or feet prior to manicuring or pedicuring service	>> Use soap and warm water; if desired, use antiseptic designed for hands and/or feet

INFECTION CONTROL PROCEDURES

Listed here are procedures for Cleaning and Disinfecting Tools, Basic Hand Washing and Blood Exposure Incidents.

Procedures for cleaning and disinfecting foot spas, basins and tubs are presented in lessons related to pedicuring.

CLEANING AND DISINFECTING TOOLS

Basic cleaning and disinfecting of tools is outlined in the sample procedure listed here. Always read and follow manufacturer's directions for the products you choose to use. Tools refers to items such as shears, combs, brushes, clips, hairpins, metal pushers, tweezers and nail clippers. This procedure outlines nonelectrical items. Follow manufacturer's directions for use with electrical tools.

TOOLS AND SUPPLIES

- Covered storage container
- Soap
- Tongs
- Single-use gloves
- Scrub brush
- Disinfectant container
- Liquid disinfectant
- Timer
- Single-use towels
- Safety glasses

CLEANING AND DISINFECTING TOOLS PROCEDURE

1. **Put on safety glasses and single-use gloves.**

2. **Clean item with warm running water:**
   - » Rinse with warm water
   - » Scrub thoroughly with soap using a disinfected nail brush
   - » Ensure entire surface of item is scrubbed—get into grooves and hard-to-clean areas

3. **Rinse away soap with warm water:**
   - » Be sure all soap is removed from item

4. **Dry item thoroughly:**
   - » Use a clean single-use towel
   - » Item is cleaned and ready to be disinfected

5. **Disinfect item by complete immersion in disinfection solution:**

   >> Use an approved EPA-registered disinfectant for the required contact time (usually 10 minutes—follow manufacturer's directions)

   >> Replace disinfectant if it has been contaminated

   >> Set a timer

   >> Open hinged items before placing and immersing in disinfectant solution

6. **Remove item with tongs or gloved hands:**

   >> Ensure required time has passed

   >> Rinse item with warm running water

   >> Pat item dry with a single-use towel

7. **Store disinfected item in a clean, dry covered container:**

   >> It is recommended that this container be labeled to clearly identify that it holds "disinfected items"

8. **Complete the disinfection procedure:**

   >> Remove gloves, turn inside-out, discard and wash your hands thoroughly with warm running water and soap

   >> Rinse and dry hands with a single-use towel (you could choose to use a fabric towel)

BASIC HAND WASHING

It all starts with basic hand washing. Regulatory agencies require basic hand washing before and after every client service. Basic hand washing is the foundation of infection control efforts and is the number one thing you can do to protect you and your clients.

TOOLS AND SUPPLIES

- Single-use towels

- Soap

- Scrub brush if needed

BASIC HAND WASHING PROCEDURE

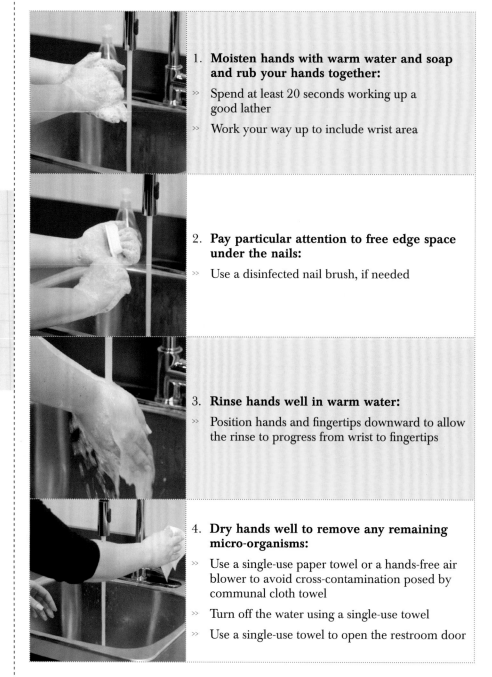

1. **Moisten hands with warm water and soap and rub your hands together:**
   - » Spend at least 20 seconds working up a good lather
   - » Work your way up to include wrist area

2. **Pay particular attention to free edge space under the nails:**
   - » Use a disinfected nail brush, if needed

3. **Rinse hands well in warm water:**
   - » Position hands and fingertips downward to allow the rinse to progress from wrist to fingertips

4. **Dry hands well to remove any remaining micro-organisms:**
   - » Use a single-use paper towel or a hands-free air blower to avoid cross-contamination posed by communal cloth towel
   - » Turn off the water using a single-use towel
   - » Use a single-use towel to open the restroom door

BLOOD EXPOSURE INCIDENT

If a blood exposure should occur, it is important that you handle the event in a confident manner.

TOOLS AND SUPPLIES

- Antiseptic
- Cotton
- Single-use towels
- Biohazard label (based on regulatory agency)
- Soap
- Bandages
- Single-use gloves
- Puncture-proof container (if needed)
- Safety glasses
- Plastic bag
- EPA-registered hospital disinfectant

BLOOD EXPOSURE INCIDENT PROCEDURE

If a blood exposure incident occurs, use the following steps:

1. **Stop the service:**
   - If the injury is severe, ask another professional to assist; put on single-use gloves

2. **Clean injured area with soap and water:**
   - Apply slight pressure to injured area with cotton to stop the bleeding
   - Cleanse area with antiseptic
   - Do not allow containers, brushes, or nozzles to touch the skin or come in contact with injured area

3. **Dress or cover injury with appropriate dressing:**
   - Cover injured area with a bandage

4. **Disinfect workstation:**
   - Place contaminated items in appropriate container for "dirty items"
   - Clean and disinfect the workstation surface, if it has been contaminated, with an approved EPA-registered hospital disinfectant (wear single-use gloves)
   - Ensure contact time is followed based on disinfectant label

5. **Discard contaminated supplies:**
   - Place contaminated supplies such as cotton and gloves (turned inside out) in an appropriate bag as directed by your regulatory agency
   - Place plastic bag in a closed trash container that has a liner bag
   - Place sharp objects (if applicable) in a puncture-proof sharps container

6. **Continue the service:**
   - Put on new pair of single-use gloves
   - Dry workstation surface that was disinfected with a single-use towel (if applicable)
   - Use new tool(s) to replace any that were contaminated

7. **After the service:**
   - Clean and disinfect tools used during the service
   - Completely immerse remaining tools in an approved EPA-registered hospital disinfectant solution (wear safety glasses and single-use gloves)
   - Consult physician if any sign of infection occurs in injury area

LESSONS LEARNED

» Cleaning standards apply to removing dirt to aid in preventing the growth of microbes. Disinfection standards require that all tools and multi-use supplies, including those that have come in contact with blood or body fluids, must be free (killed or destroyed) from certain microbes. Sterilization standards mean that all microbes must be killed or destroyed.

» Tools and multi-use supplies that have not been in contact with blood or body fluids require the use of an approved EPA-registered disinfectant while tools that have been in contact with blood or body fluids require the use of an approved EPA-registered hospital disinfectant.

» Infection control procedures used in the salon include cleaning and disinfecting tools, basic hand washing and blood exposure incident procedures.

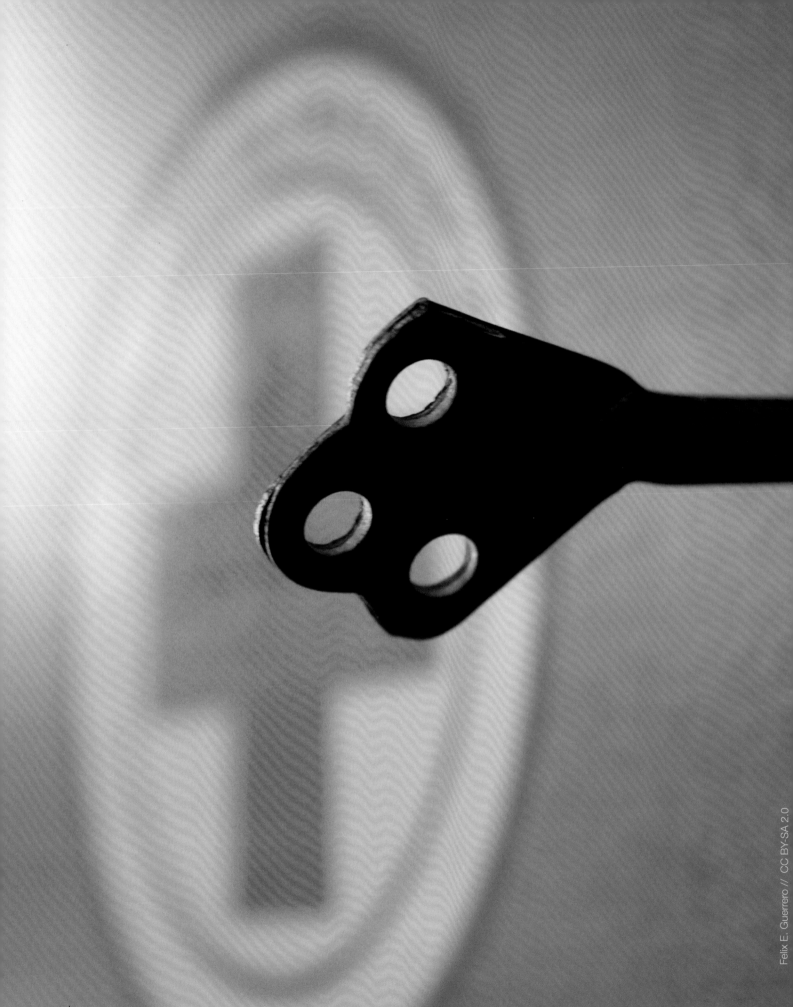

Have you ever performed first-aid techniques?

102ᶜ.3 |
FIRST
AID //

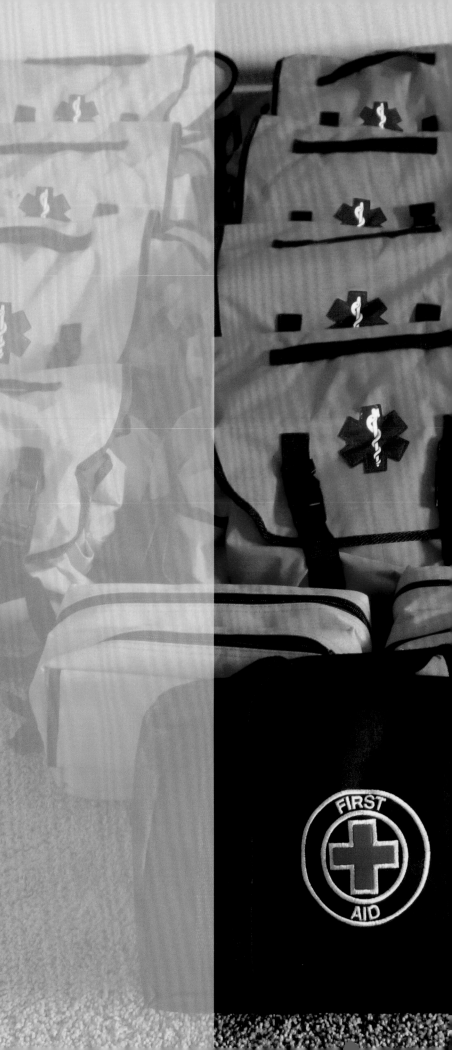

INSPIRE //

The safety, protection and welfare of the clients you serve are the reasons you are licensed as a professional.

ACHIEVE //

Following this lesson on *First Aid*, you'll be able to:

›› State first-aid techniques for bleeding and wounds

›› Identify first-aid techniques for chemical and heat or electrical burns

›› Describe first-aid techniques for choking

›› Explain first-aid techniques for fainting

›› Express first-aid techniques for eye injury

FOCUS //
FIRST AID

Bleeding and Wounds

Burns

Choking

Fainting

Eye Injury

Most states have enacted **Good Samaritan laws** to encourage people to help others in emergency situations.

These laws give legal protection to people who provide emergency care to ill or injured persons. They require that the Good Samaritan use common sense and a reasonable level of skill not to exceed the scope of the individual's training in emergency situations.

As a licensed professional, you are in contact with many people during your career. Being prepared will help make the most of a serious situation. Basic first-aid techniques for the workplace, or at home, follow.

BLEEDING AND WOUNDS

1. Place a clean cloth or gauze and gloved hand over the wound. Apply firm, steady pressure for at least five minutes.

2. Call 9-1-1 or other emergency personnel if bleeding is severe.

3. Elevate an injured arm or leg above the level of the victim's heart if practical.

4. When bleeding stops, secure the cloth with a bandage. **Do not** lift the cloth completely from the wound to check if bleeding has stopped. Instead, visually inspect the flow of blood through the cloth. Be sure the bandage is not too tight. It may cut off circulation.

Never use a tourniquet unless you cannot control the bleeding. Tourniquets may result in subsequent medical amputation.

Have emergency personnel check the victim for shock if necessary.

COVER WOUND; **APPLY** PRESSURE

ELEVATE INJURED LIMB ABOVE HEART

WHEN BLEEDING STOPS, **APPLY** BANDAGE

NEVER USE A TOURNIQUET

BURNS

CHEMICAL BURNS

1. Rinse away all traces of chemicals while moving away any contaminated clothing from the burn area.

2. Cover the burn loosely with a clean, dry cloth.

3. Refer person to medical personnel if necessary.

HEAT OR ELECTRICAL BURNS

1. If the skin is not broken, immerse the burned area in cool (not ice) water or gently apply a cool compress until pain is relieved. Bandage with a clean, dry cloth.

2. Do not break a blister if one forms. Do not apply ointments or creams.

3. If skin is broken or if burns are severe:

   » Call 9-1-1 or other emergency personnel.

   » Do not clean the wound or remove embedded clothing.

   » Cover the burn loosely with a clean, dry cloth.

CHOKING

1. Determine if the victim can speak or cough and is getting sufficient air. Do not interfere with the victim's attempts to cough the obstruction from the throat. If the victim cannot speak, or is not getting sufficient air, have someone call 9-1-1 while you perform abdominal thrusts on the victim.

2. Stand behind the victim and wrap your arms around their stomach.

3. Make a thumbless fist with one hand and place that fist just above the navel and well below the ribs, with the thumb and forefinger side toward the victim.

4. Perform an upward abdominal thrust on the victim by grasping this fist with the other hand and pulling it quickly toward you with an inward and slightly upward movement. Repeat if necessary.

NOTE: These instructions apply to victims over one year of age. Treatment of infants is not outlined in this lesson.

DETERMINE IF VICTIM CAN TALK OR COUGH

WRAP YOUR ARMS AROUND VICTIM FROM BEHIND AND MAKE A THUMBLESS FIST

PERFORM AN UPWARD ABDOMINAL THRUST ON THE VICTIM

DISCOVER**MORE**

You may have heard to apply butter or petroleum jelly to a burned area. The truth is that these products should never be applied to a burn because they could trap heat in the tissue and cause more damage or increase the chance of infection.

FAINTING

1. Lay the victim down on their back and make sure they have plenty of fresh air.

2. Reassure the victim and apply a cold compress to their face.

3. If the victim vomits, roll them on their side and keep the windpipe clear.

NOTE: Fainting victims typically regain consciousness almost immediately. If this does not happen, the victim could be in serious danger, and you should call 9-1-1 as soon as possible.

EYE INJURY

CHEMICAL

1. Hold the eyelids apart and flush the eyeball with lukewarm water for 15 to 30 minutes. Be careful not to let runoff water flow into the other eye.

2. Place a gauze pad or cloth over both eyes and secure with a bandage.

3. Get to an eye specialist or emergency room immediately.

CUT, SCRATCH OR EMBEDDED OBJECT

1. Place a gauze pad or cloth over both eyes and secure with a bandage.

2. Do not try to remove an embedded object.

3. Get to an eye specialist or emergency room immediately.

SALON**CONNECTION**

Safety Data Sheet

A separate **Safety Data Sheet (SDS)**, formerly known as a Material Safety Data Sheet (MSDS), for potentially hazardous products used in the salon, should be kept readily available in a file in case of an emergency. The SDS provides information on the contents of products, including potential hazards, which may be helpful if a certain product causes an allergic reaction or injury.

The safety, protection and welfare of the clients you serve are the reasons you are licensed as a professional. Remember that your health and safety are important issues as well. Make sure you know the procedures necessary for a clean, healthy, safe environment.

LESSONS LEARNED

Stop the bleeding for a minor cut by placing a clean cloth or gauze and gloved hand over the wound and applying firm, steady pressure for five minutes; call emergency personnel if bleeding is severe.

First-aid techniques for chemical burns include rinsing away all traces of chemicals, covering the burn loosely and referring the person to medical attention if necessary. For heat or electrical burns, if the skin is not broken, immerse the burned area in cool water, then apply a cool compress; call emergency personnel if the skin is broken or the burn is severe.

If a choking victim cannot speak or cough, have someone call 9-1-1 while you perform an upward abdominal thrust on the victim using a thumbless fist placed just above the navel and well below the ribs; repeat if necessary.

If fainting occurs, lay the victim on their back and allow plenty of fresh air; reassure the victim, apply a cold compress to their face and roll them on their side if vomiting occurs. If the victim doesn't regain consciousness almost immediately, call 9-1-1.

If a chemical eye injury occurs, flush the eyeball with lukewarm water for 15 to 30 minutes; place a gauze pad over both eyes, secure with a bandage and get to an eye specialist or emergency room immediately. If an eye injury involves a cut, scratch or embedded object, place a gauze pad over both eyes, secure with a bandage, do not try to remove an embedded object and get to an eye specialist or emergency room immediately.

What do you think is the most amazing function your body performs?

102ᶜ.4

BUILDING
BLOCKS OF THE
HUMAN BODY

102ᶜ.4 | BUILDING BLOCKS OF THE HUMAN BODY

INSPIRE //

Understanding the building blocks of the human body is important because it will help you be more aware of why the body acts and responds the way it does, and the power you have to affect it as a salon professional.

ACHIEVE //

Following this lesson on *Building Blocks of the Human Body*, you'll be able to:

>> Identify the structure of cells

>> State the structure and function of five types of tissue

>> Explain the function of the primary organs of the human body

>> Express the names of 10 body systems and their relationship to cells, tissues and organs

FOCUS //

BUILDING BLOCKS OF THE HUMAN BODY

Cells

Tissues

Organs

Body Systems

Is the image to the left the work of a popular new artist, or is it a close-up view of cells in the human body? It's actually a magnified view of human body cells. The human body is truly amazing.

The study of the human body can be divided into two general categories: **Anatomy, the study of the organs and systems of the body; and physiology, the study of the functions these organs and systems perform.** The study of structures that can be seen with the naked eye is called gross anatomy. The study of structures too small to be seen except through a microscope is called histology or microscopic anatomy.

To understand anatomy and physiology, you need to be aware of the building blocks of the human body:

- Cells

- Tissues

- Organs

- Body Systems

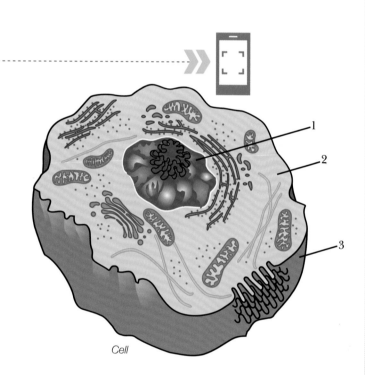

Cell

CELLS

Your knowledge of muscles, nerves, bones and all bodily systems needs to start at the level of the single cell. **Cells are the basic units of living matter (life).** Cells are composed of **protoplasm** (**PRO**-to-plazm), a gel-like substance containing water, salt and nutrients obtained from food. Cells vary in size, shape, structure and function, but most have certain characteristics in common.

Most cells contain three basic parts:

1. **The nucleus (NU-kle-us), or control center, of cell activities**

2. **The cytoplasm (SI-to-plazm), or production department of the cell, where most of the cell's activities take place**

3. **The cell membrane, or outer surface of the cell, which encloses the protoplasm**

The nucleus is located in the cytoplasm, and both are surrounded by the cell membrane. Cells with common properties or functions combine to form the various tissues of the body.

To grow and remain healthy, cells need adequate supplies of food, oxygen and water, proper temperature and the ability to eliminate waste products. If these criteria are not present, cell growth will be impaired. As each cell absorbs food, it grows in size and divides, creating two new cells. This activity is called **mitosis**. The chemical process in which cells receive nutrients (food) for cell growth and reproduction is known as **metabolism** (me-**TAB**-e-lism). There are two phases of metabolism:

1. **Anabolism** (ah-**NAB**-oh-lizm), **the process of building up larger molecules from smaller ones.** During this phase, the body stores water, food and oxygen for the body.

2. **Catabolism** (kah-**TAB**-oh-lizm), **the process of breaking down larger molecules or substances into smaller ones.** This phase causes a release of energy within the cell, necessary for the performance of specific body functions, including muscular movements and digestion.

DISCOVER**MORE**

Cell Cycle

0-4 hours – 1st stage – the cell grows and develops
6-8 hours – 2nd stage – DNA is replicated
2-5 hours – 3rd stage – cell grows and produces proteins
1 hour – DNA is divided and separates, the cell divides and mitosis occurs

The time estimates above are averages for most cells in the body. Not all cells divide at the same speed. For example, brain and liver cells do not typically divide at all. Liver cells may go through mitosis to repair minor damage, but may take a long time to complete the process.

TISSUES

Groups of cells of the same kind make up tissues. There are five primary types of tissue in the human body:

1. **Epithelial** (ep-i-**THE**-le-el) tissue that covers and protects body surfaces and internal organs

2. **Connective tissue** that supports, protects and holds the body together

3. **Nerve tissue** that coordinates body functions in addition to carrying messages to and from the brain and spinal cord

4. **Muscular tissue** that contracts, when stimulated, to produce motion

5. **Liquid tissue** that carries food, waste products and hormones

SALON**CONNECTION**

Anatomy in Action

Understanding the human body, right down to cell division, will help guide you in the salon to know how a client's skin, hair and nails may react or respond to products, treatments or services.

ORGANS

Organs are separate body structures that perform specific functions. They are composed of two or more different tissues. Organs of primary importance include:

1. The **brain**, which controls all body functions

2. The **eyes**, which control vision

3. The **heart**, which circulates the blood

4. The **lungs**, which supply the blood with oxygen

5. The **stomach** and **intestines**, which digest food

6. The **liver**, which removes the toxic byproducts of digestion

7. The **kidneys**, which eliminate water and waste products

8. The **skin**, the body's largest organ, which forms the external protective layer of the body

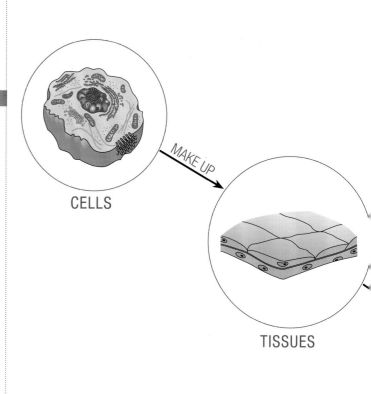

CELLS

MAKE UP

TISSUES

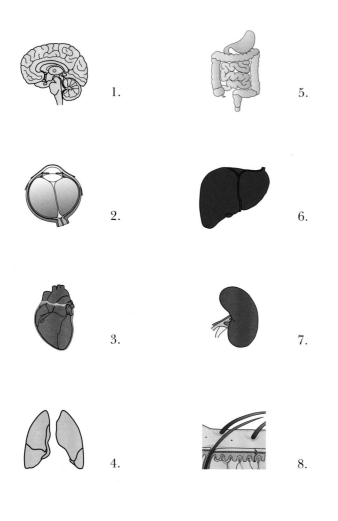

1.

2.

3.

4.

5.

6.

7.

8.

BODY SYSTEMS

A system is a group of body structures and/or organs that, together, perform one or more vital functions for the body. Various lessons in this program will provide an overview of the body systems. The 10 body systems, with a brief description of their functions, are listed here for reference:

SKELETAL – Provides framework of the body

MUSCULAR – Moves the body

CIRCULATORY – Circulates blood through the body

NERVOUS – Sends and receives body messages

DIGESTIVE – Supplies food to the body

EXCRETORY – Eliminates waste from the body

RESPIRATORY – Controls breathing of the body

ENDOCRINE – Controls growth and general health and reproduction of the body

REPRODUCTIVE – Allows living organisms to procreate

INTEGUMENTARY – Controls the sebaceous (oil) and sudoriferous (sweat) glands

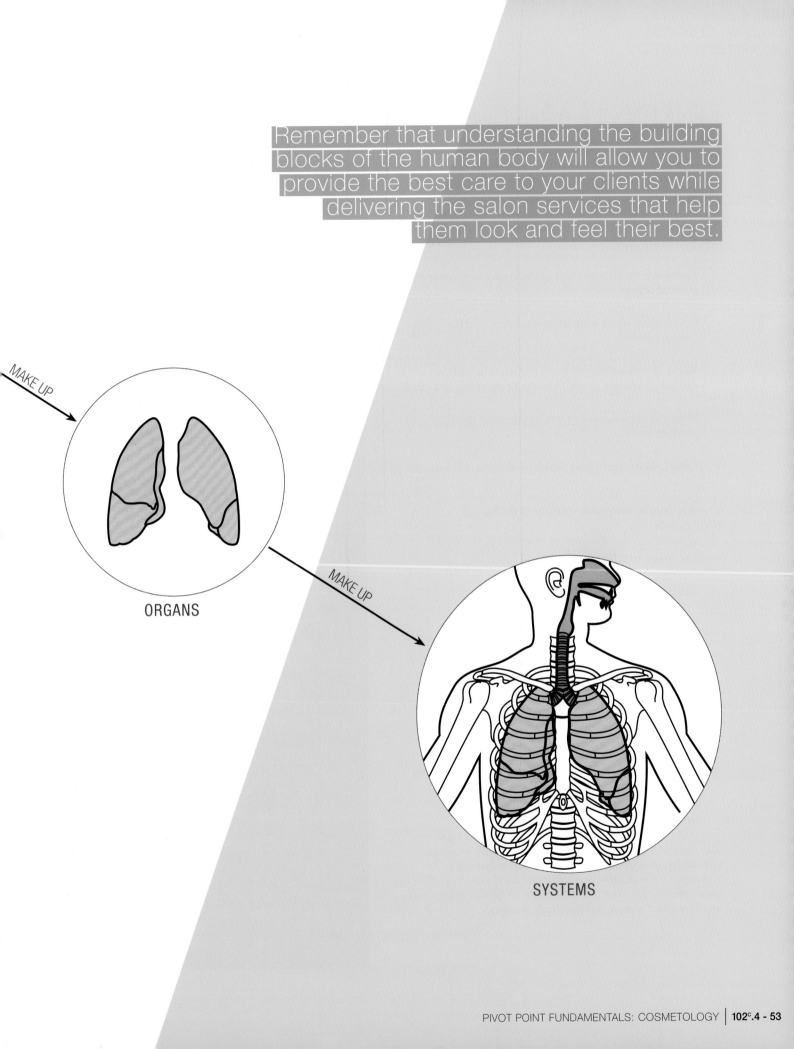

Remember that understanding the building blocks of the human body will allow you to provide the best care to your clients while delivering the salon services that help them look and feel their best.

MAKE UP

ORGANS

MAKE UP

SYSTEMS

LESSONS LEARNED

Cells consist of a nucleus, cytoplasm and cell membrane.

Tissues are groups of the same kinds of cells, and they function as five types:

>> Epithelial, which cover and protect body surfaces and internal organs

>> Connective, which support, protect and hold the body together

>> Nerve, which coordinate body functions in addition to carrying messages to and from the brain and spinal cord

>> Muscular, which contract when stimulated to produce motion

>> Liquid, which carry food, waste products and hormones

The functions of the primary organs of the human body include:

>> The brain, which controls all body functions

>> The eyes, which control vision

>> The heart, which circulates the blood

>> The lungs, which supply the blood with oxygen

>> The stomach and intestines, which digest food

>> The liver, which removes the toxic byproducts of digestion

>> The kidneys, which eliminate water and waste products

>> The skin, the body's largest organ, which forms the external protective layer of the body

The names of the body systems include skeletal, muscular, circulatory, nervous, digestive, excretory, respiratory, endocrine, reproductive and integumentary, and they relate to each other in the sense that cells make up tissues, tissues make up organs and organs make up body systems.

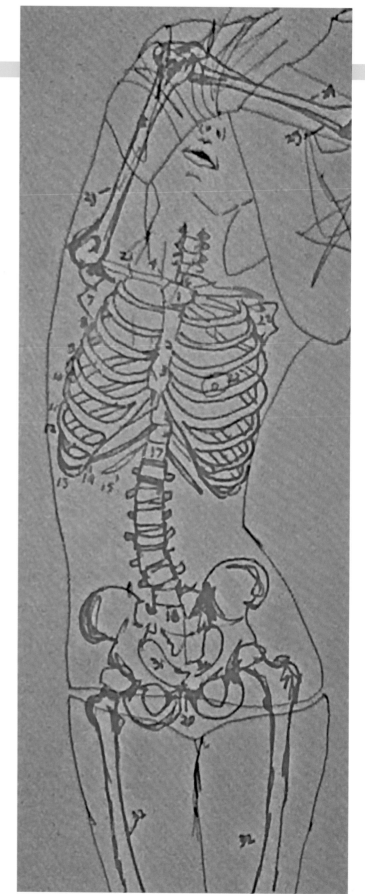

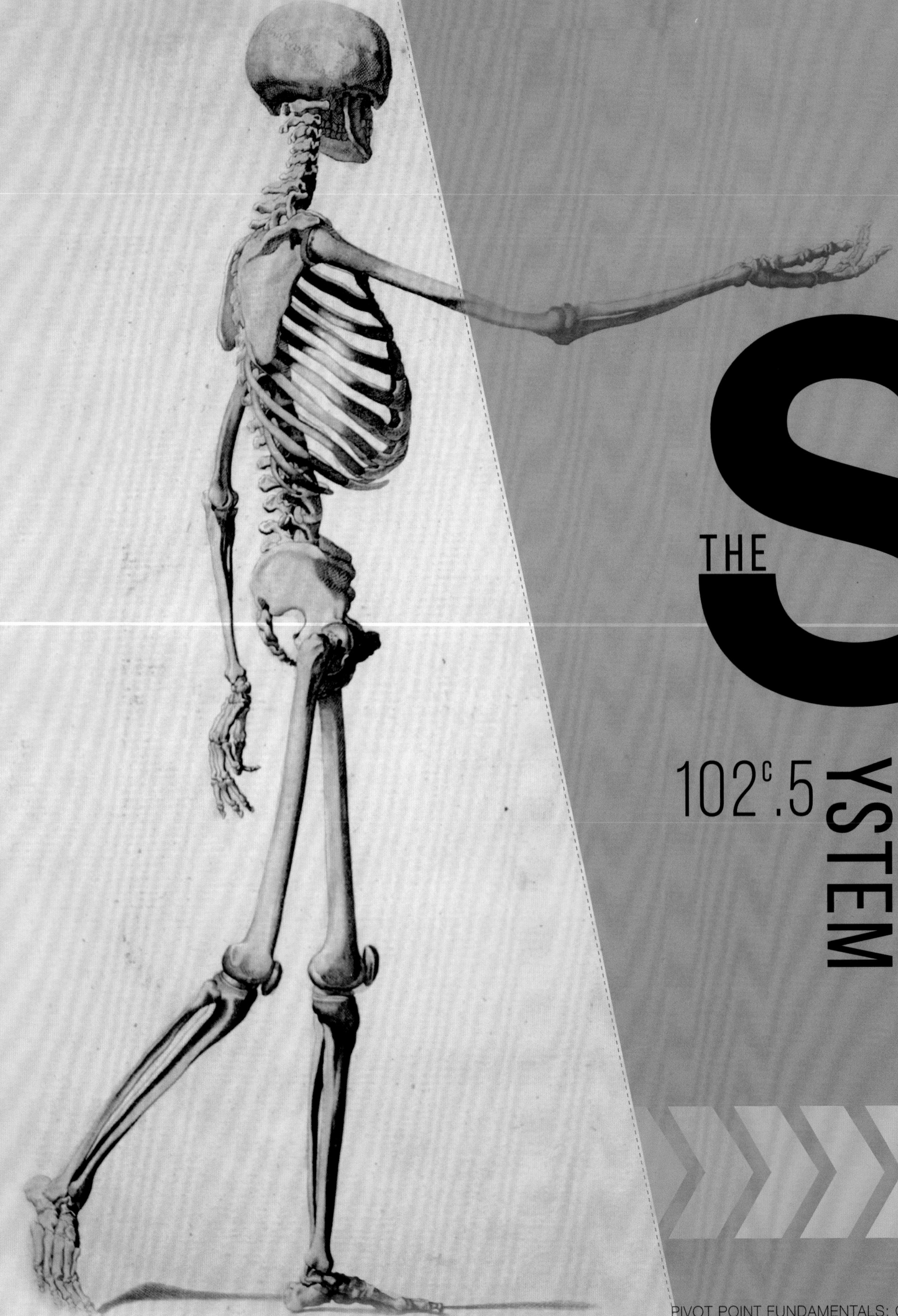

THE **S**

KELETAL
YSTEM

102^c.5

INSPIRE **//**

Knowledge of the skeletal system is fundamental for providing quality, comprehensive salon services that respect and care for the client completely.

ACHIEVE **//**

Following this lesson on *The Skeletal System*, you'll be able to:

>> Identify the structure and function of the skeletal system

>> Recap the name and location of bones of the skull affected by massage

>> Offer examples of the name and location of bones of the neck, back, chest and shoulder

>> Go over the name and location of bones of the arm, wrist and hand

>> Summarize the name and location of bones of the leg, ankle and foot

FOCUS **//**

THE SKELETAL SYSTEM

Structure and Function of the Skeletal System

Study of the Bones

102ᶜ.5
THE SKELETAL SYSTEM

Well-wishers typically say "break a leg" to actors and musicians before they go on stage to perform. What do you think this expression really means?

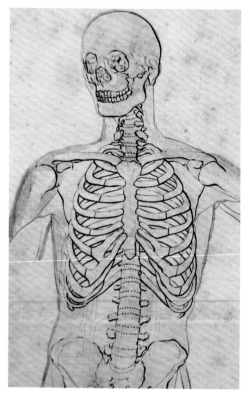

STRUCTURE AND FUNCTION OF THE SKELETAL SYSTEM

The skeletal system is the physical foundation of the body and is composed of 206 bones of different shapes and sizes. Bones are attached to others at movable joints such as elbows and knees or immovable joints found in the pelvis and skull. A joint is the point at which two or more bones are joined together.

Osteology (as-te-**AL**-e-je) **is the study of bone**. "Os" is the technical term for bone. Bones are described as either long, flat or irregular in shape.

>> **Long bones** are found in the arms and legs.

>> **Flat bones** are plate-shaped and located in the skull, scapula and sternum.

>> **Irregular bones** are found in the wrist, ankle and spinal column (the back).

Bone is composed of $2/3$ mineral matter and $1/3$ organic matter and produces red and white blood cells and stores calcium. You might have thought of bone as the hardest part of the body, but in reality, tooth enamel is the hardest substance of the body.

The functions of the skeletal system include:

1. **Supporting the body by giving it shape and strength**

2. **Surrounding and protecting internal organs**

3. **Providing a frame to which muscles can attach**

4. **Allowing body movement**

Amazing Facts About Bones...

>> Babies are born with 300 bones, but adults have only 206 bones.

>> More than half of the bones in the human body are in the hands and feet.

>> Humans and giraffes have the same number of bones in their necks.

>> Only about 3% of all animals possess a backbone or spine.

>> If you drink a lot of milk and get plenty of sunshine, your bones can grow to be stronger than concrete.

DISCOVER**MORE**

Human bones grow continually from birth until our mid-20s.
The skeleton's bone mass is at its maximum density around the age of 30.

STUDY OF THE BONES

Knowledge of the bones of the head, face, neck, arms, hands, legs and feet is essential for designing flattering hairstyles and for the proper application and use of products and cosmetics.

THE SKULL

The skull, the skeleton of the head, encloses and protects the brain and primary sensory organs. Bones of the skull are divided into two groups: the eight bones of the cranium and the 14 bones of the facial skeleton.

Cranium

Of the eight bones that compose the cranium, only **six bones are affected by scalp massage** and are frequently referred to when directions are given for sculpting and designing techniques.

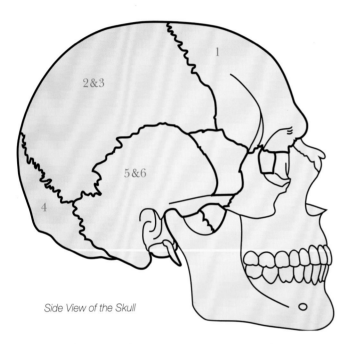

Side View of the Skull

ID	BONE	PRONUNCIATION	DESCRIPTION
1.	Frontal	FRON-tal	Extends from the top of the eyes to the top of the head to form the forehead
2&3.	Parietal	pah-RI-e-tal	2 bones that form the crown and upper sides of the head
4.	Occipital	ak-SIP-et-al	Forms the back of the skull, indenting above the nape area
5&6.	Temporal	TEM-poh-ral	2 bones located on either side of the head, directly above the ears and below the parietal bones

The remaining two bones of the cranium have no part in either massage or hair design techniques and are not labeled on the illustration.

>> The **sphenoid** (**SFE**-noid) is located behind the eyes and nose and connects all the bones of the cranium.

>> The **ethmoid** (**ETH**-moid) is the spongy bone between the eyes that forms part of the nasal cavity.

Human Skull

Facial Skeleton

Of the 14 bones that compose the facial skeleton, only nine are involved in facial massage.

Front View of the Skull

ID	BONE	PRONUNCIATION	DESCRIPTION
1.	Mandible	MAN-di-bel	Lower jaw and the largest bone of the facial skeleton
2-3.	Maxillae	mak-**SIL**-e	2 bones of the upper jaw
4-5.	Nasal	NA-zel	2 bones which join to form the bridge of the nose
6-7.	Zygomatic or Malar	zi-go-**MAT**-ik	2 bones that form the upper cheek and the bottom of the eye socket
8-9.	Lacrimal	LAK-ri-mal	Smallest 2 bones of the facial skeleton; form the front part of the inner-bottom wall of the eye socket

The remaining five bones of the facial skeleton are unaffected by facial massage and are not shown on the illustration.

» The **turbinal** (TUR-bi-nal) are the two spongy bones that form the sides of the nasal cavity.

» The **vomer** (VO-mer), or **nasal system,** is the bone in the center of the nose that divides the nasal cavity.

» The **palatine** (PAL-ah-tin) are the two bones that form the roof of the mouth and the floor of the eye sockets.

The shape and size of all bones of the skull, and their relationship to one another, will help you determine the most flattering use of makeup and hair designs for clients.

NECK BONES

ID	BONE	PRONUNCIATION	DESCRIPTION
1-7.	Cervical Vertebrae	SUR-vi-kel VURT-e-bray	7 bones that form the top part of the spinal column; involved in extended scalp massage
8.	Hyoid	HI-oid	U-shaped bone at the base of the tongue; supports the muscles of the tongue

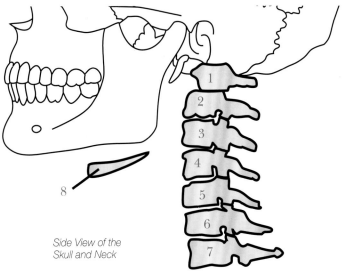

Side View of the Skull and Neck

SALON**CONNECTION**

Posture

Posture is very important for your bone health. The way that you position yourself while standing or sitting is your posture. While working in the salon, be sure you are not slouching. Keeping your bones in good alignment allows your muscles to work correctly.

Neck Bones

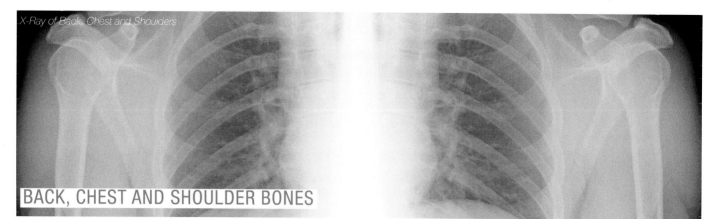

X-Ray of Back, Chest and Shoulders

BACK, CHEST AND SHOULDER BONES

The **chest**, or **thorax**, is the bony cage that protects the heart, lungs and other internal organs.

ID	BONE	PRONUNCIATION	DESCRIPTION
1.	Thoracic Vertebrae	tho-**RAS**-ik **VURT**-e-bray	12 vertebrae in the chest region that form the central region of the spine
2.	Sternum	**STUR**-num	Breastbone; long, narrow, flat plate that forms the center of the front of the chest
3-14.	Ribs		12 pairs of curved bones which form the rib cage of the upper body
15.	Clavicle	**KLAV**-i-kel	Collarbone; forms the area from the throat to the shoulder on the right and left side
16.	Scapula	**SKAP**-yu-lah	Shoulder blade; large, flat bone extending upward from the middle of the back, on the right and left side, to the joint, where it attaches to the clavicle

Front View of Back,
Chest and Shoulders

DISCOVER**MORE**

Like your skin, the human body's bones are also constantly worn down and remade, to the point where every 7 years you essentially have a new bone.

ARM, WRIST AND HAND BONES

ID	BONE	PRONUNCIATION	DESCRIPTION
1.	Humerus	HU-mur-us	Largest bone of the upper arm; extends from the elbow to the shoulder
2.	Radius	RAY-de-us	Small bone on the thumb side of the lower arm or forearm
3.	Ulna	UL-nah	Small bone on the little-finger side of the lower arm
4.	Carpals	KAR-pels	8 small bones held together by ligaments to form the wrist or carpus
5.	Metacarpals	met-ah-KAR-pels	5 long, thin bones that form the palm of the hand
6.	Phalanges	fah-LAN-jes	14 bones that form the digits or fingers; each finger has 3 phalanges, while the thumb has only 2

Side View of Arm, Wrist and Hand

DISCOVERMORE

The area of our body with the most «·········· bones is the hand, fingers and wrist, where there are 54 bones.

LEG, ANKLE AND FOOT BONES

ID	BONE	PRONUNCIATION	DESCRIPTION
1.	Femur	FEE-mur	Thigh bone; longest bone in the body
2.	Patella	pah-TEL-lah	Kneecap; sits over the front of the knee joint
3.	Tibia	TIB-ee-ah	Shinbone; inner and larger of the 2 lower leg bones, extending from the knee to the ankle
4.	Fibula	FIB-u-lah	Outer and narrower of the 2 lower leg bones, extending from the knee to the ankle
5.	Talus	TA-lus	Anklebone; sits above the heel bone and forms the lower part of the ankle; talus, tibia and fibula form the ankle joint
6.	Tarsals	TAHR-suls	7 bones that make up the mid-foot and rear foot, including talus, calcaneus (heel), navicular, 3 cuneiform bones, and the cuboid
7.	Metatarsals	met-ah-TAHR-suls	5 long, slender bones (1 for each digit) that connect the phalanges to the tarsals
8.	Phalanges	fah-LAN-jes	14 bones that form the digits; 2 phalanges in the big toe and 3 in the 4 other toes

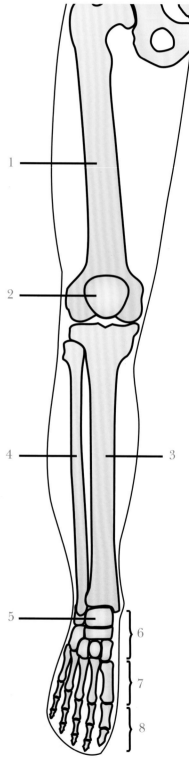

Front View of Leg, Ankle and Foot

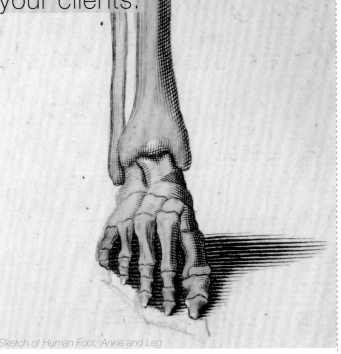

Understanding how bones in the skeletal system are interconnected will help you make the best possible judgments when recommending and delivering services to your clients.

Sketch of Human Foot, Ankle and Leg

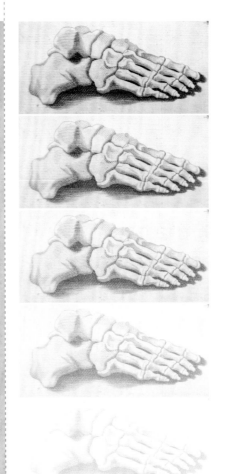

Sketch of Human Foot

LESSONS LEARNED ≪

The skeletal system supports the body, surrounds and protects internal organs, provides a frame to which muscles can attach and allows body movement.

The skull consists of eight bones in the cranium, with six of those affected by scalp massage (frontal, parietal, occipital, temporal), and 14 bones in the facial skeleton, with nine of those involved in facial massage (mandible, maxillae, nasal, zygomatic and lacrimal).

Review the neck bones (cervical vertebrae and hyoid) and recognize that seven of these bones (cervical vertebrae) are often involved in extended scalp massage.

Review the back, chest and shoulder bones (thoracic vertebrae, sternum, ribs, clavicle and scapula).

Review the arm, wrist and hand bones (humerus, radius, ulna, carpals, metacarpals and phalanges).

Review the bones in the leg (femur, patella, tibia and fibula) and the foot (tibia, fibula, tarsals, metatarsals and phalanges).

EXPLORE //

How many muscles do you think are at work when you take one step?

INSPIRE //

An understanding of muscles will help you develop beneficial facial and massage techniques.

FOCUS //

THE MUSCULAR SYSTEM

Structure and Function of the Muscular System

Study of the Muscles

7

THE MUSCULAR SYSTEM

102ᶜ.6

ACHIEVE //

Following this lesson on *The Muscular System*, you'll be able to:

>> Identify the structure and function of the muscular system

>> State the direction of massage movements used to affect muscles during massage

>> Describe the methods used to stimulate muscular tissue

>> Label the name, location and function of scalp and face muscles affected by massage

>> Call out the name, location and function of muscles of the neck and back

>> List the name, location and function of the muscles of the shoulder, chest, arm and hand

>> State the name, location and function of muscles of the leg and foot

Muscles of the Human Body

102ᶜ.6
THE MUSCULAR SYSTEM

Amazing Facts About Muscles...

It takes 17 muscles to smile and 43 to frown.

When you're cold, your muscles contract involuntarily, which sends out energy to warm up your body.

It takes half as long to gain muscle as it does to lose it.

Salon professionals, like doctors and nurses, are licensed to touch a client. Whether you are shampooing or massaging, you have the privilege of bringing relaxation, well-being and personal enhancement to others. Study of the muscles will help you do just that.

STRUCTURE AND FUNCTION OF THE MUSCULAR SYSTEM

Myology (mi-**OL**-o-je) **is the study of the structure, function and diseases of the muscles. Muscles are 40% to 50% of the body's weight.** Muscles are fibrous tissues that contract, when stimulated by messages carried by the nervous system, to produce movement.

The functions of the muscular system include:

>> Movement of body

>> Involvement in functions of other body systems

>> Support of the skeleton

>> Contouring of the body

There are two types of muscle tissue:

1. The **voluntary** or **striated** (**STRI**-at-ed) muscles respond to commands regulated by will.

2. The **involuntary** or **non-striated** muscles respond automatically to control various body functions including the functions of internal organs.

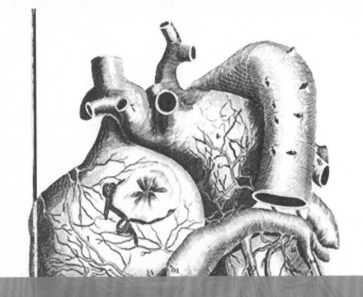

The cardiac (heart) muscle is the muscle of the heart itself and is the only muscle of its type in the human body. This rugged muscle functions involuntarily.

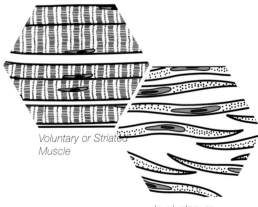

Voluntary or Striated Muscle

Involuntary or Non-Striated Muscle

The same muscles may function both voluntarily and involuntarily. For example, eye muscles respond to a conscious command to blink, but they also blink automatically to maintain eye moisture. **The salon professional is primarily concerned with the voluntary muscles of the head, face, neck, arms, hands, legs and feet.**

DISCOVER**MORE**

The exact number of muscles varies based on whether you are counting by individual muscle or parts of a single muscle, with the count ranging from 500 to 850 muscles.

The three parts of the muscle are:

1. The **origin** is the nonmoving (fixed) portion of the muscle attached to bones or other fixed muscle. The term skeletal muscle refers to muscle attached to bone.

2. The **belly** is the term applied to the midsection of the muscle.

3. The **insertion** is the portion of the muscle joined to movable attachments: bones, movable muscles or skin.

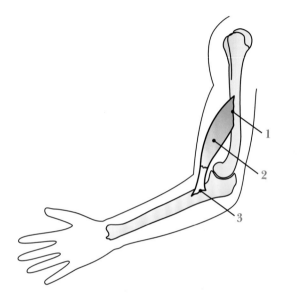

Stimulation of muscular tissue can be achieved by using the following methods:

» Massage

» Electric Current (high-frequency and faradic current)

» Temperature

   ▪ Dry (heating lamps, sun)

   ▪ Moist (steamers, warm steam towels)

   ▪ Cold (ice packs)

» Nerve Impulses (through nervous system)

» Chemicals (certain acids and salts)

Muscles produce movement through contraction (tightening) and expansion (relaxing).
When a contraction occurs, one of the muscle attachments (insertion) moves while the other (origin) remains fixed. All muscles (except those of the face) are attached at both ends to bone or another muscle. Facial muscles are only attached at one end.

SPECIAL TERMINOLOGY

The following common terms describe what a muscle does or where it is located.

ANTERIOR (an-**TER**-e-er) – in front of
POSTERIOR (pos-**TER**-e-er) – behind or in back of

SUPERIORIS (su-per-e-**OR**-es) – located above or is larger
INFERIORIS (in-**FIR**-e-or-es) – located below or is smaller

---

LEVATOR (le-**VA**-ter) – lifts up
DEPRESSOR (de-**PRES**-er) – draws down or depresses

DILATOR (**DI**-la-ter) – opens, enlarges or expands

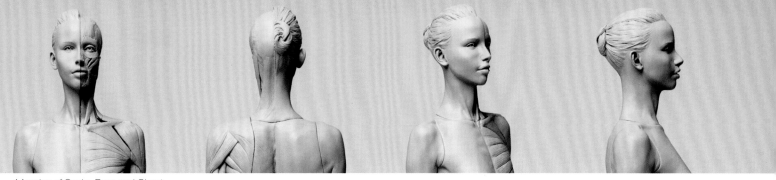

Muscles of Scalp, Face and Chest

STUDY OF THE MUSCLES

The scalp and face muscles are of primary interest as you perform scalp and neck massages and facials. The salon professional will also often employ general massage techniques to the scalp and neck just before or during a shampoo. **Muscles affected by massage are generally massaged from the insertion attachment to the origin attachment.** The professional who performs facials must know the position of the muscles in the face. Light facial massage, used when applying certain facial treatment products, should follow the muscle line.

SCALP AND FACE MUSCLES

The **epicranium** (ep-i-**KRA**-ne-um) consists of all the structures above the cranium, including muscle, skin and aponeuroses. The **epicranius** (ep-i-**KRA**-ne-us) or **occipitofrontalis** (ok-**SIP**-ih-to-fron-**TA**-les) is a broad muscle formed by two muscles joined by the **aponeurosis** (ap-o-noo-**ROH**-sis) tendon.

Scalp Muscles

ID	MUSCLE	PRONUNCIATION	DESCRIPTION	FUNCTION
1.	Frontalis	fron-**TA**-les	Extends from the forehead to the top of the skull	Raises the eyebrows or draws the scalp forward
2.	Occipitalis	ok-sip-i-**TAL**-is	At the nape of the neck	Draws the scalp back

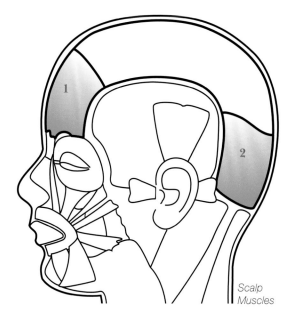

Scalp Muscles

Ear Muscles

ID	MUSCLE	PRONUNCIATION	DESCRIPTION
1.	Auricularis Anterior	aw-rik-ya-**LA**-ris an-**TER**-e-er	In front of the ear
2.	Auricularis Superior	aw-**RIK**-ya-la-ris su-**PER**-e-or	Above the ear
3.	Auricularis Posterior	aw-rik-ya-**LA**-ris pos-**TER**-e-er	Behind the ear

The three muscles of the ear are used to move the auricula (aw-**RIK**-ya-la), the visible part of the ear.

Ear Muscles

Eye and Nose Muscles

ID	MUSCLE	PRONUNCIATION	DESCRIPTION	FUNCTION
1.	Corrugator	**KOR**-e-gat-er	Between the eyebrows	Controls the eyebrows, drawing them in and downward
2.	Levator Palpebrae Superioris	le-**VA**-ter **POL**-pe-bra su-per-e-**OR**-es	Above the eyelids	Raises the eyelid
3.	Orbicularis Oculi	or-bik-ye-**LAR**-es **AK**-yu-le	Circles the eye socket	Closes the eyelid
4.	Procerus	pro-**SER**-us	Between the eyebrows; across the bridge of the nose	Draws brows down; wrinkles the area across the bridge of the nose

Four muscles located inside the nose, called the **nasalis, dilator naris posterior, dilator naris anterior** and **depressor septi**, control contraction and expansion of the nostrils.

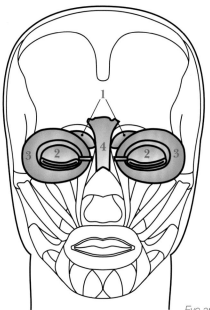

Eye and Nose Muscles

Mouth Muscles

ID	MUSCLE	PRONUNCIATION	DESCRIPTION	FUNCTION
1.	**Orbicularis Oris**	or-bik-ye-**LAR**-es **O**-ris	Circles the mouth	Contracts, puckers and wrinkles the lips, as in kissing or whistling
2.	**Quadratus Labii Superioris** aka: Levator Labii Superioris	kwod-**RA**-tus **LA**-be su-per-e-**OR**-es le-**VA**-ter **LA**-be su-per-e-**OR**-es	Consists of 3 parts located above the upper lip	Raises both the nostrils and the upper lip, as in expressing distaste
3.	**Quadratus Labii Inferioris** aka: Depressor Labii Inferioris	kwod-**RA**-tus **LA**-be in-**FIR**-e-or-es de-**PRES**-er **LA**-be in-**FIR**-e-or-es	Below the lower lip	Pulls the lower lip down or to the side, as in expressing sarcasm
4.	**Mentalis**	men-**TAL**-us	Tip of the chin	Pushes lower lip up and/or wrinkles the chin, as in expressing doubt
5.	**Risorius**	re-**SOR**-e-us	Corner of the mouth	Draws the mouth up and out, as in grinning
6.	**Caninus** aka: Levator Anguli Oris	kay-**NEYE**-nus le-**VA**-ter **AN**-gu-li **O**-ris	Above the corners of the mouth	Raises the angle of the mouth, as in snarling
7.	**Triangularis** aka: Depressor Anguli	tri-an-gu-**LAR**-us de-**PRES**-er **AN**-gu-li	Below the corners of the mouth	Draws the corners of the mouth down, as in expressing sadness
8.	**Zygomaticus**	zi-go-**MAT**-ik-us	Major and minor; outside the corners of the mouth	Draws the mouth up and back, as in laughing
9.	**Buccinator**	**BUK**-si-na-ter	Between the jaws and cheek	Compressing the cheek to release air outwardly, as in blowing

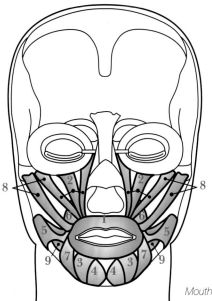

Mouth Muscles

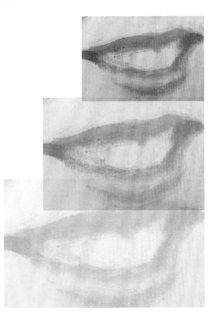

Mastication Muscles

ID	MUSCLE	PRONUNCIATION	DESCRIPTION	FUNCTION
1.	Temporalis	tem-po-**RA**-lis	Above and in front of the ear	Opening and closing the jaw, as in chewing (mastication)
2.	Masseter	**MAS**-se-ter	Covers the hinge of the jaw	Aids in closing the jaw, as in chewing (mastication)

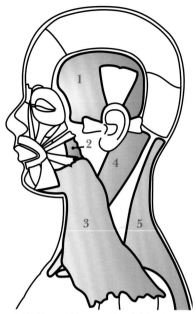

Side View of Face and Neck Muscles

NECK AND BACK MUSCLES

ID	MUSCLE	PRONUNCIATION	DESCRIPTION	FUNCTION
3.	Platysma	plah-**TIZ**-mah	Extends from the tip of the chin to the shoulders and chest	Draws the lower lip and corner of the mouth sideways and down, partially opening the mouth, as in surprise or fright
4.	Sternocleido-mastoid	stur-no-**KLI**-do-mas-**TOID**	Extends along the side of the neck from the ear to the collarbone	Causes the head to move from side to side and up and down, as in nodding yes or no
5.	Trapezius	trah-**PE**-ze-us	Flat, triangular; covers the upper and back part of the neck and shoulders	Aids in drawing the head back and elevating the shoulder blades
6.	Latissimus Dorsi	lah-**TIS**-i-mus **DOR**-se	Flat, triangular; covers the lumbar (lower back) region and lower half of the thoracic region	Aids in swinging of the arms

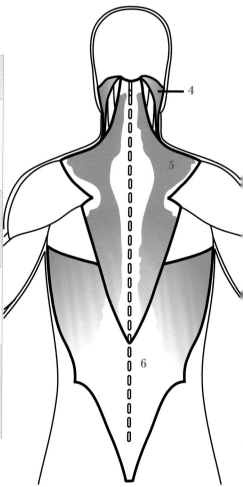

Posterior View of Neck and Back Muscles

DISCOVER**MORE**

Muscle memory is developed by practicing an action over and over again. Muscles have the ability to fine-tune with each practice, becoming more accurate at what they do. This is why practice is so important to athletes and dancers. Practice will help make your work more efficient.

SHOULDER, CHEST, ARM AND HAND MUSCLES

Shoulder, Chest and Arm Muscles

ID	MUSCLE	PRONUNCIATION	DESCRIPTION	FUNCTION
1a. 1b.	Pectoralis Major Pectoralis Minor	pek-to-**RAL**-us **MEY**-jer pek-to-**RAL**-us **MAHY**-ner	Extend across the front of the chest	Assist in swinging the arms
2.	Serratus Anterior	ser-**RA**-tus an-**TER**-e-er	Under the arm	Helps in lifting the arm and in breathing
3.	Deltoid	**DEL**-toid	Triangle-shaped; covers the shoulder	Lifts the arm or turns it
4.	Biceps	**BI**-ceps	Primary muscle in the front of the upper arm	Raises the forearm, bends the elbow and turns the palm of the hand down
5.	Triceps	**TRI**-ceps	Extends the length of the upper arm to the forearm	Controls forward movement of the forearm
6.	Supinator	**SU**-pi-nat-or	Runs parallel to the ulna	Turns the palm of the hand up
7.	Pronator	**PRO**-nat-or	Runs across the front of the lower part of the radius and the ulna	Turns the palm of the hand downward and inward
8.	Flexor	**FLEX**-er	Mid-forearm, on the inside of the arm	Bends wrist and closes the fingers
9.	Extensor	eks-**TEN**-sor	Mid-forearm, on the outside of the arm	Straightens the fingers and wrist

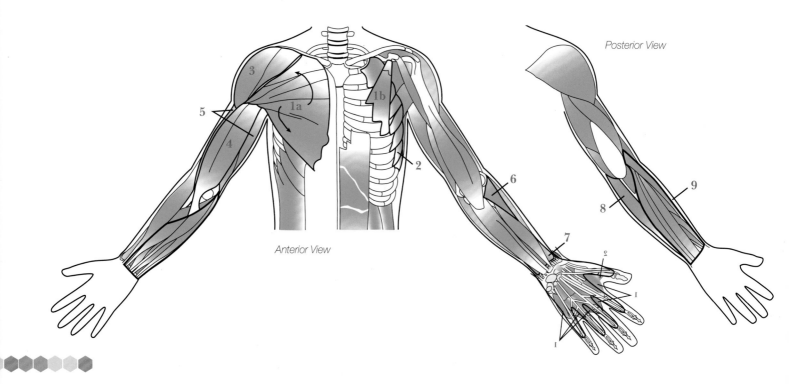

Anterior View

Posterior View

Hand Muscles

A number of small muscles stretch over the fingers, connect the joints and provide dexterity.

ID	MUSCLE	PRONUNCIATION	DESCRIPTION	FUNCTION
1.	Abductor	ab-**DUK**-tor	Stretches over fingers	Separates the fingers
2.	Adductor	ad-**DUK**-tor	Stretches over fingers	Draws the fingers together
3.	Opponens	op-**PON**-ens	Palm of hand	Causes the thumb to move toward the fingers, giving the ability to grasp or make a fist

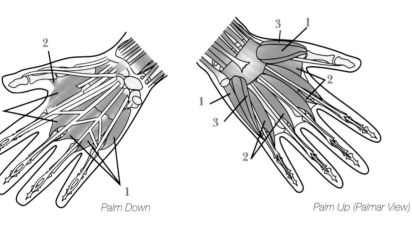

Palm Down

Palm Up (Palmar View)

DISCOVER**MORE**

To help ease a muscle cramp, you can do several things such as massaging, stretching or icing the muscle, warming the muscle or taking a bath with Epsom salt.

For a cramp in the calf or in the back of the thigh (hamstring), try putting your weight on the affected leg and bending your knee slightly, or sit or lie down with your leg out straight, and pull the top of your foot toward your head. For a cramp in the front of the thigh (quadriceps), hold onto a chair to steady yourself and pull your foot toward your buttock.

See www.webMD.com for additional information.

LEG AND FOOT MUSCLES

Leg Muscles

ID	MUSCLE	PRONUNCIATION	DESCRIPTION	FUNCTION
1.	Tibialis Anterior	tib-ee-**AHL**-is an-**TER**-e-er	Covers the front of the shin	Bends the foot upward and inward
2.	Gastrocnemius	gas-truc-**NEEM**-e-us	Back of the leg attached to the lower rear surface of the heel	Pulls the foot down
3.	Peroneus Longus	per-oh-**NEE**-us **LONG**-us	Originates in the upper ⅔ of the outer fibula	Causes the foot to invert and turn outward
4.	Peroneus Brevis	per-oh-**NEE**-us **BREV**-us	Originates in the lower third of the fibula	Bends the foot down and out
5.	Soleus	**SO**-lee-us	Originates in the upper portion of the fibula from just below the knee to the heel	Bends the foot down
6.	Extensor Digitorum Longus	eck-**STEN**-sur dij-it-**TOHR**-um **LONG**-us	Outside of the lower leg	Bends the foot up and extends the toes
7.	Extensor Hallucis Longus	eck-**STEN**-sur ha-**LU**-sis **LONG**-us	Between the tibialis interior and extensor digitorum longus	Extends the big toe and flexes the foot

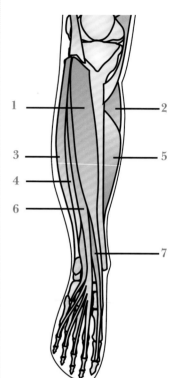

Anterior View of Leg Muscles

Foot Muscles

ID	MUSCLE	PRONUNCIATION	DESCRIPTION	FUNCTION
8.	Flexor Digiti Minimi Brevis	**FLEK**-sur dij-it-ty **MIN**-eh-mee **BREV**-us	Along the base of the small toe	Flexes the joint of the small toe
9.	Flexor Digitorum Brevis	**FLEK**-sur dij-ut-**TOHR**-um **BREV**-us	Across the ball of the foot beneath the toes	Flexes the toes
10.	Abductor Hallucis	ab-**DUK**-tohr ha-**LU**-sis	Runs along the interior border of the foot	Moves the big toe away from the other toes
11.	Abductor Digiti Minimi	ab-**DUK**-tohr dij-it-ty **MIN**-eh-mee	Runs along the outside border of the foot and connects to the heel	Moves the smallest toe away from the other toes

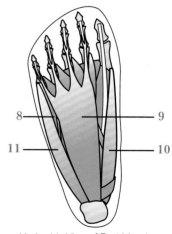

Underside View of Foot Muscles

Avoid Muscle Strain

No matter which direction you choose in your professional pursuit, you will be standing or sitting for long periods of time. You will need to find ways to relieve pressure and avoid muscle strain. For example, if you stand, shift your weight from time to time, or try to get up once an hour after a long time sitting. Use your muscles appropriately when you lift or reach for items to avoid muscle strain.

It is important to remember that the study of the muscular system will serve as a foundation for client care and services.

LESSONS LEARNED

The muscular system composes approximately 40% to 50% of the body's weight. The functions of the muscular system include supporting the skeleton, producing body movements, contouring the body and being involved in the function of other body systems, such as digestive and circulatory.

Muscles affected by massage are generally massaged from the insertion attachment to the origin attachment. Muscular tissue can be stimulated by using methods that include massage, electric current, temperature, nerve impulses and chemicals.

>> The structure and function of the scalp and face muscles can be identified by reviewing the appropriate charts and illustrations in this lesson.

>> The structure and function of the neck and back muscles can be identified by reviewing the appropriate charts and illustrations in this lesson.

>> The structure and function of the shoulder, chest, arm and hand muscles can be identified by reviewing the appropriate charts and illustrations in this lesson.

>> The structure and function of the leg and foot muscles can be identified by reviewing the appropriate charts and illustrations in this lesson.

Whose hearts do you think beat faster, women's or men's?

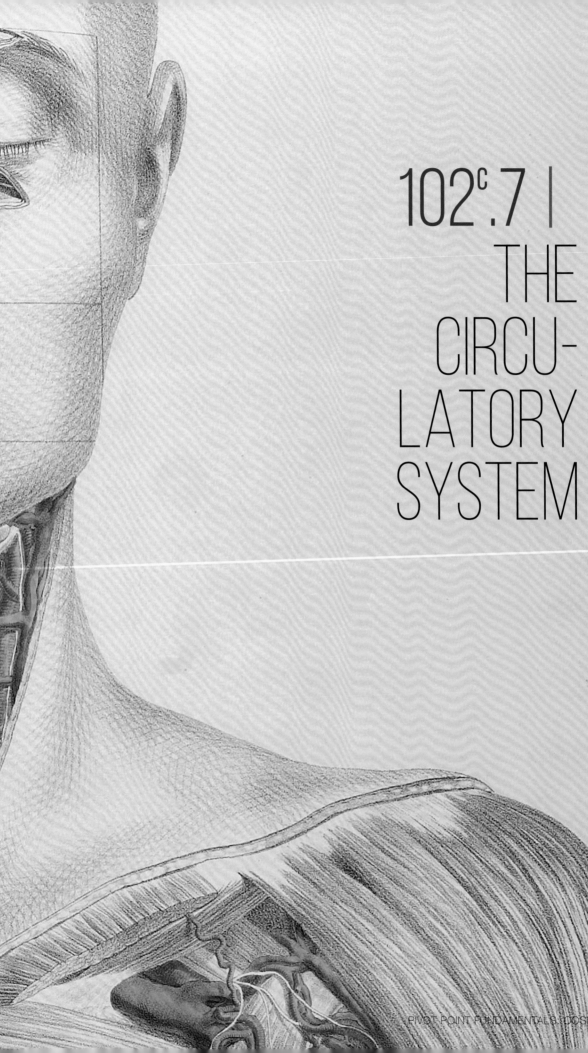

102ᶜ.7 |
THE CIRCU-
LATORY
SYSTEM

INSPIRE //

Knowing more about how the body works will help you provide the best care to your clients while delivering the salon services that help them look and feel their best.

ACHIEVE //

Following this lesson on *The Circulatory System*, you'll be able to:

>> State the structure and function of the cardiovascular system
>> Express how the heart forces blood to move through the circulatory system
>> Identify the purpose of the blood within the human body
>> Describe the blood vessels that circulate blood through the human body
>> Offer examples of names of arteries and veins in the human body
>> Explain the main function of the lymph-vascular system

FOCUS //

THE CIRCULATORY SYSTEM

The Cardiovascular System

The Lymph-Vascular System

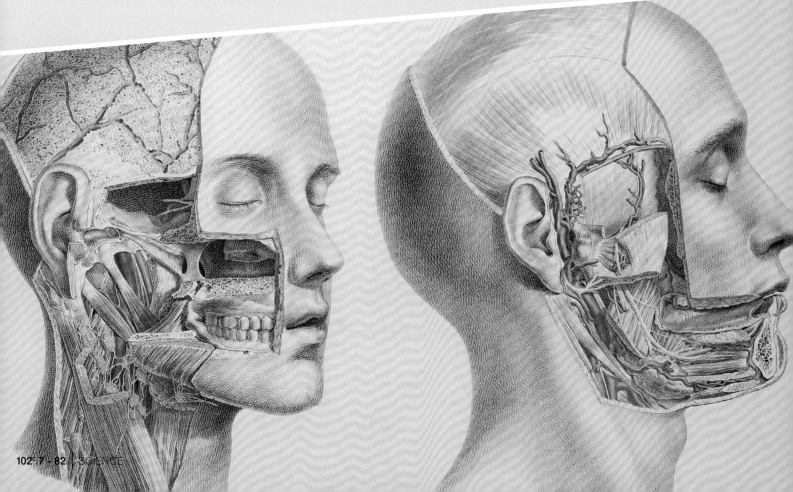

102ᶜ.7 | THE CIRCULATORY SYSTEM

Amazing Facts About the Circulatory System...

The heart beats about 100,000 times a day.

The heart beats around 3 billion times in the average person's life.

Within a tiny droplet of blood, there are some 5 million red blood cells.

It takes about 20 seconds for a red blood cell to circle the whole body.

The **circulatory** or **vascular system** controls the circulation of blood and lymph through the body. As a salon professional, you will use massage treatments that will directly influence or stimulate the circulatory system. The circulatory system is divided into two interrelated subsystems called:

1. The cardiovascular or blood-vascular system

   - Responsible for the circulation of blood

   - Includes the heart, arteries, veins and capillaries

2. The lymph-vascular system or lymphatic system

   - Responsible for the circulation of lymph

   - Includes lymph nodes (gland-like structures) and lymphatic vessels

The cardiovascular system, using arteries, veins and capillaries as blood-carrying vessels, combines with the lymph-vascular system to maintain steady circulation of the blood.

THE CARDIOVASCULAR SYSTEM

THE HEART

The heart, a cone-shaped muscular organ located in the chest cavity, is normally about the size of a closed fist. The rugged muscle of this organ, entirely encased in a membrane called the **pericardium** (per-i-**KAR**-de-um) (**1**), contracts and relaxes to force blood to move through the circulatory system.

The interior of the heart contains four chambers:

» **The upper chambers consist of the right atrium (AY-tree-um) (2) and the left atrium (3). The lower chambers consist of the right ventricle (VEN-tri-kel) (4) and the left ventricle (5).**

ID	MUSCLE/CHAMBER	PRONUNCIATION
1.	Pericardium	per-i-**KAR**-de-um
2.	Right Atrium	**AY**-tree-um
3.	Left Atrium	**AY**-tree-um
4.	Right Ventricle	**VEN**-tri-kel
5.	Left Ventricle	**VEN**-tri-kel

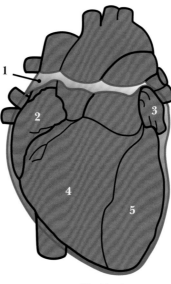

The Heart

THE BLOOD

Blood is the sticky, salty fluid that circulates through the body, bringing nourishment and oxygen to all body parts and carrying toxins and waste products to the liver and kidneys to be eliminated.

» On average, an adult has 8 to 10 pints of blood flowing through their circulatory system.

» The function of the blood is to:

▪ Transport oxygen, waste, nutrients and hormones

▪ Protect the body from the threat of infections and disease-causing bacteria, and, by using platelets that cause clotting of the blood, limit loss of blood

▪ Regulate the temperature, pH balance and blood pressure of the body

Plate 15.

Fig 1.

The average resting
heart rate is 60 to 100
beats per minute,
according to impulses
received from the
sympathetic nervous
system and the vagus
(10th cranial) nerve, which
regulate the heartbeat.

The blood consists of red and white corpuscles, platelets and plasma. The first two components, referred to as the blood cells, compose the semisolid part of the blood, along with the blood platelets. Additional details regarding these blood cells include:

1. **Red blood cells (RBCs) are also called erythrocytes** (e-**RITH**-ro-sitz) **or red corpuscles.** These cells carry oxygen and contain a protein called hemoglobin.

   ▪ **Hemoglobin** (**HE**-mo-glo-bin) attracts oxygen molecules through a process known as **oxygenation** (ok-si-je-**NA**-shun), which means "to combine with oxygen."

   ▪ The blood appears bright red in color when oxygen is being carried.

   ▪ As the red blood cell moves through the body, it releases oxygen molecules and collects molecules of carbon dioxide.

   ▪ When oxygen is low, the blood appears deep scarlet red.

2. **White blood cells (WBCs) are also called leukocytes** (**LOO**-ko-sitz) or white corpuscles. White blood cells:

   ▪ Fight bacteria and other foreign substances

   ▪ Increase in number when infection invades the body

3. **Blood platelets** (**PLAT**-letz) **or thrombocytes** (**THROM**-bo-sitz) **are responsible for the clotting of blood,** starting the process of coagulation (clotting) when they are exposed to air or rough surfaces (bruised skin).

4. **Plasma is the fluid part of the blood in which red and white blood cells and blood platelets are suspended, to be carried throughout the body by this liquid's flow.** Plasma makes up about 55% of the blood and consists of about 90% water.

Blood Vessels

Blood vessels are any vessels through which blood circulates through the body. There are three types of blood vessels:

» **Arteries** are tubular, elastic, thick-walled branching vessels that:

   ▪ Carry pure blood (blood containing oxygen and which is bright red in color) from the heart through the body

   ▪ Branch into smaller-diameter blood vessels called arterioles (ar-**TEER**-ee-ohls) that lead to capillaries

» **Veins** are tubular, elastic, thin-walled branching vessels that:

   ▪ Carry impure blood (blood containing carbon dioxide and which is dark red in color) from the capillaries to the heart

   ▪ Contain cup-like valves to prevent backflow

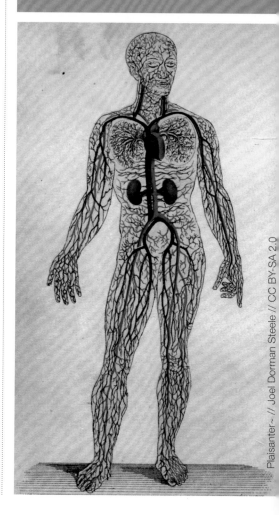

SALON**CONNECTION**

Varicose Veins

Varicose veins are bulges that might form if veins stretch and lose their elasticity. Salon professionals may experience varicose veins due to long periods of standing. Preventative measures such as support hose or socks and appropriate-size shoes are recommended.

- Are positioned closer to the outer surface of the body than arteries

- Receive blood back from the capillaries through small-diameter blood vessels called venules (**VEN**-yools)

>> **Capillaries** are small vessels that:

- Take nutrients and oxygen from the arteries to the cells

- Take waste products from the cells to the veins

Blood Flow Through the Heart

The process of blood traveling from the heart, throughout the body and back to the heart is referred to as systemic or general circulation and is described here:

>> Oxygen-poor blood enters the right atrium of the heart through the **superior vena cava** and **inferior vena cava**.

>> From the right atrium, blood is pumped through the **tricuspid** (tri-**KUS**-pid) valve into the right ventricle.

>> From the right ventricle, blood is pumped into the **pulmonary** (**PUL**-mo-ner-e) **artery**.

>> Blood travels through the pulmonary artery to the lungs, where it is oxygenated. This phase of the circulation of blood is referred to as **pulmonary circulation**.

>> From the lungs, the newly oxygenated blood returns to the heart via the pulmonary vein and enters the heart's left atrium.

>> Blood is pumped from the left atrium to the left ventricle by the bicuspid valve or mitral valve.

>> From the left ventricle, blood pumps through the aortic valve into the aorta.

>> Blood then flows from the aorta to other arteries, arterioles, capillaries, venules and veins as it circulates through the body, only to return and begin the circulatory process once again.

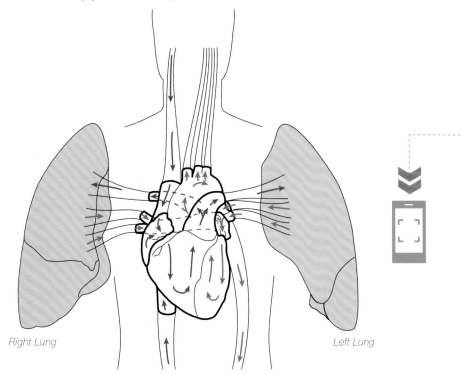

Right Lung

Left Lung

Blood Flow Through the Heart

ARTERIES AND VEINS OF THE FACE, HEAD AND NECK

ID	ARTERY/VEIN	PRONUNCIATION	DESCRIPTION
1.	Common Carotid Artery (CCA)	kah-**ROT**-id	Split into the internal and external carotid arteries; supplies blood to head, face and neck
2.	Internal Carotid Artery (ICA)	kah-**ROT**-id	Branch of common carotid artery; supplies blood to brain, eyes and forehead
	Supraorbital	su-prah-**OR**-bi-tal	Branch of internal carotid artery; supplies blood to parts of the forehead and eyes
	Infraorbital	in-fra-**OR**-bi-tal	Branch of internal carotid artery; supplies blood to the muscles of the eye region
3.	External Carotid Artery (ECA)	kah-**ROT**-id	Branch of common carotid arteries; splits into smaller arteries; supplies blood to skin and muscles of the head
4.	Internal Jugular Vein (IJV)	**JUG**-u-lur	Vein that returns all blood from the head, face and neck to the heart
5.	External Jugular Vein (EJV)	**JUG**-u-lur	Returns all blood from the head, face and neck to the heart
6.	Occipital	ak-**SIP**-et-el	Branch of the external carotid artery; supplies blood to back of the head, up to the crown
7.	Posterior Auricular	pos-**TER**-e-or aw-**RIK**-u-lur	Branch of the external carotid artery; supplies blood to scalp, above and behind the ears
8.	Superficial Temporal	su-pur-**FI**-shul **TEM**-po-ral	Branch of external carotid; branches into smaller arteries; supplies blood to sides and top of the head
	Frontal	**FRON**-tal	Branch of superficial temporal artery; supplies blood to the forehead
	Parietal	pah-**RI**-e-tal	Branch of superficial temporal artery; supplies blood to crown and sides of the head
	Middle Temporal	**TEM**-po-ral	Branch of superficial temporal artery; supplies blood to temples
	Transverse	trans-**VERS**	Branch of superficial temporal artery; supplies blood to the masseter muscle
	Anterior Auricular	an-**TER**-e-er aw-**RIK**-u-lur	Branch of superficial temporal artery; supplies blood to anterior part of the ear
9.	External Maxillary aka: Facial Artery	eks-**TUR**-nal **MAK**-si-ler-e	Breaks into smaller branches; supplies blood to lower portion of the face, including the mouth and nose
	Submental	sub-**MEN**-tal	Branch of external maxillary artery; supplies blood to chin and lower lip
	Inferior Labial	in-**FIR**-e-or **LA**-be-al	Branch of external maxillary artery; supplies blood to lower lip
	Angular	**ANG**-gu-lar	Branch of external maxillary artery; supplies blood to sides of nose
	Superior Labial	su-**PER**-e-or **LA**-be-al	Branch of external maxillary artery; supplies blood to upper lip and septum

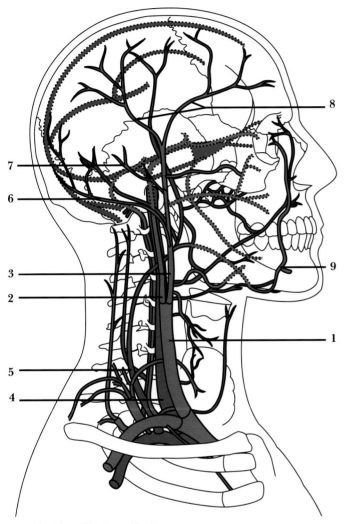

Side View of the Face, Head and Neck

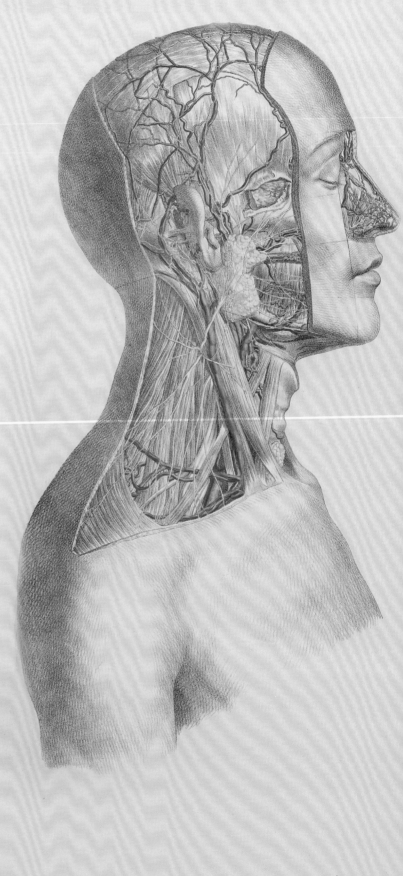

ARTERIES OF THE HAND AND ARM

ID	ARTERY	PRONUNCIATION	DESCRIPTION
1.	Ulnar	**UL**-nur	Supplies blood to little-finger side of the forearm and the smaller arteries in the hand
2.	Radial	**RAY**-dee-ul	Supplies blood to thumb side of the arm and hand

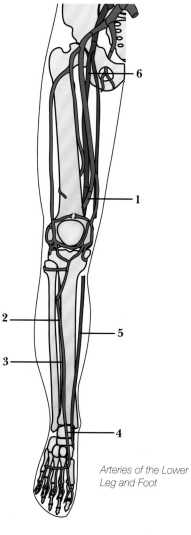

Arteries of the Hand and Arm

ARTERIES AND VEINS OF THE LOWER LEG AND FOOT

ID	ARTERY/VEIN	PRONUNCIATION	DESCRIPTION
1.	Popliteal	pop-lih-**TEE**-ul	Supplies blood to knee joint and muscles in the thigh and calf
2.	Anterior Tibial	an-**TER**-e-er **TIB**-ee-al	Supplies blood to just below the knee; passes down between the tibia and fibula to branch off into smaller arteries into the skin and muscles in the lower leg
3.	Posterior Tibial	pos-**TER**-e-or **TIB**-ee-al	Supplies blood beneath calf muscle to the skin, muscles and other tissues of the lower leg
4.	Dorsalis Pedis	**DOR**-sul-is **PEED**-is	Supplies blood to upper surface of the foot
5.	Saphenous Vein	sa-**FEEN**-us	Transports blood from veins in the foot to the femoral artery
6.	Femoral Vein	**FEM**-er-uhl	Transports blood to the heart and lungs for oxygenation

Arteries of the Lower Leg and Foot

THE LYMPH-VASCULAR SYSTEM

The **lymph-vascular system** (also referred to as the **lymphatic system**) is the second subsystem of the circulatory system and is responsible for picking up and returning leaked tissue fluid and plasma proteins to the cardiovascular system.

Other functions of the lymph-vascular system include:

>> Transporting nourishment from the blood to body cells and tissues

>> Carrying away from the tissues the products of metabolism and chemical change such as carbon dioxide, bacteria and certain fats from digestion

>> Helping maintain fluid balance

>> Distributing germ-fighting white blood cells to help develop immunity

Lymph is a colorless liquid produced as a byproduct in the process of plasma passing nourishment to capillaries and cells that travels through lymph vessels—thin-walled, valved structures—which help maintain blood volume and pressure.

Lymph nodes filter foreign particles from the lymph vessels. Swollen or tender lymph nodes indicate infection in the body.

>> Lymph nodes act as barriers to infection from one part of the body to another.

>> As the lymph nodes take on this protective task, they may swell and cause pain.

>> Lymph nodes most often affected in this way are in the neck and under the arms.

>> Many other circumstances may be causing the swelling. Consult a doctor at the first sign of any swelling in these areas.

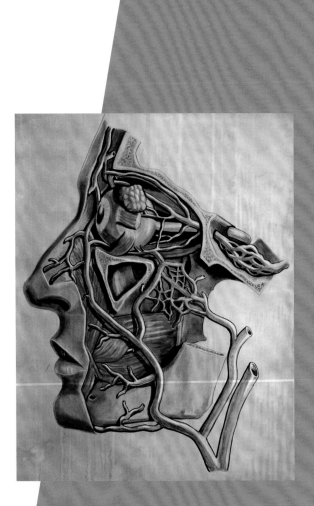

DISCOVER**MORE**

Unlike the blood flow in the circulatory system, the lymphatic system does not possess any pumping organ for the movement of lymph through its network of channels. Pressure created from muscle movement and the heartbeat assists the smooth movement of lymph fluid.

Remember,
as a salon
professional,
you have the
ability to directly
influence or
stimulate the
circulatory system
by using massage
treatments.

LESSONS LEARNED

The cardiovascular system is composed of the heart, arteries, veins and capillaries and is responsible for the circulation of blood.

The heart forces blood to move through the circulatory system by contracting and relaxing.

The purpose of the blood within the human body is to carry nourishment and oxygen to all body parts and carry toxins and waste products to the kidneys and liver to be eliminated.

The blood vessels that circulate blood through the human body are arteries, veins and capillaries.

Review the labeled artery and vein illustrations in this lesson.

The main function of the lymph-vascular system is to pick up leaked tissue fluid and plasma proteins and return them to the cardiovascular system.

102^c.8 | THE NERVOUS SYSTEM

EXPLORE //

How many thoughts do you think you have in any given day?

>>

INSPIRE //

Your knowledge of the nervous system and how it responds to massage movements will help you, as a salon professional, relax and soothe your clients' tight and fatigued muscles.

ACHIEVE //

Following this lesson on *The Nervous System*, you'll be able to:

>> Describe the structure and function of the central nervous system

>> Explain the structure and function of the peripheral nervous system

>> Offer examples of names of nerves found in the peripheral nervous system

>> Describe the structure and function of the autonomic nervous system

FOCUS //

THE NERVOUS SYSTEM

The Central Nervous System

The Peripheral Nervous System

The Autonomic Nervous System

Amazing Facts About the Nervous System...

>> The speed of message transmission to the brain can be as high as 250 miles per hour.

>> Sphenopalatine ganglioneuralgia is the scientific name for brain freeze.

>> It is thought that a yawn works to send more oxygen to the brain, therefore working to cool it down and wake it up.

>> Most people dream about 1-2 hours a night and have an average of 4-7 dreams each night.

The study of the nervous system is called neuroscience. The nervous system coordinates and controls the operation of the human body.

The nervous system is divided into three subsystems:

1. The central or cerebrospinal nervous system

2. The peripheral nervous system

3. The autonomic nervous system

Primary components of the nervous system include the brain, spinal cord and nerves. The components of the nervous system, operating in harmony, receive and interpret stimuli and send messages from the nerve cell to the appropriate tissues, muscles and organs.

THE CENTRAL NERVOUS SYSTEM

The central or cerebrospinal nervous system is composed of the brain, spinal cord and spinal and cranial nerves. The central nervous system is responsible for all voluntary body action.

THE BRAIN AND SPINAL CORD

The **brain** controls the nervous system. For that reason, the brain is referred to as the command center. The average adult human brain weighs between 45 and 49 ounces.

The **spinal cord**, composed of long nerve fibers, originates in the base of the brain and extends to the base of the spine. The spinal cord holds 31 pairs of spinal nerves that branch out to muscles, internal organs and skin.

THE PERIPHERAL NERVOUS SYSTEM

The **peripheral** (pe-**RIF**-ur-al) nervous system is composed of sensory and motor nerves that extend from the brain and spinal cord to other parts of the body. This network of nerve cells carries messages to and from the central nervous system.

Nerve cells:

>> Like other cells, the **nerve cell** or **neuron** (**NU**-ron) has a nucleus, cytoplasm (**SI**-to-plazm) and membrane.

>> Nerve cells differ in appearance from other cells due to long and short threadlike fibers called axons and dendrites that extend from the cell.

   ▪ Axons (**AK**-sonz) (**1**) take information away from the cell body in the form of nerve impulses

   ▪ Dendrites (**DEN**-dritz) (**2**) bring information to the cell body

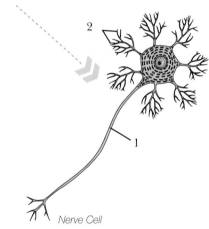

Nerve Cell

TYPES OF NERVES

Nerves or nerve tissues perform two basic functions.

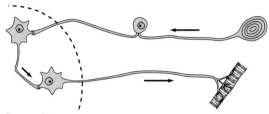

Sensory Nerve

>> **Sensory** or **afferent nerves** carry messages to the brain and spinal cord.

   ▪ **Receptors** (sensory nerve endings) send sensory messages like touch, temperature, sight, sound, taste, smell, pain and pressure to the brain for processing.

Motor Nerve

>> **Motor** or **efferent nerves** carry messages from the brain to the muscles and glands.

   ▪ When the brain sends a message, motor nerves receive the message and cause a muscle to contract or expand.

   ▪ Motor nerves cross over from one side of the body to the other at the top of the spinal cord.

   ▪ Signals from the right side of the brain go to the left side of the body and vice versa.

Sensory and motor nerves can work together or independently. For example, if you want to pick up a pen, the brain simply sends a message to the motor nerves of your hand. This is a conscious decision. You are in control of your hand movement. However, remember the last time you accidentally touched a hot curling iron? Your sensory nerves sent a rapid message to your brain, transmitting the sensation you experienced. Your brain immediately responded by sensing pain and sending impulses back to motor nerves to move your hand away. This interaction of sensory and motor nerves is called a **reflex action**.

DISCOVER**MORE**

The dendrite system is similar to over a million interstate highways traveling back and forth from nerve cell to nerve cell. Certain activities, such as harmful narcotic drugs or a prolonged lack of oxygen, can close the highways down, never to open again.

FACE, HEAD AND NECK NERVES

Two of the 12 pairs of cranial nerves exert primary control in the areas of the face, head and neck: the trifacial (trigeminal or 5th cranial) nerve and the facial (7th cranial) nerve

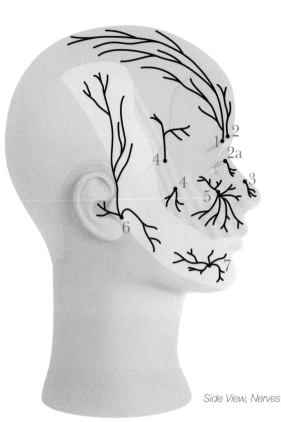

Side View, Nerves

Trifacial Nerve

The largest of the cranial nerves, the **trifacial (trigeminal or 5th cranial) nerve, is the chief sensory nerve** primarily responsible for transmitting facial sensations to the brain and for controlling the motor nerve function of chewing (mastication). The trifacial nerve divides into three main branches.

The **ophthalmic** (of-**THAL**-mik) branch is the main nerve branch to the top ⅓ of the face, which further divides into:

ID	NERVE	PRONUNCIATION	DESCRIPTION
1.	Supraorbital	soo-pra-**OR**-bi-tal	Extends to the skin of the upper eyelid, eyebrow, forehead and scalp
2.	Supratrochlear	soo-pra-**TRO**-klee-ur	Extends to the skin of the upper side of the nose and between the eyes
2a.	Infratrochlear	in-fra-**TRO**-klee-ur	Emerges on the skin of the upper eyelid and side of the nose
3.	Nasal	**NA**-zal	Extends to the tip and lower side of the nose

The **maxillary** (**MAK**-si-ler-e) branch is the main nerve branch to the middle ⅓ of the face, which further divides into:

ID	NERVE	PRONUNCIATION	DESCRIPTION
4.	Zygomatic	zi-go-**MAT**-ik	Extends to the side of the forehead, temple and upper part of the cheek
5.	Infraorbital	**IN**-fra-or-bi-tal	Extends to the lower eyelid, side of the nose, upper lip and mouth

The **mandibular** (man-**DIB**-u-lur) branch is the main nerve branch to the lower ⅓ of the face and further divides into:

ID	NERVE	PRONUNCIATION	DESCRIPTION
6.	Auriculotemporal	aw-**RIK**-u-lo-**TEM**-po-ral	Extends to the ear and to the area from the top of the head to the temple
7.	Mental	**MEN**-tal	Extends to the lower lip and chin

Facial Nerve

The facial (7th cranial) nerve emerges from the brain at the lower part of the ear and is the primary motor nerve of the face. The facial nerve controls muscles of facial expression and sensation from the skin and tongue. Of its many branches, six are of particular importance.

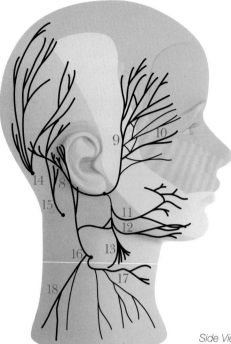

Side View, Nerves

ID	NERVE	PRONUNCIATION	DESCRIPTION
8.	Posterior Auricular	pos-**TER**-e-er aw-**RIK**-u-lur	Extends to the muscles behind and below the ear
9.	Temporal	**TEM**-po-ral	Extends to the muscles of the temple, the side of the forehead, the eyebrow, eyelid and upper cheek
10.	Zygomatic (Upper and Lower)	zi-go-**MAT**-ik	Extends to the upper muscles of the cheek
11.	Buccal	**BUK**-al	Extends to the muscles of the mouth
12.	Marginal Mandibular	mahr-**JUH**-nal man-**DIB**-u-lur	Extends to the muscles of the chin and lower lip
13.	Cervical	**SUR**-vi-kal	Extends to the muscles on the side of the neck and platysma muscle

Other cervical nerves originate in the spinal cord with branches into the back of the head and neck.

ID	NERVE	PRONUNCIATION	DESCRIPTION
14.	Greater Occipital	ak-**SIP**-et-el	Extends up the back of the scalp to the top of the head
15.	Lesser Occipital	ak-**SIP**-et-el	Extends into the muscles at the back of the skull
16.	Greater Auricular	aw-**RIK**-u-lur	Extends into the side of the neck and external ear
17.	Cervical Cutaneous	**SUR**-vi-kal ku-**TA**-ne-us	Extends into the side and front of the neck to the breastbone

The 11th cranial nerve is affected when using massage movements during a facial.

ID	NERVE	PRONUNCIATION	DESCRIPTION
18.	Accessory	ac-**CES**-sory	Extends into the sternocleidomastoid and trapezius muscle

ARM AND HAND NERVES

The primary nerves found in the arm and/or hand transmit sensations to the brain and carry impulses from the brain to the muscles.

ID	NERVE	PRONUNCIATION	DESCRIPTION
1.	Ulnar	**UL**-nur	Extends down the little-finger side of the arm into the palm of the hand
2.	Radial	**RAY**-de-ul	Extends down the thumb side of the arm into the back of the hand
3.	Median	**ME**-de-un	Extends down the mid-forearm into the hand
4.	Digital	**DIJ**-i-tul	Extends into the fingers of the hand //

Arm and Hand Nerves

LOWER LEG AND FOOT NERVES

The nerves of the leg and foot help move the body through the actions of the legs, feet and toes while maintaining balance when the body is moving or at rest.

ID	NERVE	PRONUNCIATION	DESCRIPTION
1.	Sciatic	sy-**AT**-ik	Begins in the lower back and runs through the buttock and down the lower limb
2.	Tibial	**TIB**-ee-al	Passes behind the knee and the common peroneal nerve
3.	Common Peroneal	per-oh-**NEE**-al	Runs alongside the sciatic nerve from the femur to the buttocks, then ventures further down on its own along the knee and behind the fibula. The nerve then splits inside the neck of the fibula into the deep peroneal and superficial peroneal.
4.	Deep Peroneal aka Anterior Tibial	per-oh-**NEE**-al an-**TER**-e-er **TIB**-e-al	A branch of the common peroneal
5.	Superficial Peroneal	su-pur-**FI**-shul per-oh-**NEE**-al	A branch of the common peroneal
6.	Dorsal	**DOR**-sul	The superficial nerve simply sits closer to the skin than the deep nerve and becomes the dorsal nerve
7.	Saphenous	sa-**FEEN**-us	Begins in the thigh
8.	Sural	**SUR**-ul	Runs down the back of the leg to the outside of the foot and little toe //

Anterior   *Posterior*

SALON**CONNECTION**

Nerves and Massage

The nerves of the face, head, neck, hands and feet may be stimulated during facials and/or massage. During massage services, movements can stimulate sensitive nerve tissues, resulting in nerve impulses that expand and contract corresponding muscles. Through this process, tight muscles can be relaxed; fatigued muscles can be soothed.

THE AUTONOMIC NERVOUS SYSTEM

The **autonomic** (aw-to-**NOM**-ik) nervous system is responsible for all involuntary body functions. The autonomic system operates the digestive, excretory, respiratory, circulatory, endocrine and reproductive systems. The circulatory system can be found in a separate lesson, while the other involuntary systems are briefly explained in this lesson.

THE DIGESTIVE SYSTEM

The digestive system, also known as the gastrointestinal system, breaks food down into simpler chemical compounds that can be easily absorbed by cells or, if not absorbed, eliminated from the body in waste products.

>> The digestive process begins as soon as food is ingested, when **enzymes** (**EN**-zimz) secreted by the **salivary** (**SAL**-i-ver-e) glands (**1**) start breaking down the food.

>> Food travels down the **pharynx** (**FAR**-ingks) (**2**) and through the **esophagus** (e-**SOF**-ah-gus) (**3**) into the stomach (**4**), propelled by a twisting and turning motion of the esophagus called **peristalsis** (per-i-**STAL**-sis). In the stomach, **hydrochloric** (hi-dro-**KLO**-rik) acids and several other enzymes further break down food.

   ▨ One of these other enzymes, pepsin, is responsible for the breakdown of protein into polypeptide (pol-e-**PEP**-tide) molecules and free amino acids, which are particularly important to the production of hair, skin and nails.

>> As partially digested food passes from the stomach into the **small intestine** (**5**), the assimilation of nutrients begins.

   ▨ Nutrients are absorbed by the **villi** (**VIL**-i), which are fingerlike projections of the intestine walls, and transported through the circulatory system to the tissues and cells of the body.

>> Undigested food passes into the **large intestine** (**6**), or colon, which stores the waste for eventual elimination through the anal canal.

   ▨ This process of digestion takes about nine hours to complete. **Happiness and relaxation promote good digestion**. Good digestion helps keep all other bodily functions on track.

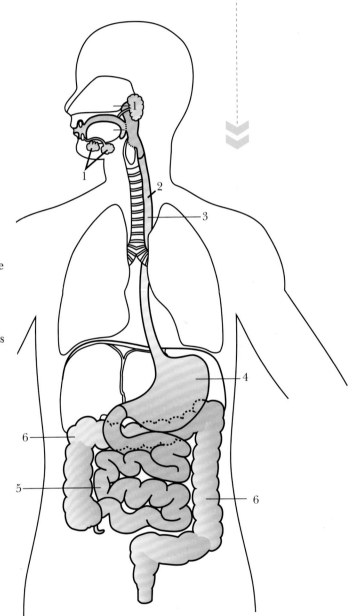

Digestive System

THE EXCRETORY SYSTEM

The excretory system eliminates solid, liquid and gaseous waste products from the body.
Organs of the excretory system include:

>> The **skin** covers nearly 20 square feet of body surface and is the body's largest organ. The skin releases water, carbon dioxide and other waste through the sweat glands.

>> The **liver** converts and neutralizes ammonia from the circulatory system to **urea** (u-RE-ah). Urea is then carried, through the bloodstream, to the kidneys for excretion.

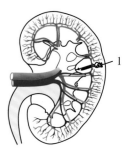

>> The **kidneys** receive urea from the liver and then pass the urea through small tubelike structures known as **nephrons** (**NEF**-ronz) (**1**). Nephrons filter waste products and water, allowing usable nutrients to be reabsorbed into the blood. Excreted waste products travel through the **ureter** (**U**-re-tur) and bladder and are eliminated from the body in urine.

Illustrations of Skin, Liver, Kidney, in Order, from Top to Bottom

THE RESPIRATORY SYSTEM

The respiratory system is made up of organs and tissues that help you breathe. **The primary functions of the respiratory system are:**

>> **The intake of oxygen to be absorbed into the blood**

>> **The exhalation of oxygen's toxic byproduct, carbon dioxide**

Both of these functions take place every time you take a breath. While it is possible to breathe through both the mouth and the nose, breathing through the nose is the healthier option. The nose contains mucus membranes, to filter out dust and dirt, and warms the inhaled air as it travels through the nasal passages.

Primary respiratory system organs:

1. The **lungs** are spongy organs composed of cells into which air enters when you inhale. These cells process oxygen for absorption into the blood and release carbon dioxide as you exhale.

2. The **diaphragm** is a muscular organ that separates the chest cavity from the abdomen. The diaphragm expands and contracts automatically, forcing air into and out of the lungs. //

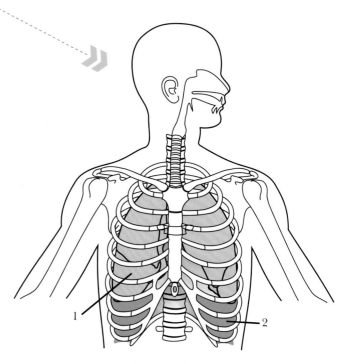

Respiratory System

THE ENDOCRINE SYSTEM

The endocrine system is composed of a group of specialized ductless glands that regulate and control the growth, reproduction and health of the body. These glands manufacture chemical substances called hormones and secrete them directly into the bloodstream. For example, the thyroid gland is a ductless gland that is responsible for making and storing hormones that help regulate the heart rate, blood pressure, body temperature and the rate at which food is converted into energy.

The endocrine system directly affects hair growth, skin conditions and energy levels. **Signs of fatigue or changes in hair growth may signal the need for medical attention.**

THE REPRODUCTIVE SYSTEM

The reproductive system is responsible for the process by which a living organism procreates. Estrogen and testosterone are two hormones produced by the reproductive system that have the ability to influence skin conditions such as acne, hair growth and hair color.

LESSONS LEARNED

» The central nervous system is composed of the brain, spinal cord and cranial nerves that are responsible for all voluntary body actions.

» The peripheral nervous system is composed of sensory and motor nerves from the brain and spinal cord that extend to other parts of the body, and its function is to carry messages to and from the central nervous system.

» Review the nerve illustrations in this lesson. Some nerves in the peripheral nervous system include trifacial nerves—such as the opthalmic branch—and facial nerves—such as the zygomatic branch.

» The autonomic nervous system operates the digestive, excretory, respiratory, circulatory, endocrine and reproductive systems. It is responsible for all involuntary body functions.

102ᶜ.9 |
PRINCIPLES OF ELECTRICITY

EXPLORE //

Have you experienced a situation where you were without electricity?

INSPIRE //

Salon professionals are expected to safely and efficiently use electrical appliances.

ACHIEVE //

Following this lesson on *Principles of Electricity*, you'll be able to:

>> Define major terms related to principles in electricity

>> Describe direct current and alternating current

>> Compare an electrical overload with an electrical short circuit

>> Explain safety measures that are related to electricity

FOCUS //

PRINCIPLES OF ELECTRICITY

Vocabulary of Electricity

Electric Current

Safety Measures

102ᶜ.9 | PRINCIPLES OF ELECTRICITY

Electricity is a powerful and important form of energy. Anyone who has ever watched lightning in a stormy sky has seen its power. Anyone who has felt an electric shock knows what that power feels like. The power of electrical energy is essential in modern life; no salon could function without it. As a salon professional, you aren't expected to develop the knowledge and skills of an electrician, just an understanding of electricity's basic principles and its important uses in your work.

VOCABULARY OF ELECTRICITY

Jump-start your understanding of electricity by keeping this list handy as you move through this lesson.

TOP 10 ELECTRICITY TERMS

1.	Electricity	A form of energy that produces light, heat and magnetic and chemical changes
2.	Electric current	The movement of electricity along a path called a conductor
3.	Load	A technical name for any electrically powered appliance
4.	Conductor	Material that allows electricity to flow through it easily
5.	Insulator	A material that does not allow the flow of electric current
6.	Amp	A unit of electric strength
7.	Volt	A unit of electric pressure
8.	Ohm	A unit of electric resistance
9.	Watt	A measure of how much electrical energy (power) is being used per second
10.	Kilowatt	1,000 watts = 1 kilowatt

ELECTRICITY AND ELECTRIC CURRENT

Electricity is a form of energy that produces light, heat and magnetic and chemical changes.

» Most of the electricity you use daily consists of a flow of tiny, negatively charged particles called **electrons**.

» The flow of electrons is called an **electric current**, which moves along a path called a conductor.

» Electrons must always be flowing to have current.

LOADS, CONDUCTORS AND INSULATORS

A salon is full of **loads** (electrically powered appliances) just waiting to be activated by the flow of electric current. Think of all the blow dryers, curling irons and clippers that need electrical energy to work.

The materials that best transport electricity are called conductors.

» The best conductors are silver and copper.

» Other metals, graphite, carbon and water-containing ions allow current to flow as well.

» Since the human body is composed of approximately 60% water, it too can be a conductor.

The purpose of a conductor is to transport current in a circuit to a load. This conductor is safely contained in an **insulator, which is a material that does not allow a current to pass through it**.

» Insulators protect you from electric current and allow you to handle electricity safely.

» Examples of insulating materials include silk, plastic, rubber, wood, glass, paper, air, brick, cloth and certain liquids such as alcohol, oil and pure distilled water.

» Most currents in the salon are carried by copper wire (conductors) insulated with varying amounts of rubber.

» You know this combination of conductor and insulator as a cord. *Cords on appliances should be kept straight and free of knots, kinks and tangles to prevent breaks.*

» **A break in any electrical cord can put you or your client in contact with an active current, causing electric shock.**

AMP

An amp or ampere is a unit of electric *strength*. The amp rating indicates the number of electrons flowing on a line.

» Your house has a power box with a certain number of amps coming to it that enables you to use all the appliances in the house. The conductors (wires) in your home have the ability to carry a limited number of amps at a time. Circuits will have 10, 20, 30 or larger amp ratings.

» When buying or remodeling an older building, you may have to have new power lines laid to run the appliances in the building. Through the years, additional uses for electricity, such as the microwave, clothes dryer, computer, etc., have increased the amp requirements for the modern home.

» One ampere equals 1,000 milliamperes.

VOLT

A volt, also called voltage, is a unit of electric *pressure*. In simple terms, a volt measures how hard the electrons are being forced or pushed by the source. AC generators force or push 120 or 240 volts in a circuit.

» Normal wall sockets of 120 volts power small appliances.

» Large motors, such as those found in clothes dryers and air conditioners, may require the higher electric pressure of 240 volts to operate properly.

» The 240-volt sockets look different from standard wall sockets in that the prongs that plug into the wall are generally round and pointed into the shape of a "v" at the end.

» This precaution reduces the danger of someone attempting to plug a 240-volt appliance into a 120-volt wall socket.

» The cord carrying 240-volt current is also much thicker, and there is a higher cost to install lines that carry higher-voltage currents.

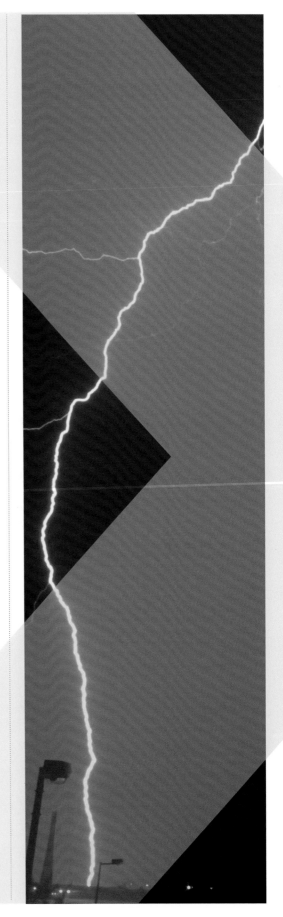

OHM

An ohm is a unit of electric *resistance*. A German physicist named Georg Ohm discovered that every conductor has a specific rate at which it will allow electrons to move through it.

» **The measure of how difficult it is to push electrons through a conductor is called resistance.**

» Three things determine the amount of resistance in a conductor: its size, its material (such as copper or aluminum) and its temperature.

  ▪ A conductor's resistance increases as its length increases or diameter decreases.

  ▪ The more conductive the materials used, the lower the conductor resistance becomes.

  ▪ A rise in temperature will generally increase resistance in a conductor.

WATT

A watt is a measure of how much electrical energy (power) is being used per second. One watt is a small amount of energy. A blow dryer can use 1,000 watts per second. A light bulb can use 25, 60 or 100 watts per second. You can use thousands of watts in a short time.

» To deal with these large numbers, the power company describes watt use in larger terms: 1,000 watts equal one **kilowatt**. With many appliances on at one time, thousands of kilowatts can be used in a short time.

» The power company defines the energy used in hourly terms.

| Amp = strength |
| Volt = pressure |
| Ohm = resistance |
| Watt = electricity used |

DISCOVER**MORE**

A generator is built to cycle at a specific rate. The rate of cycling, or frequency (hertz), is measured in cycles per second. In the United States, generators are built at a frequency of 60 cycles per second, or 60 hertz (60 Hz). The nameplate of an appliance will indicate the frequency of the source into which the appliance must be plugged to operate safely.

Appliances from other countries have different hertz (Hz) or cycle ratings and cannot be operated in the U.S. without an adapter. The same is true of appliances made for the U.S. but taken out of the country.

SALON**CONNECTION**

Electric Bill

If you turned on a 500-watt dryer and let it run for 8 hours, you would have used 4,000 (500 x 8 = 4,000) watt hours (or 4 kilowatt hours) of power. You pay the electric company so many cents per kilowatt hour used. Energy conservation is important to the salon. When not in use, appliances should be turned off and stored safely.

❯ ELECTRIC CURRENT

Electric current exists in two forms:

1. **DC, or direct current, in which electrons move at an even rate and flow in only one direction.**

2. **AC, or alternating current, in which electrons flow first in one direction and then in the other.**

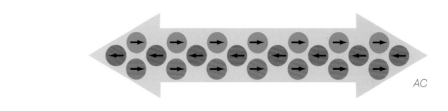

DC

AC

Special instruments can be used to change alternating current (AC) to direct current (DC) or direct current to alternating current.

›› An **inverter** changes direct current (DC) to alternating current (AC). An example of an inverter at work is the mobile phone charger in your car. A car battery runs on a direct current, and the mobile phone cord (and plug) converts the DC to AC to charge the mobile phone.

›› A **rectifier** changes alternating current (AC) to direct current (DC). An example of using a rectifier would be the block that's between the wall plug (AC) and your computer that transforms AC to DC to charge the computer's battery. The block (rectifier) is sometimes referred to as a power adapter for the computer.

The nameplate of an appliance tells:

›› Frequency (Hz) needed
›› Volts needed (120 or 240V)
›› Watts appliance consumes per second (100W, 200W, etc.)

It may also have a UL or Underwriters Laboratories designation. A **UL rating** means the appliance has been certified to operate safely under the conditions the instructions specify. Look for these ratings on your tools.

SOURCES OF ELECTRIC CURRENT

Electrons cannot move through a conductor without help. A **source** provides the force to move the electrons in the conducting material. Two common sources of electric current are batteries and generators.

›› A **battery** has a positive terminal (+) and a negative terminal (-) and produces direct current only.

›› A **generator** is the power source most often used in a salon. Generators produce alternating current. When you want to turn on a dryer, you plug it into a wall socket. The wall socket itself is not the source of current. The source is the generator, a machine many miles away, which uses mechanical energy to produce a flow of electrons. The generator pumps huge numbers of electrons into power lines that bring electricity to homes and businesses.

HOW ELECTRIC CURRENT IS PRODUCED

Two conditions must exist for electric current to be produced.

» First, as you just read, there must be a source.

  ▪ Generator producing alternating current

  ▪ Battery producing direct current

» Second, there must be a closed path, called a **circuit**, through which the electrons travel.

▪ A **closed circuit** is a path of electron flow from the source to operate an appliance.

» When this path is broken, it is called an **open circuit**. If you plug in a blow dryer and turn it on, and air begins to flow, you have an example of a closed or completed circuit. When you turn the switch off, the circuit breaks and is now an open circuit.

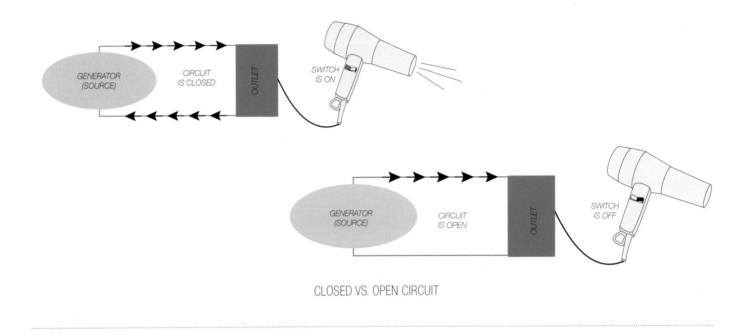

CLOSED VS. OPEN CIRCUIT

There are two ways circuits can be connected to power loads.

» **Parallel wiring** allows the user to power several loads at different times or at once. With parallel wiring, a blow dryer and curling iron can be plugged into the same circuit. Each can be run alone, or both can be run at once. In the salon, only parallel wiring should be installed.

» **Series wiring** forces the user to have all loads running at the same time since the circuit travels from one load to the next.

  ▪ An example of series wiring would be many connected strings of Christmas tree lights. If one string of lights is malfunctioning, the electric current cannot flow to the next string. The malfunction causes an open circuit, and none of the strings work.

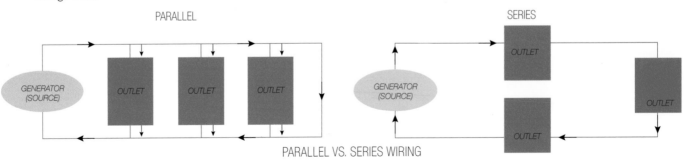

PARALLEL VS. SERIES WIRING

OVERLOAD AND SHORT CIRCUIT

When a building is constructed, an electrician normally wires it with a certain number of circuits (each capable of carrying 20 or 30 amps). When you turn on an appliance, such as a blow dryer, the appliance causes current to flow on the line to meet its power needs. A problem can occur when too many appliances are put on one circuit and are operated at the same time. More current flows than the line is designed to carry. This situation is called an **overload**. Although there are safety devices to detect overloading, they can fail. If they do, the lines of the circuit will heat up and may burn.

In general, it takes 1 amp on the circuit to operate every 100 watts of an appliance. So, to operate a 1,000-watt blow dryer, a 10-amp circuit is required.

» If you operated a 1,000-watt dryer on a 5-amp circuit, it would overload.

» **Fires can occur when an extension cord with multiple plugs is used to attach four or five appliances to one wall socket.** If all the appliances are turned on, that extension cord (if not rated for the amps flowing) can melt and burn in seconds. Hiring a qualified electrician is essential to install adequate wiring.

» The number of amps demanded by each appliance (dryers, air conditioner, washer) during a normal working day must be determined to safely predict the number of amps a salon needs.

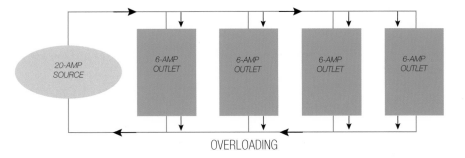

OVERLOADING

102°.9 // PRINCIPLES OF ELECTRICITY

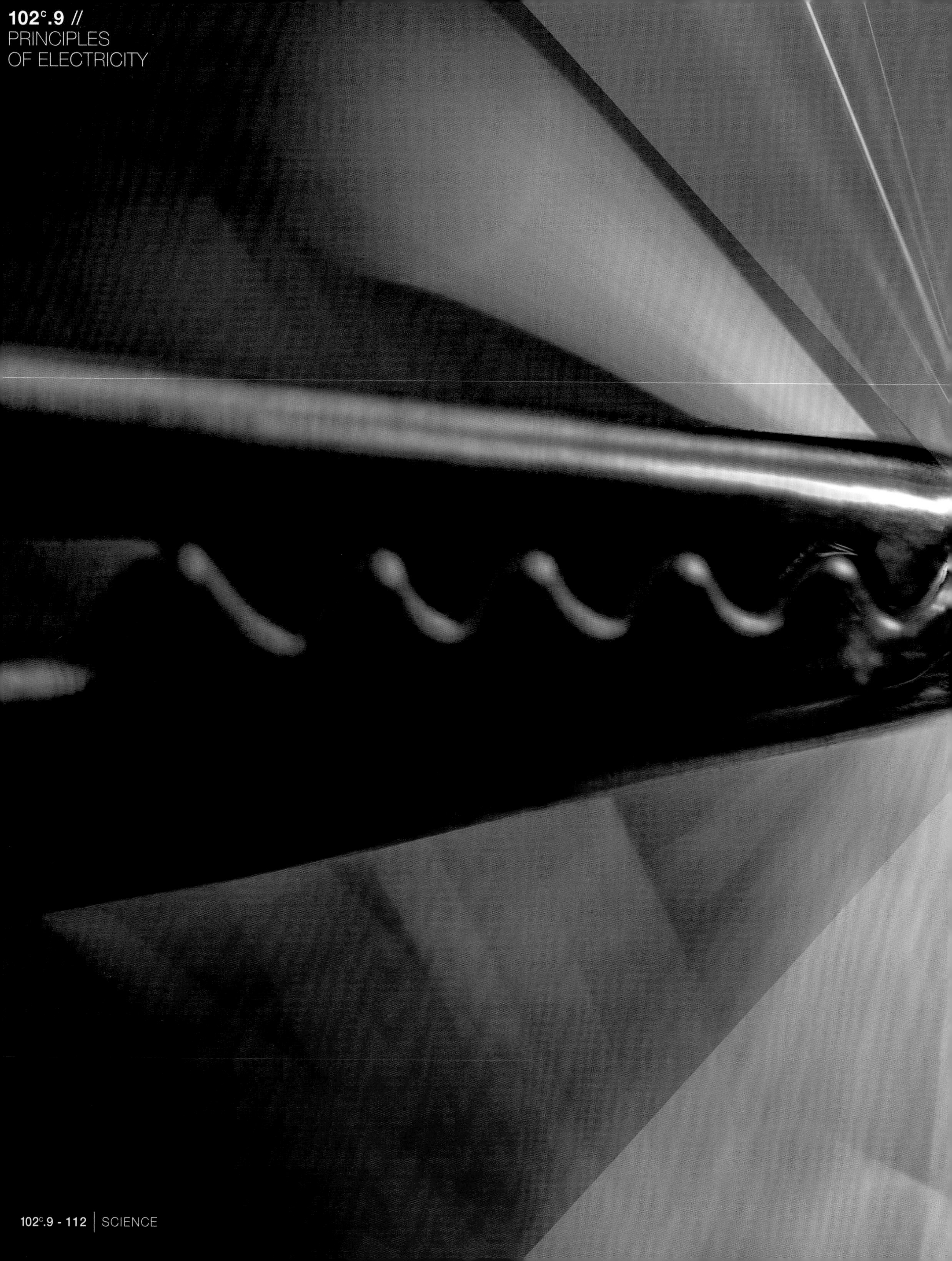

A second problem that frequently occurs in the salon is called a short circuit. A **short circuit** can occur anytime a foreign conductor comes in contact with a wire carrying current to a load (appliance).

» A classic short circuit occurs when someone tries to plug in an appliance and gets a finger between the wall socket and the plug. The finger becomes the foreign conductor and receives the electric current instead of the appliance for which the current was intended.

» Dropping an appliance into water will cause the current to flow through the water, which in this case is a foreign conductor. If you tried to retrieve the appliance while it was still on, you would be electrocuted. With dry hands, remove the plug from the wall socket first.

» Short circuits occur commonly in thermal styling tool cords. Twisting and bending cords can eventually break the copper wires. If you touch the break, you'll get an electric shock.

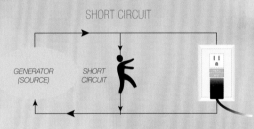

SHORT CIRCUIT

GENERATOR
(SOURCE)

SHORT
CIRCUIT

»» Alert!
Electric shock can be fatal.

❯ SAFETY MEASURES

Because of the possibility of overloads and short circuits, safety devices are installed in many appliances and buildings. Two of these devices, fuses and circuit breakers, connect directly to the circuits in the power box, the carefully insulated location where the electric current enters a building from a generator or power plant. From the power box, many circuits continue throughout the building.

FUSE

A fuse is a safety device that contains a fine metal wire that allows current to flow through it. If an overload occurs (too much current flowing), the fuse will heat up and the wire will melt, breaking the circuit and cutting the flow of electricity. Fuses cannot be reused. A new fuse of the same amp rating (10, 20 or 30) must be installed.

Installing a new fuse:

1. Turn off all appliances operating on that circuit.

2. Go to the power box and turn off the main power handle on the side of the box. (Wearing insulated rubber gloves is recommended.)

3. Remove the burned-out fuse and replace it with a new one.

4. Close the box and switch on the main power handle.

SALON**CONNECTION**

Power Box

It will be wise to become familiar with the power box in the salon.

- Know where it is and how to operate it safely.

- If the salon still has fuses, it's a good idea to have extra fuses on hand.

- Each circuit should be clearly labeled, and you should have a flashlight available in case it is dark when a circuit breaks.

Circuit Breakers

GROUNDING

Today, most electrical outlets are polarized. These polarized outlets feature two slots of different sizes and are designed so the slot for the neutral wire is wider than the slot for the hot wire, making it difficult to insert an electrical plug the wrong way. When used with a polarized plug or prong, these outlets provide protection by keeping the electric current directed. This is referred to as a 2-plug or prong system.

A 3-plug or prong system features grounded outlets with a round hole for the grounding conductor in addition to the two vertical slots. The circle slot is connected to a ground wire. The 3-plug system offers the most protection when it comes to grounding.

2-Prong Electrical Cord

3-Prong Electrical Cord

CIRCUIT BREAKER

A **circuit breaker** is simply a reusable safety device that breaks the flow of current when an overload occurs. It contains two pieces of metal that make contact with each other. Like a fuse, these pieces of metal conduct electric current unless too much current flows on the line. If the flow is too high, there is a heat-sensing device that causes the two pieces to separate, and the circuit is broken. Most new buildings use the circuit breaker, which works like a switch. Instead of burning out, the circuit breaker turns the switch off. You just need to turn it back on to make the circuit work again.

To restore power when circuit breakers are being used:

1. Turn off appliances.

2. Go to the power box and open it.

3. Find a row of switches that look just like wall light switches.

4. Look for a switch that has a color marker (red or yellow) showing. Turn this switch completely to the off position, then immediately to the on position. This resets the breaker. The circuit is now operating. If the problem continues, there may be more serious issues. Contact an electrician to diagnose the problem.

A ground fault circuit interrupter (GFCI) outlet is recommended for installation in any area where water and electricity could come into contact. A GFCI can sense current leakage in an electric circuit and will interrupt power if there is contact with water, preventing electric shock. Make sure appliances used near water are unplugged when not in use.

(GFCI information adapted with permission from the Electrical Safety Foundation International.)

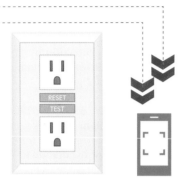

SAFETY GUIDELINES FOR USING ELECTRICAL EQUIPMENT, CORDS, PLUGS AND OUTLETS

Category	Guideline
Electrical Equipment	Read instructions carefully before using electrical equipment.
	Ensure electrical equipment is UL (Underwriters Laboratories) certified.
	Disconnect all electrical equipment when not in use.
	Inspect electrical equipment on a timely basis and make sure it is in good working order.
	Do not handle electrical equipment with wet hands.
	Avoid contact with water and metal surfaces when using electrical equipment.
	Do not leave a client unattended if they are connected to electrical equipment.
	Do not attempt to repair electrical equipment yourself; contact a certified electrician.
Electrical Cords, Plugs and Outlets	Disconnect cords by pulling on the plug, not the cord.
	Use only one plug in each outlet to avoid overloading the circuit breaker.
	Use a power strip with a surge protector if more than one plug is needed in an area.
	Keep electrical cords off the floor and away from everyone's feet to prevent tripping.
	Do not place electrical cords in traffic areas or place things on top of electrical cords.
	Never clean around electrical outlets when equipment is plugged in.
	Never remove the circular prong of a 3-prong plug to make it work in a 2-prong outlet.
	Avoid short-circuiting electrical cords by making sure they don't become twisted.
	Keep all cords, plugs and outlets in good repair.

FIRE

When working with electricity, knowing how to prevent and manage fires can prevent injury or even save lives. Follow specific safety guidelines and practice the protocols listed here.

FIRE SAFETY GUIDELINES

Prevention of fires	If a fire results from an overload of an electric circuit
Use and store flammable materials properly.	Do not put water on it.
Post and comply with local fire codes.	Immediately pull the cord from the socket while wearing protective covering, such as rubber gloves.
Inspect fire safety devices, such as fire extinguishers, smoke alarms and sprinkler systems, frequently.	Smother the fire with a rug, a heavy towel or a powder, such as cornstarch or laundry detergent.
Dispose of or repair frayed or exposed wires.	Locate and use a fire extinguisher.

In the event of being trapped in a smoke-filled room or building	To exit safely through a door
Open the windows for air.	Feel the door, and if it is not hot, open it slowly.
Stay low to the ground and exit immediately if possible.	If there is no smoke on the other side of the door, stay low and proceed to the nearest exit.
Check all doors for heat and signs of fire before opening.	If the door is hot or smoke is seeping from beneath it, do not open the door.
	Line the bottom of the door with wet towels to prevent heat and smoke from entering the room.
	Find a safe exit, or if you are trapped, call 9-1-1 and tell the operator your location.
	Stay on the phone and follow the operator's instructions.
	Remain calm until you are rescued.

Fire Extinguisher

Fire Extinguishers

Electrical fires cannot be extinguished with water, so fire extinguishers are necessary in the salon or spa. This is because water is a good conductor of electricity, and adding water to an electrical fire increases the risk of electric shock.

Guidelines for electrical fires include:

» Use Class C fire extinguishers, which contain non-conductive agents.

» Install fire extinguishers approximately four feet from the floor in areas with potential hazards and in areas close to an exit.

» Position the extinguishers in areas where they are easily accessible, where chemicals are kept and in the kitchen area.

» Inspection of fire extinguishers should be frequent and performed by all employees, instructors and students.

» To inspect fire extinguishers, do the following:

1. Check that the pressure indicator is in the green or "ready" zone.

2. Ensure that the lock pin is firmly in place.

3. Check that the discharge nozzle is free from obstruction.

4. Check the extinguisher for dents, corrosion or evidence of tampering. Ensure that all individuals can properly operate the fire extinguisher.

5. If there is ever any doubt that the extinguisher is functioning properly, call your local fire department and ask for assistance.

For fire extinguisher use, remember **PASS**:

■ **P**ull the pin on the handle.

■ **A**im the hose at the base of the fire from at least six feet away.

■ **S**queeze the handle to begin the flow of the chemical.

■ **S**pray chemical discharge back and forth over the fire.

Understanding the basics of electricity will enable you to serve your clients more efficiently and safely.

LESSONS LEARNED

Key terms of the principles of electricity include electricity, electric current, load, conductor, insulator, amp, volt, ohm, watt and kilowatt.

In direct current, the electrons flow in one steady direction. In alternating current, electrons flow first in one direction and then in the other.

An electrical overload occurs when too many appliances are put on one circuit and are operated at the same time, while an electrical short circuit occurs when a foreign conductor comes in contact with a wire carrying current to an appliance.

Safety measures include fuses, circuit breakers, grounding, ground fault circuit interrupters and being familiar with the use of fire extinguishers.

ELECTRICITY IN COSMETOLOGY

What do you think has been the greatest advancement in electricity in your lifetime?

INSPIRE //

Knowing more about
the benefits of electric
current used in salon and
spa services broadens
your awareness of the
potential value for clients.

ACHIEVE //

Following this lesson on *Electricity in Cosmetology*, you'll be able to:

>> Explain the three kinds of effects that can be produced by electric current

>> Describe the benefits that can be created by special electric current used during electrotherapy and light therapy treatments

>> State the four types of electric current available for the salon professional's use

>> Compare the use of visible and invisible light

FOCUS //

ELECTRICITY IN COSMETOLOGY

Effects of Electric Current

Electrotherapy

Light Therapy

Now that you understand the principles of electricity, you can take a look at how it is used in the salon.

KNOW YOUR EQUIPMENT

Photo Example	Equipment	Description	Example
	Thermal	Used to generate heat	Curling irons, heat lamps, color machines, manicure heaters, facial steamers and scalp steamers, which produce moist heat at a constant temperature
	Mechanical	Has a motor	Clippers and massagers
	Combination	Generates heat and produces a flow of air	Hood dryers and blow dryers

EFFECTS OF ELECTRIC CURRENT

Electric current can produce three kinds of effects during cosmetology services. They are **heating effects, mechanical or magnetic effects and electrochemical effects.**

HEATING EFFECTS

Every conductor has some resistance to the flow of current through it.

» The more resistance, the more drag or friction there will be in the line, which equals increased heat.

» A curling iron, a light bulb and a blow dryer all create heating effects because they contain special conductors (heating elements) that heat up when current flows through them.

» A low setting simply cuts the amount of current allowed to pass through the special conductor. This fact explains why a blow dryer can have a "cold" setting. The cold setting stops all flow of current to the heating element but still allows current to flow to the blower.

MECHANICAL OR MAGNETIC EFFECTS

As you've learned, electrical generators push alternating current through the conductor.

» Alternating current flows first one direction and then the other.

» Manufacturers of mechanical equipment—clippers, massagers, electrodes, etc.—design motors with magnetic fields that have positive and negative poles.

» When the current travels through the conductor and into the magnetic field of the motor, a push-pull effect is created as the negative and positive charges interact.

» This push-pull effect causes the motor to turn, creating a mechanical motion like the rotating blades of a fan.

ELECTROCHEMICAL EFFECTS

Electrochemical effects are created when electric current travels through a water-based solution (a liquid conductor) to produce relaxing or stimulating results.

ELECTROTHERAPY

Electrotherapy is the use of a specific electric current or piece of equipment for corrective and therapeutic benefits on the skin. These benefits include:

» Skin firming

» Deep firming

» Deep cleansing

» Germicidal cleansing

» Hydration

» Deeper product penetration

It is important to know what skin treatments are promoted to do, so you are familiar with their potential in the salon.

There are four types of current you should know:

» Galvanic

» EMS (Electric Muscle Stimulation), also known as faradic

» Microcurrent, also known as sinusoidal

» High-frequency, also known as Tesla

Galvanic and high-frequency are the most popular and widely used in the salon and spa environment.

Alert!
A person with any potentially restrictive medical condition should always consult a physician before receiving electrotherapy treatment.

To be safely used in electrotherapy, galvanic, EMS, microcurrent and high-frequency current must be reduced from the 120 volts of electric power carried through a wire conductor to a level safely handled by the human body.

» A portable appliance known as a wall plate accomplishes this reduction of power.

» The wall plate is available in various sizes and styles and plugs into the stationary wall outlet.

» The current conductors used in electrotherapy applications are plugged into and operated through the wall plate, allowing voltage regulations as necessary for a particular treatment or current.

A current conductor called an **electrode** is used to bring the current from the appliance to the client's skin. The most common electrodes are:

1. A comb electrode (for use on the scalp)

2. A rake electrode (for use on the scalp)

3. A wrist electrode (worn by the salon professional)

4. A carbon electrode (for the client to hold)

5. A massage roller electrode (for application to the client by the salon professional)

An electrode is the only safe contact point through which the current can pass to the client.

A **contraindication** is a certain condition that suggests it is inadvisable to perform a procedure. It is extremely important to properly assess your client's health prior to any electrical treatment. Do not perform electrotherapy if your client has any of the following conditions:

■ Pregnancy

■ Heart condition and/or a pacemaker

■ Epilepsy

■ High blood pressure

■ Open cuts, abrasions or sores

■ Diabetes

■ Dilated (couperose) capillaries

■ Metal plates, pins in body or dental braces

Exercise caution when treating clients who are using strong acne medications such as Retin-A, Accutane® or antibiotics, who have hypersensitive skin or who may be claustrophobic. In addition, do not perform high-frequency treatment on a client who reports a loss of skin sensation.

Alert!
Do not use the galvanic current over an area that has many broken capillaries.

GALVANIC CURRENT

Galvanic current has an electrochemical effect and is the oldest form of electrotherapy in the salon.

» **Galvanic current is a direct current (DC) that has a chemical effect caused by passing the current through particular acidic or alkaline solutions and/or by passing the current through body tissues and fluids.**

» Because galvanic current is a direct current, and generally only alternating current is available in the salon, a special appliance is necessary to convert the salon's alternating current to the direct current.

All electrotherapy applicators have a negatively charged electrode (called a **cathode**) and a positively charged electrode (called an **anode**).

» The cathode is usually black in color or displays a large "N" or negative sign (-).

» The anode, usually colored red, displays a large "P" or a positive sign (+).

If the electrodes are not visibly marked as negative or positive, test for polarity.

» You can determine polarity by separating the tips of the applicators and submerging the tips only into a glass of water. Salt water is best, but tap water will do. Keep tips from touching each other.

» Slowly turn up the galvanic current using the wall plate's regulator.

» The negative electrode will create more and smaller bubbles than the positive electrode.

Phoresis

The process of forcing an acid (+) or alkali (-) into the skin by applying current to the chemical is called **phoresis**, and is probably the most typical application of galvanic current. Phoresis is sometimes referred to as bleaching the skin.

Anaphoresis

Anaphoresis uses a negative pole (cathode) or electrode to force negatively charged (alkaline) solutions into the skin without breaking the skin. This method is used for a process called **desincrustation**, a treatment in which sebum is broken down or blackheads are liquefied, as in deep-pore cleansing.

The **negative pole of galvanic current** is believed to have the following temporary effects on the area of the body to which it is applied:

» Produces an alkaline reaction, which can force alkaline solutions to penetrate the skin.

» Increases the blood flow by expanding the vessels to aid circulation.

» Softens tissues.

» Stimulates nerves.

Cataphoresis

Cataphoresis uses a positive pole (anode) or electrode to force positively charged (acidic) solutions into the skin without breaking the skin. This method is used for a process called **iontophoresis** (eye-on-to-fo-**REE**-sis), a treatment used to infuse (acidic) water-based products for deeper penetration into the skin.

The **positive pole of galvanic current** is believed to have temporary effects opposite those produced by the negative pole, including:

» Produces an acidic reaction, which can force acidic solutions to penetrate the skin.

» Slows the blood flow by contracting the vessels to decrease redness or inflammation when applied to simple blemishes on the skin.

» Hardens tissues, closing pores after facial treatment.

» Soothes nerves.

Galvanic Current Electrotherapy

The salon professional applies the active electrode to the client. The active electrode is connected to either the positive or the negative pole, depending on the therapeutic reaction desired.

» The client holds the inactive electrode, which is connected to the opposite pole.

» Both the active and inactive electrodes should be wrapped lightly in moist cotton. While the comfort level for the current will vary from one client to the next, generally the current should not exceed two milliamperes. Be sure to follow manufacturer's instructions.

EMS, ELECTRIC MUSCLE STIMULATION (FARADIC CURRENT)

Electric muscle stimulation (EMS) is an alternating current (AC), interrupted to produce a mechanical, non-chemical reaction. EMS stimulates nerve and muscle tissue. Possible benefits from the application of EMS could include:

» Improved blood circulation
» Improved muscle tone
» Stimulation of hair growth
» Increased glandular activity

Used chiefly to cause muscle contractions during scalp and facial massage, EMS can be soothing and relaxing and is believed to help preserve muscle tone.

EMS Indirect Method

The most frequently used application of EMS is **indirect method** electrotherapy. In the indirect method:

» The salon professional usually wears a wristband with a moistened electrode.

» The second electrode is wrapped in moist cotton and either held by the client or, better, attached to the client's lower neck between the shoulders.

» The salon professional's fingers are then placed on the client's face before the current is turned on to prevent shock.

» When the current reaches the desired level, a facial massage is given, with particular focus on motor points.

» The current is gradually decreased and finally turned off completely before the salon professional's fingers are removed.

EMS Direct Method

The **direct method** of application, used less often for EMS, places both electrodes on the client's skin, **making certain the electrodes never touch.**

» The current is turned on and slowly increased only after the electrodes are in place.

» In this application, the current travels through the motor nerves between the two electrodes, causing muscle stimulation.

MICROCURRENT (SINUSOIDAL CURRENT)

Microcurrent is an alternating current (AC) with a mechanical effect, much like EMS, that produces muscle contractions. Machines that cause muscle contraction are illegal in some areas. Read your area's rules and regulations.

» Microcurrent electrotherapy is performed by using the indirect method of application.

» Some users believe microcurrent to be superior to EMS because microcurrent penetrates more deeply and can provide greater stimulation to the treated area.

» For this reason, it is most often preferred to EMS for middle-age and older clients.

» Treatments using microcurrent generally last no longer than 30 minutes.

Alert!
Microcurrent should not be used on unhealthy and/or broken skin.

HIGH-FREQUENCY CURRENT (TESLA)

High-frequency current, known as Tesla or the "violet ray," is an alternating current that can be adjusted to different voltages to produce heat.

» Because the Tesla current is a high-oscillation current, its use does not produce muscle contractions.

» Use of the Tesla current can result in relaxation or stimulation, depending on method of application.

There are three methods for using high-frequency current:

1. When using high-frequency **direct application**, the salon professional applies the electrode directly to the client's scalp or face.

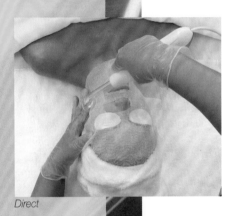
Direct

2. When using high-frequency **indirect application**, the salon professional hands the glass electrode to the client before activating the current to avoid the electrical shock that could result in passing an active current from one person to another. The client then holds the activated electrode while the salon professional manually stimulates the area being treated. The current is turned off before the client returns the electrode to the salon professional after the treatment.

3. In high-frequency **general electrification**, the salon professional hands the electrode to the client before activating the current. The power is switched on, and the client experiences a generalized tingling or vibration.

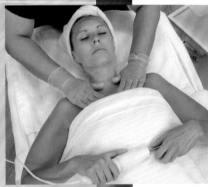
Indirect

To create soothing or relaxing effects, the electrode must be kept in direct contact with the areas being treated. To stimulate an area through rapid vibration, during a direct application, gauze is placed over the skin, and the electrode is applied over gauze. The slight separation of the electrode from the skin creates a mild, stimulating sensation called a spark gap.

Possible benefits from the application of the high-frequency or Tesla current could include:

» Improved blood circulation

» Increased rate of metabolism

» Increased sebaceous (oil glands) glandular activity

Cosmetology Uses for High-
Frequency Current

**Dry Skin Facial Treatment –
Indirect Application**

1. Cleanse client's face.

2. Have the client hold the glass
   rod electrode.

3. Place the tips of your fingers against
   skin on client's face before turning
   on the high-frequency current.

4. Turn on the current, slowly
   increasing strength. Perform usual
   facial massage movements, being
   careful not to lift fingers from
   client's skin.

5. Massage according to
   manufacturer's directions, in most
   cases for no more than 15 minutes
   per treatment. Your fingertips may
   tingle slightly during contact. This
   is normal. Turn off current before
   removing your fingers from client's
   face to avoid shock.

6. Complete facial treatment.

**Mild Acne and/or Blackhead Facial
Treatment – Direct Application**

1. Cleanse client's face.

2. Apply the facial electrode directly
   to the skin and turn on current.

3. Move the electrode gently across
   skin, in small circular rotations,
   while slowly increasing strength
   of the current.

4. Repeat until entire face has been
   covered at least once, but do
   not exceed 5 minutes for the
   entire treatment.

5. Turn the current down slowly until
   it's turned off completely.

6. Remove the electrode from your
   client's skin and proceed with the
   rest of the facial.

Dry Scalp – Indirect Application

1. Apply moisturizing scalp
   treatment cream.

2. Have client hold glass rod electrode.

3. After putting your hand on the
   client's scalp, turn on the current.

4. Perform normal scalp massage,
   being careful not to break contact
   with the client, while gradually
   increasing current.

5. Time treatment according
   to manufacturer's directions,
   massaging entire scalp.

6. Turn off the current, maintaining
   contact with client.

7. Complete scalp treatment.

**Scalp Treatment – Direct
Application**

1. Apply moisturizing non-alcohol-
   based scalp treatment cream.

2. Apply scalp electrode (rake) to scalp
   and turn on current.

3. Using push-pull movements,
   manipulate rake electrode over
   entire scalp while slowly increasing
   strength of current.

4. Continue treatment for
   approximately 5 minutes.

5. Turn off current.

6. Remove electrode rake from scalp
   and complete scalp treatment.

THE SLIGHT
SEPARATION
OF THE
ELECTRODE
FROM THE
SKIN CREATES
A MILD,
STIMULATING
SENSATION
CALLED A
SPARK GAP.

ELECTROTHERAPY PRECAUTIONS

General	Galvanic/EMS/Microcurrent	High-Frequency
» Always read the manufacturer's directions and follow them carefully.	» It is usually recommended that galvanic current should not exceed 2 milliamperes.	» Begin each treatment with a mild current, increasing strength slowly.
» Electrodes should never touch each other.	» Make sure the current is off before beginning indirect application and before breaking contact with client at the end of the treatment.	» Keep client out of contact with metal during treatment.
	» Microcurrent treatment should never exceed 30 minutes.	» Limit treatment duration to approximately 5 minutes for direct application and 8-15 minutes for indirect application.
	» Limit galvanic treatment duration to approximately 4-7 minutes and 3-5 minutes for sensitive skin.	» If you use cream during scalp or other high-frequency treatments, be sure the cream contains no alcohol. Alcohol-based creams may be flammable and could be ignited by a spark.
		» Turn the current on only after the client is holding the electrode.
		» Turn the current off before removing the electrode from clients contact.

HEAT ENERGY

Heat always moves from a hotter body to a cooler body and can be transferred from one object to another in one of three ways:

1. Conduction – The transfer of heat via direct contact

2. Convection – The transfer of heat via liquid or gas

3. Radiation – The transfer of heat through a vacuum (empty space)

Effects of Heat

Mild heat:

» Relaxes the muscles.

» Causes blood circulation to increase.

» Helps salon professionals perform many hair and skin care services.

Intense heat:

» Destroys cells and tissues.

» Can be observed when you are burned and a blister forms. This is a chemical breakdown of the skin (called pyrolysis).

LIGHT THERAPY

Light therapy is the production of beneficial effects such as reducing acne through treatments using light rays or waves.

» Radiation is the transfer of heat energy through an empty air space (a vacuum).

» Heat energy is simply movement of electrons.

When heat energy is transferred by radiation:

» Electrons move in wave-like patterns.

» Waves of electrons are called electromagnetic radiation.

» Waves can be long or short.

» Waves are measured from the crest of one wave to the crest of the next.

▪ This measurement is a wavelength.

▪ The range of all the wavelengths that can be produced by radiant energy is called the electromagnetic spectrum.

▪ The shorter the wavelength, the more energy the wave is carrying.

▪ X-rays have a short wavelength.

▪ TV and radio broadcasts are examples of long wavelengths of radiant energy.

▪ Heat lamps used in chemical services have long wavelengths as well.

Short Wavelength

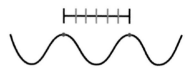

Long Wavelength

Laser, light-emitting diode (LED) and intense pulse light (IPL) are used in medical devices to treat a variety of skin conditions.

» Laser is an acronym for "light amplification simulation emission of radiation."

» Laser devices can remove blood vessels, excessive hair, tattoos or wrinkles without destroying skin tissue.

» LED devices are primarily used to reduce acne (blue light), increase circulation (red light), reduce inflammation (yellow light) or reduce hyperpigmentation (green light).

» IPL devices are used to treat spider veins, wrinkles, hyperpigmentation, excessive hair and rosacea.

Follow regulatory guidelines when using laser, LED and IPL.

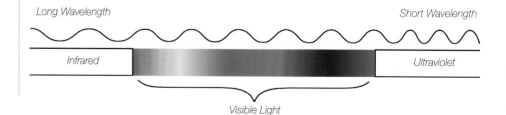

Long Wavelength *Short Wavelength*

Infrared *Ultraviolet*

Visible Light

VISIBLE LIGHT

The portion of the electromagnetic spectrum humans can see is called visible light.

» This range of wavelengths produces visible color.

» When these waves hit an object, they are either absorbed or reflected. Our eyes pick up the reflected waves and interpret them as color.

White light is referred to as combination light. This visible light can be broken into its individual wavelengths by a prism.

» A prism is a three-sided glass object.

» If white light (sunlight or light from a light bulb) passes through a prism, the wavelengths are separated and become visible to the eye as seven colors: red, orange, yellow, green, blue, indigo and violet.

» Raindrops can act as prisms by breaking up white light into those seven colors to create a rainbow.

» **The wavelengths that produce red are the longest waves of the visible spectrum.**

» The wavelengths that produce violet are the shortest.

In the past, two kinds of light in the salon produced white light: fluorescent and incandescent. And now another type, LED, is also available as a white light source.

Fluorescent Light

Fluorescent light is an economical and long-lasting light source.

» Depending on its design, fluorescent light can create blue tones or cool casts in the objects it lights.

» In the salon, fluorescent light can create hair-coloring problems, unless natural sunlight is available, or the fluorescent bulbs are balanced for daylight.

Incandescent Light

To balance the tones of light in the salon, incandescent light is incorporated.

» Incandescent light is provided by an ordinary light bulb.

» Normally, incandescent light produces redder tones or warmer casts in the objects it lights.

LED Light

LED lamps have a lifespan and electrical efficiency that is several times better than incandescent lamps, and significantly better than most fluorescent lamps.

» LED lamps come to full brightness without need for a warm-up time.

» LED lamps are close to being adopted as the mainstream light source due to falling prices and because 40- and 60-watt incandescent bulbs are being phased out.

Light Through a Prism

INVISIBLE LIGHT

Salon professionals use invisible light to produce physical effects in the skin. Since this range of light is not visible to the human eye, you can be overexposed to invisible light in natural sunlight without knowing it.

Over half of sunlight is composed of invisible rays beyond red, which are called infrared. A small percentage of natural sunlight is composed of invisible rays beyond violet, which are called ultraviolet (UV).

Small doses of infrared or ultraviolet light can produce beneficial effects. Using either ultraviolet or infrared light to treat the skin is called light therapy.

DISCOVER**MORE**

LED lights don't burn out the way that incandescents do. Instead, they undergo "lumen depreciation," gradually growing dimmer and dimmer over time. (Lumens are units of brightness for a light source.) Many LED lights have an average life expectancy of 20,000 hours, while a comparable incandescent light has an average life expectancy of 1,000 hours.

Infrared Light

Just as infrared rays produce pure heat rays, any infrared light produces heat. Heat lamps or infrared bulbs can be purchased for use in processing chemical services. Position the lamps according to the manufacturer's instructions.

Benefits of using infrared light during a facial include:

» Increased circulation

» Increased skin gland secretions

» Relaxation of muscles

» Stimulation of cell and tissue activity

Exposure times range from 5 to 15 minutes. The light must be placed at least 30 inches from the client's face. Eye pads or protective eye forms need to be used to cover the client's eyes.

Salon owners strive to create a balance of LED, incandescent and fluorescent lighting in the salon design. Balanced lighting systems can have a pleasant psychological effect on staff and clients and create a natural light to effectively evaluate hair color. Fluorescent light can be irritating to some people, while incandescent light can create excessive heat.

SALONCONNECTION

Salon Lighting – Aim to Please

The directional aim of your lighting can be just as critical as the light source mix in rendering different results on the skin and hair. A mix of crisp white to slightly cool overhead light and warmer eye-level lighting from a sconce can provide optimum task lighting while diminishing shadows.

General rules include aiming recessed or track lights at 30-degree angles and keeping the distance between fixtures the same measure as from the client's head to the light source above. At Minardi NYC, bulbs are placed 16 inches below the 10-foot ceilings to create a wash of "umbrella" uplighting against the ceiling. Just keep in mind: when designing the lighting plan from the ground up, most states regulate how many watts you're allowed per square foot, so check your state regulations.

No single lighting scheme works for every salon; each space demands its own plan. Experiment with a blend of wattages, fixture heights, lighting sources and temperatures to present the salon, and its clients, in the very best light.

Adapted from www.behindthechair.com, "Light Ideas: Eight Illuminating Tips" by A. K. Sterling. Visit behindthechair.com and search articles to read more about lighting in top salons.

Ultraviolet Light

Ultraviolet light, also known as actinic light, has a shorter wavelength and can be more damaging than infrared light.

» **Ultraviolet light, or UV, has positive and negative effects on the skin, depending on the exposure time.**

» **Small doses of UV light can tan the skin and may help the body produce vitamin D.**

» **UV light is germicidal and can kill bacteria that cause skin infections.**

- UV light may promote healing and is used in the treatment of acne.

» UV can also produce harmful chemical effects on the skin.

» Skin can be sunburned, eyes can be damaged and hair can be photochemically damaged by UV light.

- Studies prove overexposure to UV light can result in skin cancer.

During facials or scalp massage, UV light can be used effectively.

» The skin or scalp should be cleansed before using ultraviolet light on the client.

» The client's eyes should be covered with protective eyewear, such as cotton eye pads, goggles, etc. The salon professional should wear protective eyewear also.

» For germicidal treatments, place the lamp at least 12 inches from the area to be treated. This distance allows the strong "short waves" to penetrate intensely.

» Expose the skin initially for 1 minute. Check for reactions. One to 5 minutes of total exposure time is often recommended.

» For larger areas, like the scalp, place the lamp 20 to 30 inches from the area. Exposure can be up to 15 minutes. This exposure time would include the normal scalp massage.

The trend of tanning beds or booths in salons poses serious questions related to client health and well-being. Dry, leathery skin, peeling, itching, wrinkling, sagging, permanent discoloration and possible skin cancers are all reactions to long exposure. **When using UV light, you and your client should wear protective eyewear.**

Understanding the basics of electricity will enable you to serve your clients more efficiently and safely, especially when working with electrotherapy and specialized electrical appliances.

LESSONS LEARNED

The three kinds of effects that can be produced by electric current include heating effects, mechanical or magnetic effects and electrochemical effects.

Benefits that can be produced by special electric current used during electrotherapy and light therapy treatments include skin firming, deep firming, deep cleansing, germicidal cleansing, hydration and deeper product penetration.

The four types of current available for use by the salon professional include galvanic; EMS, also known as faradic; microcurrent, also known as sinusoidal; and high-frequency, also known as Tesla.

When considering visible and invisible light, salon owners balance visible light in the form of LED, incandescent and fluorescent lighting. Invisible light is used to produce physical effects in the skin through infrared and UV light.

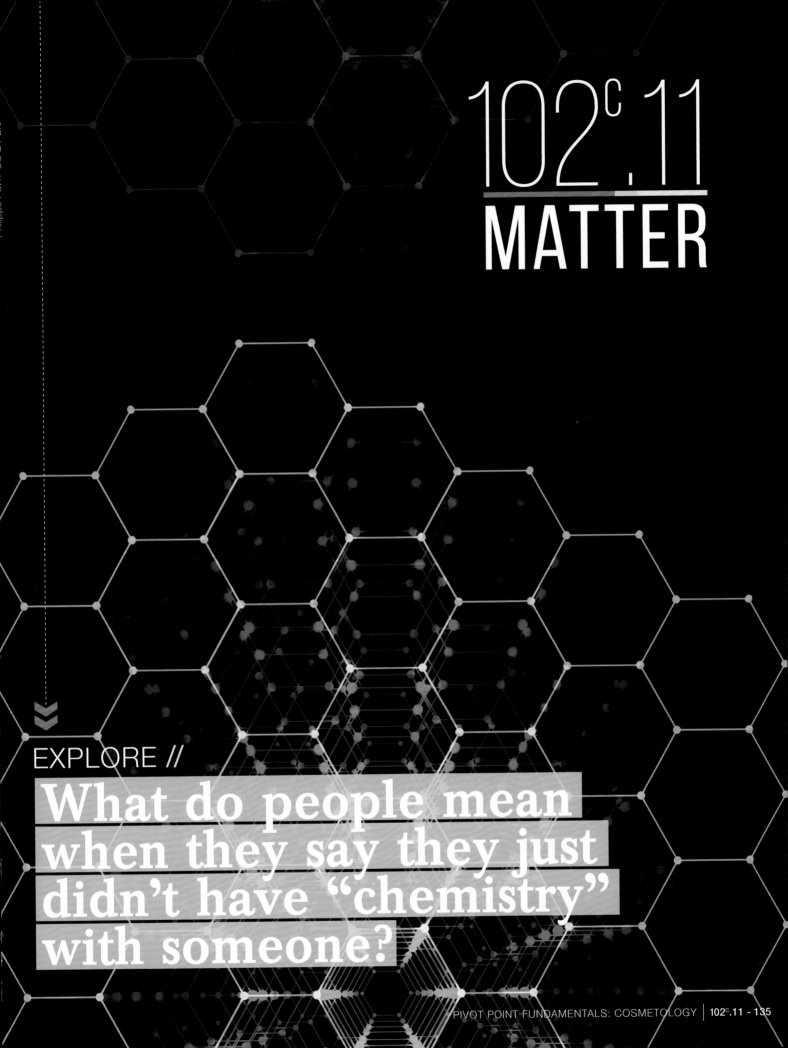

EXPLORE //

What do people mean when they say they just didn't have "chemistry" with someone?

INSPIRE //

Clients will return if you have a basic understanding of how chemistry can elevate your work to higher levels.

ACHIEVE //

Following this lesson on *Matter*, you'll be able to:

>> Define matter and its forms
>> Compare physical changes with chemical changes of substances
>> List the five elements of hair
>> Describe the effects of side bonds when performing physical and chemical services in the salon
>> Construct a chart to illustrate the hair's chemical structure

FOCUS //

MATTER

Properties of Matter
Physical and Chemical Changes
Elements
Chemical Bonds

Many of you may remember the experiment with candy and a bottle of soda pop that went viral. Dropping a few candies into a bottle of soda pop resulted in a foaming surprise. The study of chemistry holds many such surprises. From improving products to making new products, chemistry serves as a foundation for creating effective results.

PROPERTIES OF MATTER

Chemistry is the scientific study of matter and the physical and chemical changes of matter. **Matter** is anything that occupies space and has weight. Look around. Matter is everywhere. Nails, hair and skin are matter. Water and even oxygen are matter. All of these things occupy physical space.

Some matter is living, and some is not. It is the presence of the element carbon that distinguishes living matter from nonliving matter. Chemistry has a special division for each kind of matter:

» **Organic chemistry** deals with all matter that is now living or was alive at one time, with carbon present, such as plants and animals.

» **Inorganic chemistry** studies all matter that is not alive, has never been alive and does not contain carbon, such as rocks, water and minerals.

Chemists are scientists who study matter, its properties and changes. Chemists study properties or characteristics, such as color, odor, weight (density), melting point or boiling point, and hardness, softness or glossiness, that define a substance. Chemists teach that matter exists in three basic forms:

» **Solid** – Matter with definite weight, volume and shape

» **Liquid** – Matter with definite weight and volume but no definite shape

» **Gas** – Matter with definite weight but indefinite volume and shape

For example:

» Hair is a solid because it has definite weight, volume and shape.

» Conditioners, perm solutions and most shampoos are liquids.

  ▪ They have weight and volume but no definite shape, which explains why liquids take the shape of the solid container into which they are poured.

» Oxygen is a colorless, odorless gas.

  ▪ It has weight, even though it may not seem to, but no definite volume or shape.

⟫ PHYSICAL AND CHEMICAL CHANGES

Matter can be changed from one form to another in two ways:

» **Physical Change** – A change in the physical characteristics of a substance without creating a new substance

■ Examples include melting ice or freezing water, crushing a can, mixing sand and water, breaking a glass or shredding paper.

» **Chemical Change** – A change in a substance that creates a new substance with chemical characteristics different from those of the original substance

■ Examples include iron changing to rust, a cake being baked, or a hair color change by mixing hair color and hydrogen peroxide.

A **physical change** in matter would be when water freezes and becomes ice. It is still water, but now it's a solid instead of a liquid.

A **chemical change** occurs when hydrogen combines with oxygen to form a new substance, water.

DISCOVER**MORE**

You might be stumped when thinking about vapor. Is it a liquid or a gas? Vapor is the gas state of a liquid that has been through a physical change. The next time you use the facial steamer, consider that the vapor you see form in the air can actually return to its liquid state when it cools to room temperature. It started as a liquid, evaporated into the air, and then when it cooled, it returned to its liquid state.

ELEMENTS

All matter, whether solid, liquid or gas, whether living or nonliving, consists of atoms, which make up elements. **Elements** are basic substances that cannot be broken down into simpler substances.

Hair comprises two solids (carbon and sulfur) and three gases (hydrogen, nitrogen and oxygen).

C	6
Carbon	
12.0107	

O	8
Oxygen	
15.999	

H	1
Hydrogen	
1.0079	

N	7
Nitrogen	
14.007	

S	16
Sulfur	
32.06	

To remember the elements found in hair, use this acronym: COHNS (carbon, oxygen, hydrogen, nitrogen and sulfur).

»

There are 118 known elements. Those above the 92nd element are synthetic and do not occur naturally. Because they form the basis of hair, nails and skin, five elements are important for the salon professional to know. These elements are carbon, oxygen, hydrogen, nitrogen and sulfur. Look at this chart to notice a few more things about elements:

ATOMIC NO.	ELEMENT	SYMBOL	CATEGORY
1	Hydrogen	H	Gas
2	Helium	He	Gas
3	Lithium	Li	Solid
6	Carbon	C	Solid
7	Nitrogen	N	Gas
8	Oxygen	O	Gas
13	Aluminum	Al	Solid
16	Sulfur	S	Solid
80	Mercury	Hg	Liquid

» The first column on the left shows each element's atomic number. You'll read more about this number later in this lesson.

» The second column lists the element.

» The third column lists the letters, or symbol, used for each element's name. These symbols are a kind of scientific shorthand, like a nickname, that makes it easier for you to identify the elements. You will see these symbols used throughout this coursebook, in other professional literature and on some product labels.

» The fourth column lists whether the element is a solid, liquid or gas.

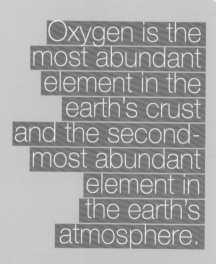

Oxygen is the most abundant element in the earth's crust and the second-most abundant element in the earth's atmosphere.

Sculpture of Atoms

ATOMS

An atom is the smallest complete unit of an element. Each element consists of a certain kind of atom different from the atoms of any other element.

Atoms have three main parts:

» Protons
» Neutrons
» Electrons

Protons and neutrons are packed together tightly to form a dense core, or nucleus, at the center of the atom. Electrons move about this nucleus on orbiting paths or shells at nearly the speed of light.

Protons have a positive electrical charge (+) and identify the atom as, for example, a hydrogen atom or an oxygen atom, etc.

Neutrons have no electrical charge– they are neutral. The neutron determines the weight of the atom.

Electrons have a negative electrical charge (-). Under certain circumstances, they make it possible for atoms to unite with other atoms to form bonds.

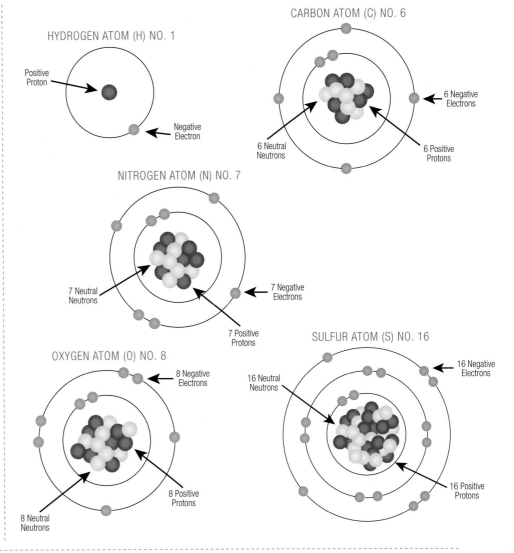

HYDROGEN ATOM (H) NO. 1

Positive Proton

Negative Electron

CARBON ATOM (C) NO. 6

6 Negative Electrons

6 Neutral Neutrons

6 Positive Protons

NITROGEN ATOM (N) NO. 7

7 Neutral Neutrons

7 Negative Electrons

7 Positive Protons

OXYGEN ATOM (O) NO. 8

8 Negative Electrons

8 Positive Protons

8 Neutral Neutrons

SULFUR ATOM (S) NO. 16

16 Neutral Neutrons

16 Negative Electrons

16 Positive Protons

Above is a diagram of the atomic structure of the five elements important to you as a salon professional. Notice how different one atom is from another in terms of number of protons, neutrons and electrons.

The atomic number indicates how many protons are in a single atom of a particular element.

» For example, the atomic number of hydrogen is 1, which means it has only 1 proton and 1 electron.
» **Hydrogen has the simplest atomic structure.**
» Carbon has an atomic number of 6, which means it has 6 protons, 6 neutrons and 6 electrons.
» Nitrogen has 7, oxygen 8 and sulfur 16.

Stable Atoms

>> The chemical behavior of an atom depends mostly on the number of electrons in its outermost orbiting path or shell.

>> Some atoms by their very structure are not missing any electrons in their outer shell.

>> These atoms are considered stable and are electrically neutral.

Unstable Atoms

If the outer shell of the atom is missing electrons, the atom is considered unstable or reactive.

>> Unstable atoms seek other atoms with which they can share electrons to complete their outer shell.

>> When they combine, they make more complex units, known as molecules.

MOLECULES

When unstable atoms combine chemically by sharing electrons, they form molecules. **A molecule is two or more atoms joined together by a chemical bond.**

>> If the atoms that combine are different—for example, an atom of hydrogen and an atom of oxygen—the resulting molecule is a compound.

>> Different atoms joined together as molecules become the smallest parts of a compound.

For example, ammonia, a colorless gas is a compound:

>> Composed of nitrogen and hydrogen

>> Used in color, perm and relaxer products to allow penetration of the hairstrand

When two hydrogen atoms, each with one electron, combine with one oxygen atom and its eight electrons, the result is a water molecule of the compound H_2O. This is an example of two gases–hydrogen and oxygen–uniting and becoming a liquid.

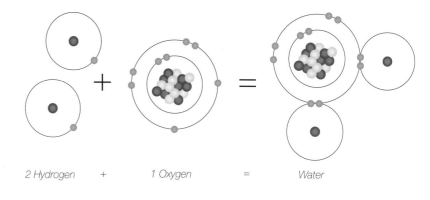

2 Hydrogen   +   1 Oxygen   =   Water

Pure Substance or Mixture?

Almost everything on earth is either a pure substance or a mixture. Pure substances are made of only one type of atom or molecule. All elements and chemical compounds are pure substances. Examples include: hydrogen, gold and salt.

A mixture contains two or more substances that are physically combined. Examples include: sand, oil and water.

O_2 means two atoms of the element oxygen have combined. O_2 is called an elemental molecule.

With an element, the atoms are the same. With a compound, the atoms are different.

CHEMICAL BONDS

You are now familiar with the diagrams of the atoms of the five elements of hair—carbon, oxygen, hydrogen, nitrogen and sulfur. These atoms combine chemically to create compounds that eventually create the protein of hair. To see how they join to form hair, you'll need to learn about chemical bonds, starting with amino acids.

AMINO ACIDS

Amino acids are compounds consisting of carbon, oxygen, hydrogen and nitrogen.

» Amino acids join together in chains to become proteins, which provide the chemicals the body needs for growth and repairing tissues.

» Although amino acids create all proteins, each protein is different because of the way it is put together.

» **Hair is a form of protein called keratin.**

» Keratin in hair contains 19 of the common amino acids.

» **Hair is made of 97% keratin protein and 3% trace minerals.**

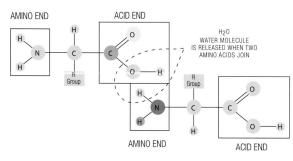

Amino Acid Compound

The chain, or the order in which the amino acids link together, makes each type of protein one of a kind. Also, the number of amino acids in the chain is important. For example, the 19 amino acids found in hair must all be present, or the structure won't be hair.

Peptide Bonds (End Bonds)

The amino acids that create protein are linked together end to end by a **peptide bond**, also known as an end bond.

» The peptide bond is the backbone of all protein molecules.

» When two amino acids are positioned end to end, the acid end of one amino acid attaches to the amino end of another amino acid.

» **The peptide bond forms when these two ends join.**

» The polypeptide bond ("poly" means many) connects thousands of amino acids lengthwise to form a chain.

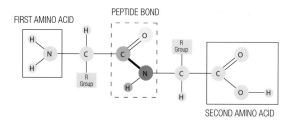

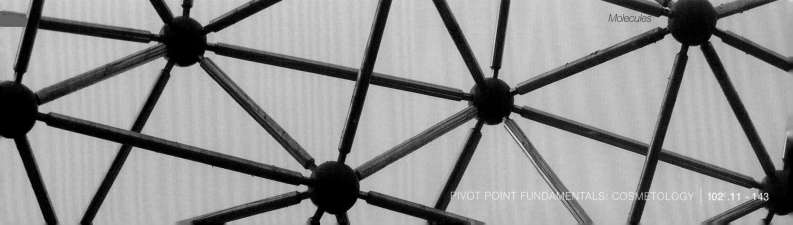

Molecules

In other words, **hair is the linking together of protein groups**. You, as a salon professional, will be altering these links. You need to know how your techniques and tools will affect your client's hair.

» **It's very important not to disturb peptide bonds.**

» For instance, if you put a sodium hydroxide relaxer under a hair dryer, the **combination of the alkaline chemicals and heat could break these critical peptide bonds and destroy the protein structure.**

» If they are broken, the protein chains separate into small fragments or revert to groups of amino acids that no longer have the characteristics of hair.

Side Bonds

When amino acids combine to form the keratin protein of hair, they take on a spiraling configuration. When these long, spiraling protein chains are placed next to each other, they can be linked together by four side bonds. The four bonds holding protein chains together behave differently, and each serves a different purpose in building hair. The four side bonds created are:

1. The hydrogen bond

2. The salt bond

3. The disulfide bond

4. van der Waals forces

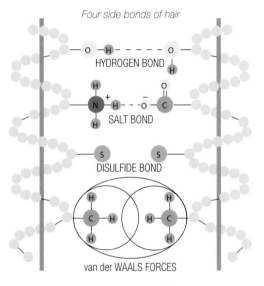

Four side bonds of hair

HYDROGEN BOND

SALT BOND

DISULFIDE BOND

van der WAALS FORCES

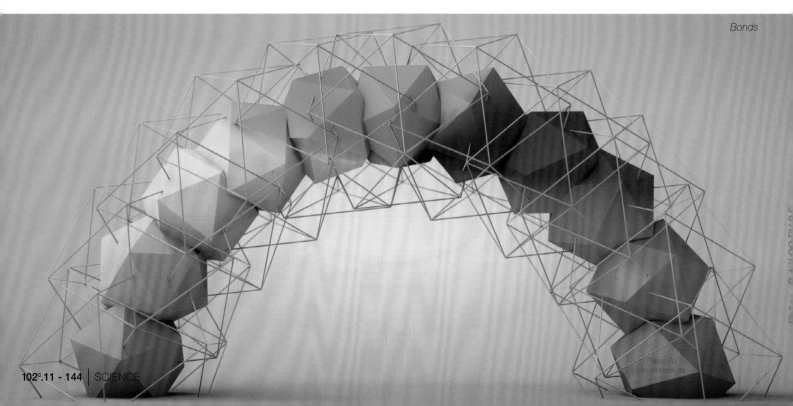

Bonds

When performing chemical services, you are affecting all these bonds. To minimize damage to the hair, it is important to understand how the four side bonds work.

The **hydrogen bond** works on the principle that unlike charges attract.

» Hydrogen bonding takes place when the hydrogen atom in one molecule is attracted to an atom of another molecule that has many negative electrons.

» **Hair has many hydrogen bonds, which are individually weak and can easily be broken by heat or water.**

» Although the attraction in these hydrogen bonds is weak, there are so many of them in the protein of hair that they tend to organize the protein chains and give hair its shape.

» **About 35% of the hair's strength is due to the millions of hydrogen bonds in its structure.**

The **salt bond** is also a result of the attraction of unlike charges.

» The negative charge in one amino acid grouping attracts the positive charge in another amino acid grouping.

» Salt bonds also help organize the protein chains.

» Salt bonds account for another 35% of the hair's resistance to change and, like hydrogen bonds, are not particularly strong.

Since both **hydrogen and salt bonds can be weakened by water**, hair can be shampooed, set on rollers and dried by heat into a new shape.

» **When hair is saturated with water, the hydrogen and salt bonds are weakened, leaving the hair more pliable.**

» Then, by wrapping it around a roller under tension and drying it, the hair takes on a new shape because new hydrogen and salt bonds are formed between the protein chains.

» This set is only **temporary because exposure to water will break the new bonds.**

» **Even the humidity in the air can break the new bonds and restore the original ones.**

» Using rollers or a blow dryer and curling iron to create a thermal design is referred to as a physical change, since it is only the physical characteristics of the hair that change.

The sulfur-containing side bond, the disulfide bond, is the most important to your work.

» **When these sulfur-type side chains join with other sulfur-type side chains, they form the disulfide bond.**

» This bond is a chemical bond that forms between protein structures.

» A lot of your chemical services, particularly perming and relaxing, directly affect the disulfide bond by either breaking the disulfide bond or reforming it in a new shape.

» This process is a chemical change and creates lasting results.

The side bond known as van der Waals forces is based on the theory that atomic groups prefer an environment with other groups that have structures similar to theirs. This type of bonding is not important for your work as a salon professional other than to know that it exists and plays a role in bonding protein chains.

SALON**CONNECTION**

Chemical Services
Chemical services play a pivotal role in salon revenue. The price for highlights averages about $91 per visit, and chemical relaxing averages $166 per visit. These averages indicate the positioning chemical services have when you compare them to a ladies' cut/blow dry service, averaged at $42.

–Data reported in 2013
American Salon Better Business Network Survey

REVIEW:
Hair's Chemical Structure

1. Hair begins with individual atoms, the smallest unit of matter.

2. These atoms unite by sharing electrons to become molecules of amino acids.

3. One end of one amino acid bonds to the opposite end of another amino acid to form the peptide or end bond.

4. The amino acids create polypeptide protein chains.

5. The individual protein chains bond, side to side, to other chains by hydrogen bonds, salt bonds, disulfide bonds and van der Waals forces.

6. The bonding of protein chains to other protein chains makes human hair.

STAGES OF HAIR FORMATION

1

ATOM

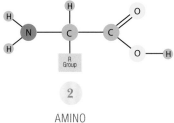

2

AMINO
ACID

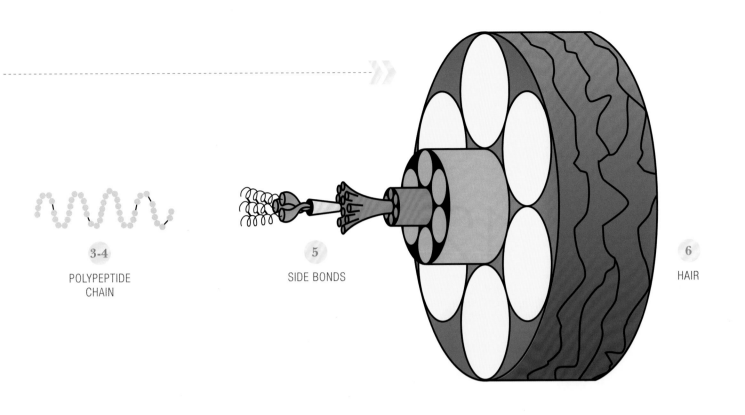

LESSONS LEARNED «

Matter is defined as anything that occupies space and exists in the forms of solid, liquid and gas.

A physical change refers to change in the physical characteristics of a substance without creating a new substance. A chemical change refers to a change in a substance that creates a new substance with chemical characteristics different from those of the original substance.

The five elements of hair are carbon, oxygen, hydrogen, nitrogen and sulfur.

The effects of side bonds when performing physical and chemical services in the salon include:

» Hydrogen and salt bonds are broken during physical services

» Disulfide bonds are broken during chemical services

An illustration of the hair chemical structure needs to include:

» Hair begins with individual atoms, the smallest unit of matter

» Atoms unite by sharing electrons to become molecules of amino acids

» One end of one amino acid bonds to the opposite end of another amino acid to form the peptide or end bond

» Amino acids create polypeptide protein chains

» Individual protein chains bond, side to side, to other chains by hydrogen bonds, salt bonds, disulfide bonds and van der Waals forces

» Bonding of protein chains to other protein chains makes human hair

102^C.12 pH

Have you ever peeled an orange and felt your skin tingle?

INSPIRE //

Salon professionals need to be knowledgeable about pH so they can select and use products that will maintain or restore the natural pH of the skin, hair and nails.

ACHIEVE //

Following this lesson on *pH*, you'll be able to:

>> Identify why it is important for salon professionals to be knowledgeable about pH
>> Explain the effects of acids and alkalis in water in relation to pH
>> Describe the pH scale and its three main categories
>> State the three ways to measure pH
>> Identify the importance of pH-balanced products

FOCUS //

pH

pH Starts With Water
The pH Scale

102ᶜ.12 | pH

Have you ever seen someone with unhealthy, dull, limp-looking hair? A lack of understanding of pH could be the cause of both conditions. In this lesson, you will learn about pH and the role it plays in the environment, products, hair, skin and nails.

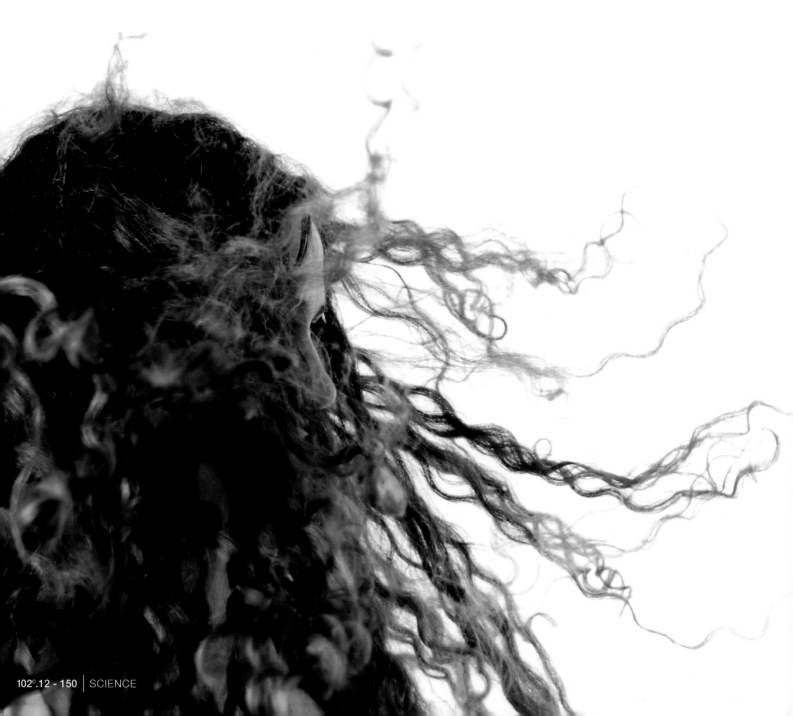

pH STARTS WITH WATER

pH stands for potential hydrogen and is a numerical measurement that indicates the acidity or alkalinity of a water-based substance. pH plays a big part in our daily lives.

» Cosmetics, hair care treatments, household cleansers, medicines, fertilizers, water purification chemicals, pet care items, and many other products must be within a certain pH range in order to work effectively.

» If pH products are not within a certain pH range, they can be damaging and possibly even deadly.

» Only solutions containing water or solutions that can be dissolved in water can be acidic or alkaline in value.

» Since many of the products in the cosmetology industry list water as the primary ingredient on their labels, there are many products that have acidic or alkaline values.

» The pH value of products is the most common method of identifying the appropriate use of a product for the hair, skin or nails.

Water Molecule
[H$_2$O]

Hydroxide
[OH-]

Hydrogen Ion
[H+]

Why do different substances have different pH values? pH starts with the behavior of water, H$_2$O.

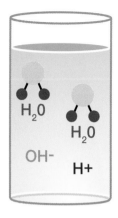

Water molecules have two hydrogen atoms and one oxygen atom. It is natural for a small percentage of the water molecules to split apart, resulting in a positive hydrogen ion, H+, and a negative hydroxide ion, OH-.

The illustration on the left represents a glass of pure, distilled water. Most of the water molecules (H_2O) stay intact, but some of them split apart, or ionize. H+ and OH- ions can also come back together to form water molecules.

Because this is pure water, the breaking apart of the H_2O molecules will always result in a 1:1 ratio of positive H+ ions and negative OH- ions. That is why pure water is considered a neutral substance—the positive and negative ions balance each other out.

ACIDS AND ALKALIS

Water is all around us and, therefore, so are acids and alkalis. Other words used to describe alkalis include alkaline, alkalinity or base.

An **acid** is a substance that increases the concentration of hydrogen ions when placed in water because it donates, or releases, H+ ions.

An **alkali** decreases the concentration of hydrogen ions when placed in water because it accepts, or combines with, H+ ions, resulting in fewer "loose" H+ ions and proportionately more OH- (hydroxide) ions. When acids and alkalis are brought together, they neutralize each other.

Acids tend to taste sour and react strongly with metals. Alkalis tend to taste bitter and feel slippery. Strong acids, such as hydrochloric acid, and strong alkalis, such as lye, can both burn.

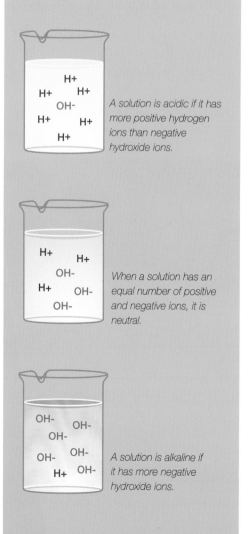

Acids and alkalis are substances that change the balance of hydrogen and hydroxide ions in water.

A solution is acidic if it has more positive hydrogen ions than negative hydroxide ions.

When a solution has an equal number of positive and negative ions, it is neutral.

A solution is alkaline if it has more negative hydroxide ions.

DISCOVER**MORE**

The human stomach contains hydrochloric acid to help digest food and kill certain bacteria, which keeps humans from getting sick. However, too much hydrochloric acid can lead to indigestion, so the acid can be neutralized with an alkali such as an indigestion tablet.

THE pH SCALE

Acids and alkalis have been around for ages, but the pH scale is relatively new; it was invented in 1909 by a Danish biochemist named Soren Sorensen. The pH scale is a quick way to understand the degree of acidity or alkalinity of a substance without needing an in-depth knowledge of the molecular changes involved.

The **pH scale** ranges from 0 to 14. Seven is the midpoint, indicating a neutral substance. Distilled water has a neutral pH of 7. pH values below 7 indicate more acidity—a higher concentration of H+ ions than OH- ions. pH values above 7 indicate more alkalinity—a higher concentration of OH- ions than H+ ions. The closer you get to 0, the stronger the acidity. The closer you get to 14, the stronger the alkalinity.

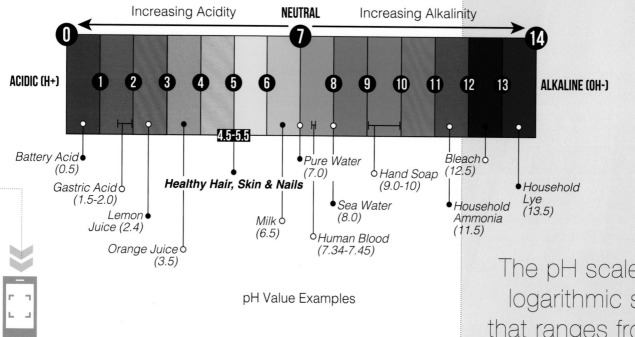

pH Value Examples

An important point to know about the pH scale is that it is a logarithmic scale. This means that each change in value along the scale is a change of 10 times: a pH of 2 is 10 times more acidic than a pH of 3, 100 times more acidic than a pH of 4, and 1,000 times more acidic than a pH of 5. Likewise, a pH of 9 is 10 times more alkaline than a pH of 8, 100 times more alkaline than a pH of 7, and 1,000 times more alkaline than a pH of 6.

The pH scale is a logarithmic scale that ranges from 0 to 14. Substances with a pH less than 7 are acidic; substances with a pH more than 7 are alkaline; and substances with a pH of 7 are neutral.

MEASURING pH

pH Meter   *Indicator Liquid*   *Indicator Paper*

There are three main ways to measure pH:

» pH meter

» Indicator liquid

» Indicator paper

The **pH meter** is the most accurate of the three methods. An electrode is placed in the substance to be measured, and an immediate pH reading appears. It can also measure the pH of the acid mantle that coats the skin and hair. **Indicator liquid** and **indicator paper** both use color changes to indicate pH. Litmus paper is a well-known type of indicator paper.

» Blue litmus paper turns red in an acid

» Red litmus paper turns blue in an alkali

Indicator paper that shows a range of color changes corresponding to different pH levels is a convenient way to establish the pH of various products. pH (nitrazine) paper is a more specialized indicator and can provide a specific pH number.

pH BALANCED

pH balanced refers to a product with a pH from 4.5 to 5.5 (average pH range of hair, skin and nails). Your task as a salon professional will be to use products that will help maintain the pH balance of the hair, skin and nails at the 4.5 to 5.5 pH range. When using alkaline products, it is important to restore the pH balance once the service is complete. Keep in mind that in order for a product to have a pH rating or be tested for pH it must contain water and/or have the ability to dissolve in water.

SALON**CONNECTION**

Salon Products and Their pH Ranges

SHAMPOOS AND CONDITIONERS

pH-Balanced Shampoo	4.5 - 5.5
Alkaline Shampoo	7.0 - 9.0
Acidifying Conditioner	2.2 - 5.5
Deep Penetrating Conditioner	3.5 - 5.5

PERMS AND RELAXERS

Acid Perm	6.9 - 7.2
Alkaline Perm	8.0 - 9.5
Sodium Hydroxide Relaxer	11.5 - 14.0
Ammonium Thioglycolate Relaxer	8.5 - 9.5
Neutralizer	2.5 - 7.0

COLORS AND LIGHTENERS

Oil Bleach	8.0 - 9.5
Powder Bleach	10.0 - 11.0
Tints	9.5 - 10.5
Hydrogen Peroxide	2.5 - 4.5

FINISHING PRODUCTS

Mousse	5.5 - 6.0
Gel	4.5 - 5.5
Hair Spray	5.0 - 6.0

SKIN PRODUCTS

Cleanser	4.5 - 5.5
Toner	5.5 - 6.0
Moisturizer	5.5 - 6.0

NAIL PRODUCTS

Polish Remover	5.0 - 6.0
Cuticle Cream	5.5 - 6.0
Hand Lotion	4.5 - 5.5

An understanding of pH is important to you because every organ and tissue of the human body is made up largely of water, including the hair, skin, nails, brain, muscles and blood. You can determine the acidity or alkalinity of all of these. Knowing whether the product is acidic or alkaline helps identify the appropriate product to use to restore the natural pH of the hair, skin and nails.

LESSONS LEARNED

›› The pH scale indicates whether a substance is acidic, neutral or alkaline to assist salon professionals in keeping the hair, skin and nails in the best condition possible.

›› Acids and alkalis are substances that change the balance of hydrogen and hydroxide ions in water.

›› The pH scale is a logarithmic scale that ranges from 0 to 14. Substances with a pH less than 7 are acidic; substances with a pH more than 7 are alkaline; and substances with a pH of 7 are neutral.

›› Salon professionals know pH values can be measured with a pH meter, indicator paper or indicator liquid.

›› Salon professionals need to be familiar with the pH of products so they know how to select and use the appropriate products when performing client services.

H AIR CARE PRODUCT KNOWLEDGE

102ᶜ.13

EXPLORE //

What's the first thing people do when they find a product they really like?

INSPIRE //

An understanding of the physical and chemical characteristics of cosmetics will help you serve clients and meet their needs.

ACHIEVE //

Following this lesson on *Hair Care Product Knowledge*, you'll be able to:

>> Identify the six general cosmetic classifications

>> Classify the differences between various shampoo, rinse and conditioner products

>> Describe the precautions that are necessary when working with various professional products and cosmetics

FOCUS //

HAIR CARE PRODUCT KNOWLEDGE

Cosmetic Classifications

Shampoos

Rinses and Conditioners

Product Information

102^c.13 | HAIR CARE PRODUCT KNOWLEDGE

The U.S. Federal Food, Drug, and Cosmetic Act of 1938 defines cosmetics as "articles intended to be rubbed, poured, sprinkled, or otherwise applied to the human body or any part thereof for cleansing, beautifying, promoting attractiveness or altering the appearance." As a salon professional, it's important to understand the physical and chemical characteristics of cosmetics in order to better serve your clients.

COSMETIC CLASSIFICATIONS

There are six general classifications assigned to categorize cosmetics used in the cosmetology industry. Knowledge of these cosmetic classifications will help you understand product labels and direct their use. These classifications are based on how well the substance combines with another as well as the physical characteristics of each.

6 COSMETIC CLASSIFICATIONS

1. Solutions
2. Suspensions
3. Emulsions
4. Ointments
5. Soaps
6. Powders

A mixture is two or more substances that are physically combined and is referred to as being immiscible or miscible. **Immiscible** refers to liquids not able to be mixed. **Miscible** refers to liquids able to be mixed together without separating.

6 COSMETIC CLASSIFICATIONS

1. **Solutions**	>> Mixtures of two or more kinds of molecules, evenly dispersed; solutions do not separate when left standing; generally clear mixtures
Solute	>> Any substance that dissolves into a liquid and forms a solution; stirring is usually required when dissolving a solute; can be either solid, liquid or gas; hydrogen peroxide would be an example of a gas mixed with a liquid to form a solution
Solvent	>> Substance that is able to dissolve another substance ■ Water is considered a universal solvent because it is capable of dissolving more substances than any other solvent. ■ Only oil and wax cannot be dissolved in water.
3 Classes of Solutions: Dilute Solution	>> Contains a small quantity of the solute in comparison to the quantity of solvent
Concentrated Solution	>> Contains a large quantity of the solute in comparison to the quantity of solvent
Saturated Solution	>> Can't take or dissolve more of the solute than it already holds at a given temperature
2. **Suspensions**	>> Mixtures of two or more kinds of molecules; have a tendency to separate when left standing and therefore need to be shaken before using An example of a suspension would be vinegar and oil as a salad dressing preparation. If left standing, the mixture of vinegar and oil separates and needs shaking before being used. Many lotions used in the cosmetology industry are suspensions. Calamine lotion is another example.
3. **Emulsions**	>> Formed when two or more immiscible substances (like oil and water) are united with the help of a binder or gum-like substance (emulsifier); the gum-like substance might be a soap General classifications are oil-in-water (perm solutions) and water-in-oil (cold creams). Most emulsions used in the cosmetology industry are classified as oil-in-water.
4. **Ointments**	>> Mixtures of organic substances and a medicinal agent, usually found in a semi-solid form; water is generally not present in this mixture Ointment-type preparations come in the form of sticks (like lipstick), pastes (like some eye shadows or blush) and mucilages (thick liquids, such as styling lotions).
5. **Soaps**	>> Mixtures of fats and oils converted to fatty acids by heat and then purified Soaps used in the cosmetology industry generally fall into the categories of deodorant soaps, beauty soaps, medicated soaps and liquid soaps.
6. **Powders**	>> Equal mixtures of inorganic and organic substances that do not dissolve in water and that have been sifted and mixed until free of coarse, gritty particles Perfume and shades of color are usually added for purposes of enhancement.

SHAMPOOS

The natural place to start a review of products related to the six cosmetic classifications is with the service most often performed... shampooing. **Hair is shampooed primarily to clean the hair and scalp and to remove all foreign matter, including dirt, sebum (natural scalp oil), cosmetics, hairspray and skin debris without adversely affecting either the scalp or the hair.**

>> Shampooing the hair is an important function, as it is often the first impression the client has of the salon and of the designer.

>> Shampooing, as part of a salon service, can be highly therapeutic if it is performed in a caring, organized and confident manner that results in a soothing, relaxing experience.

>> The shampoo sets the climate for all future services.

Hair should be shampooed as often as necessary depending on how quickly the scalp and hair become soiled. Frequency varies from individual to individual.

>> **Improper or irregular cleansing allows a breeding place for disease-causing bacteria** and can lead to scalp disorders and even hair loss.

>> Generally, oily hair needs to be shampooed more often than normal or dry hair.

>> Strong alkaline shampoos are not recommended as they may make the hair dry and brittle.

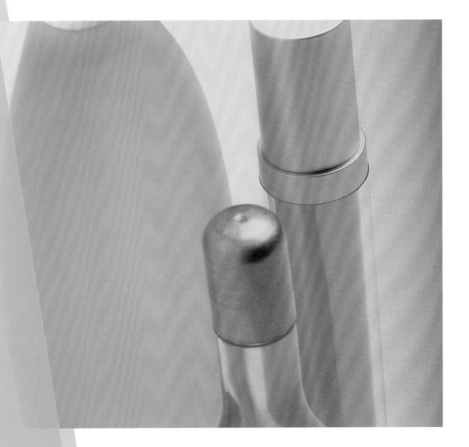

Solute, Solvent or Solution

To help you understand the difference between a solute, a solvent and a solution, consider what happens when you mix a pack of instant hot cocoa and a cup of hot water.

>> The dry cocoa would be the solute because it dissolves into a liquid to form a solution.

>> The water would be the solvent because it dissolves another substance.

>> The cocoa itself would be called the solution.

HOW SHAMPOO WORKS

Even though the hair fiber beyond the scalp is dead (i.e., biologically inactive), the acid mantle (a mixture of secretions from the sebaceous glands and perspiration from the sweat glands) helps maintain the hair and scalp at its natural pH of 4.5 to 5.5, allowing a shiny, alive appearance.

» These scalp secretions can be spread by simply running the fingers through the hair or by brushing or combing.

» Failure to remove these scalp secretions on a regular basis will allow a buildup of oily film.

» The oily film is an emulsion: a combination of oil, sweat, dead epidermal cells and dirt particles.

Most shampoo is water-based and contains an ingredient known as a **surfactant** or cleansing agent. **Surfactants, also called surface active agents, are used to remove oil from the hair.**

» A surfactant is necessary because water alone cannot attack and dissolve oil.

» For example, if you just wet the remains of a greasy dinner plate of spaghetti, the water simply beads up. Once you add soap, the grease breaks up and is easily washed away. It is necessary to add detergents, soaps or other surface active agents (surfactants) to do the job.

The molecule of a surfactant is a two-part molecule. **It has a water-loving (hydrophilic) part and an oil-loving (lipophilic) part.**

» During a shampoo, the water-loving part is attracted to water, while the oil-loving part is attracted to oil on the hair.

» The resulting "push-pull" action causes the oil to "roll up" into droplets, which are then lifted into the water and washed away.

» By removing the oil from the hair shaft and scalp, the water can wet the hair and scalp and the debris can be washed away.

SURFACTANT

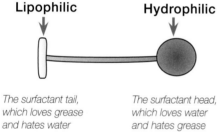

Lipophilic

Hydrophilic

The surfactant tail, which loves grease and hates water

The surfactant head, which loves water and hates grease

SHAMPOO ACTION

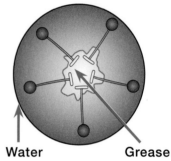

Water   **Grease**

THE ROLE OF WATER

Water plays an important part in the success of your shampoo. Water can be classified as either hard or soft, depending on the amount and kinds of minerals present.

» Hard water, well water, contains certain salts of calcium, magnesium and other metals that prevent the shampoo from lathering. It can be softened by a chemical process.

» Soft water contains very small amounts of minerals and is preferred for shampooing as it lathers more freely.

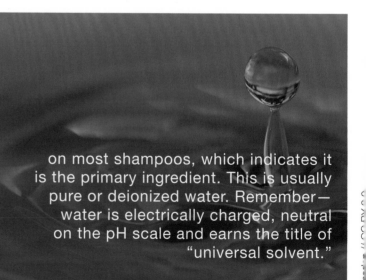

on most shampoos, which indicates it is the primary ingredient. This is usually pure or deionized water. Remember— water is electrically charged, neutral on the pH scale and earns the title of "universal solvent."

Water (H_2O) makes up approximately 60% of the human body and covers 75% of the earth's surface.

Water Purification

Water boiled at a temperature of 212° Fahrenheit (100° Celsius) will destroy most microbial life. However, sedimentation and filtration are two methods used in the purification of water.

>> During sedimentation, undesirable substances, such as clay, sand, etc., sink to the bottom.

>> Then, during filtration, the undesirable substances pass through a porous substance.

>> Chlorine is added to kill bacteria and complete the purification process.

TYPES OF SHAMPOOS

Many varieties of shampoos are available today to the salon professional. It is important that you familiarize yourself with all of them to learn which will bring the best results to your individual clients. Remember to always read and follow the recommended directions for successful results.

TYPES OF SHAMPOOS	
1. All-Purpose Shampoos	» Contain a low alkaline content and a low concentration of surface active agents » Designed to cleanse the hair without correcting any special condition » Do not strip color; very mild; some even include anti-fungal and anti-dandruff agents
2. pH-Balanced Shampoos	» Formulated to have the same pH as the hair and skin (4.5 to 5.5) » Can be used on almost all types of hair » Referred to as acid-balanced (non-stripping) shampoos within the industry when discussing hair color » Made especially to cleanse chemically treated hair without removing permanent hair coloring or toners (use on bleached and dry, damaged hair)
3. Plain Shampoos	» Usually strong and contain a high alkaline or soap base » Can be used successfully on virgin hair in good condition, but are not recommended for chemically treated or damaged hair » Always follow with an acid rinse to restore the acid balance of the client's hair and scalp
4. Soapless Shampoos	» Able to lather without harsh alkaline ingredients; also called sulfate-free shampoos » Made by a process in which the oils from synthetic detergents have been treated with sulfuric acid, resulting in substances known as wetting agents » Effective in both soft and hard water and rinse out easily
5. Medicated Shampoos	» May be available from a local beauty supply house, but often can be obtained only by prescription from a client's doctor » Contain ingredients designed to treat scalp and hair problems or disorders
6. Clarifying Shampoos	» Often have a higher alkalinity in order to be able to remove residue, chlorine, minerals or product buildup » Used often before chemical services
7. Anti-Dandruff Shampoos	» Formulated for either a dry or an oily scalp, and contain an anti-fungal or germicidal ingredient and conditioners to control dandruff conditions or other scalp conditions that could breed infections » Always follow manufacturer's directions, massage the scalp vigorously and rinse thoroughly
8. Strengthening Protein Additive Shampoos	» Contain both a surfactant and conditioner; not only cleanse but condition » Designed to help strengthen the hair through the addition of artificial or hydrolyzed protein derivatives that strengthen damaged areas of the hair by depositing protein fragments along the hair shaft

9. Aerosol Dry Shampoos	>> Product packaged under pressure and blended with a propellant (gas) inside a container, which is usually a can
	>> Used by clients wanting to expand the time between shampoos and add texture
	>> Work by absorbing oil at the roots
	>> Aerosols provide a unique advantage of dispensing the product without the user having to come in contact with the product other than on the application area; however, most aerosol products are flammable (potentially explosive) and an environmental nuisance to discard
10. Non-Aerosol Powder Dry Shampoos	>> Used by clients wanting to expand the time between shampoos and add texture; formulated for clients who are bedridden and cannot wet their hair
	>> Some contain orris root powder that absorbs oil and distributes oil as the product is brushed through the scalp and hair
	▪ After applying the powder, brush it out of the hair with a long-bristled brush until all traces of powder are removed
	▪ Between strokes, wipe the brush with a clean towel
	>> Do not give powder dry shampoo before a chemical service
11. Liquid Dry Shampoos	>> Used to cleanse the scalp and hair when the client is unable to receive a normal shampoo; effective in cleaning wigs and hairpieces because ordinary shampoos deteriorate the wefting (base material to which the hair is sewn)
	▪ Shampoo loosens the dirt and oil from the hair and scalp or weft when applied with saturated cotton
	▪ Basic procedure is to apply the solution to the scalp and small strands of hair or weft, rubbing briskly along each section
	▪ Follow the application by blotting with a towel; any remaining solution will evaporate
	>> Very drying to the hair and should be used only when necessary
	>> Highly flammable and should be used with caution; always use in a well-ventilated room away from open flames or appliances; never smoke cigarettes or allow clients to smoke when using liquid dry shampoos
12. Conditioning Shampoos	>> Contain small amounts of animal, vegetable or mineral additives that coat the cuticle layer of the hair, resulting in surface benefits such as shine and manageability
	>> Additives like protein or biotin improve the tensile strength, elasticity and porosity and will usually be removed with the next shampoo
13. Neutralizing Shampoos	>> Developed to restore the hair to its 4.5 to 5.5 pH by neutralizing any remaining alkaline values
	>> Used generally in conjunction with a chemical relaxing service
14. Color Shampoos	>> Temporary color molecules that adhere to the outer cuticle of the hair and deposit color
	>> Effects of these shampoos, available in enhancing and vivid colors, last from shampoo to shampoo
15. Thinning Hair Shampoos	>> Formulated as gentle shampoos, with a lighter molecular weight that does not cause damage or weigh hair down
	>> May also contain ingredients to provide a healthy environment for the maximum amount of hair growth

Healthy Hair

The wide variety of shampoos available has one desired result—a satisfied customer with healthy hair. It is essential for you, as a salon professional, to realize that not all shampoos that claim pH balance are necessarily acid balanced.

» A pH-balanced shampoo has the natural 4.5 to 5.5 pH of the hair and scalp. If the natural acidic conditions are maintained during a shampoo, the cuticle scales are kept in a more compact state, and therefore a minimal amount of swelling of the cuticle fibers occurs.

» Hair is strongest at a pH of 4.5 to 5.5 because it is compact and least swollen.

» If the pH of a shampoo is too alkaline (or too acidic), the hair fiber can swell. This swelling weakens the hair, making it more susceptible to other forms of distress, such as dryness and cuticle damage.

» Strong, compact hair is more pleasing in appearance and easier to manage.

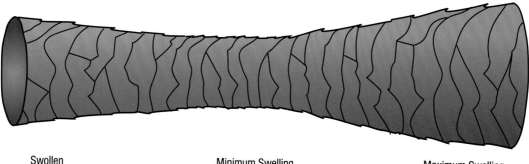

Swollen	Minimum Swelling	Maximum Swelling
pH 3 or less	*pH 4-6*	*pH 8 or greater*

COSMETIC APPEARANCE is the luster or shine of the hair. If the layers of the outer cuticle stand away from the hair shaft, the hair will appear rough and dull.

POROSITY refers to the ability of the hair to absorb moisture, liquids or chemicals.

MANAGEABILITY is determined by how easily a comb can pass through wet or dry hair.

ELASTICITY is the ability of the hair to stretch and return to its natural shape without breaking. Healthy hair can be stretched about 50% when wet and up to 20% when dry. Tensile strength measures the amount of tension that can be applied before the hair breaks.

RINSES AND CONDITIONERS

Hair becomes chemically and mechanically damaged through daily care.

>> The tools of your profession—thermal styling irons, blow dryers, teasing combs, brushes and even rollers—can cause a degree of damage to hair.

>> Hair's chemical composition is changed with perm and color services. Bonds are broken that can never be rejoined. Once the natural bonds in the hair are broken, nothing can be done to actually reconnect them and repair the hair.

>> Other factors that can affect hair condition are the environment and products such as alkaline shampoos.

It is your responsibility to be aware of products that can strengthen hair, add body and protect it from further damage. Scientists have formulated products that can smooth rough hair cuticles, add protein molecules to the hair shaft and add humectants (moisturizers) to replace moisture to dry hair. It is important for you to investigate these products, to help preserve the favorable look and condition of your clients' hair and to prepare their hair properly for chemical services. To achieve this, it is important for you to know why and when each product type is used and the results you can expect to achieve.

RINSES

Rinses affect mostly the surface of the hair. Rinses are usually applied to the hair and rinsed off immediately.

>> Rinses sometimes leave a coating that surrounds each hair strand.

>> Some rinses can actually be detrimental to the hair because they contain ingredients that "build up" on the hair's surface. This "buildup" can make the hair feel limp, attract dirt and make it difficult to control.

>> Rinses are applied to the hair to help close the cuticle and make hair feel soft and manageable.

There are several effective rinses on the market today. Many rinses (and conditioners) are formulated for specific types of hair by chemists who specialize in the study of hair. At one time, however, all rinses had to be prepared in the salon or by the consumer at home. Rinses you should be familiar with include the following.

1. **Vinegar and Lemon (Acid)**

   » The vinegar rinse is mixed by using two tablespoons of white vinegar with a pint of tepid water.

   » Lemon rinse uses the strained juice of two lemons or 15 drops of concentrated lemon extract. Adjust with water to a pH of 4.5 to 5.5.

   » Acid rinses usually have a very low pH (2 to 3) and are designed to dissolve soap scum, untangle and separate the hair and add sheen. Soap scum, caused by the combination of the minerals in the water and the fatty acids of soap, is the residue remaining on the surface of the hair after shampooing.

   » An acid rinse can also be used to counteract the alkalinity present after a chemical service.

2. **Cream rinses soften and add luster, making tangled hair easier to comb.**

   » A cream rinse is creamy in appearance and adheres to the hair shaft, even after ordinary rinsing, thus leaving the hair with a soft feel and much easier to comb and handle.

   » Cream rinses are only slightly acidic and do not have the same function as acid rinses.

   » In selecting a cream rinse, be sure to select one with a proper pH level for your needs.

3. **Medicated rinses are designed with ingredients that control minor dandruff and scalp conditions.**

   » Can usually be applied with cotton or poured over the scalp followed by a one-minute scalp massage, but be sure to follow manufacturer's instructions.

   » Active ingredients, such as benzalkonium chloride, lauryl isoquinolinium bromide and polysorbate leave the hair lustrous and manageable.

CONDITIONERS

Conditioning is an important step in your clients' hair needs. Sometimes a client's hair may be in great condition and only require a rinse to smooth the cuticle. But in many cases the hair has been dried out and damaged by strong alkaline shampoos, chemical damage or heat styling. Any amount of heat can damage the cuticle layer over time, leaving a rough, dry feeling. In these cases, a conditioning treatment may be needed.

Conditioners usually penetrate deep into the hair, so they are formulated differently from rinses.

>> In order to achieve maximum penetration, they are usually kept on the hair for a specific length of time.

>> The length of time a conditioner should be left on the hair depends on its formulation and purpose.

>> Sometimes the addition of heat is recommended to open the cuticle, which allows for better penetration. Read the manufacturer's instructions before applying.

Remember, hair "damage" generally refers to bonds (disulfide, etc.) that have been broken through the application of chemical services or thermal styling.

>> Conditioners don't actually repair broken bonds, but rather fortify the damaged areas of the hair and protect it against further damage from chemical services or heat.

>> Conditioners may also alter the way hair behaves, giving it less stretch or reducing the relaxation of a set.

>> Conditioners provide a temporary remedy for existing hair problems.

CONDITIONERS	
1. Instant Conditioners	>> Coat the hair shaft and restore moisture and oils, but do not penetrate into the cortex or replace keratin in the shaft >> Usually have a vegetable oil base, an acidic pH and are not recommended for fine and limp hair >> Generally left on the hair for 1 to 2 minutes, then rinsed off
2. Normalizing Conditioners	>> Usually contain a vegetable protein and have an acidic pH, which causes the cuticle to close after alkaline chemical services >> Generally applied for approximately 2 minutes and rinsed off
3. Body-Building Conditioners *Body-Building Agents (Protein, Polymers)* *Low pH Constricts Fiber*	>> Required when hair is fine and limp and contains too much moisture to maintain a good style >> The formula, with protein, will penetrate into the damaged hair shaft and deposit proteins into the cortex; proteins displace the excess moisture, providing more body to the hair, which modifies the delicate moisture/protein balance and makes the hair more manageable and able to hold a style for a longer period of time >> Protein conditioners may be used before chemical services to help ensure their success >> Usually left on about 10 minutes; always follow manufacturer's instructions
4. Moisturizing Conditioners *H₂O* *Emollients* *Humectants*	>> Contain hydrolyzed animal proteins and are recommended for dry, brittle hair that has been mechanically or chemically damaged >> The humectants (moisturizing ingredients) in a moisturizing conditioner will penetrate into each hair shaft to bind and hold moisture in the hair; these conditioners form a thin film on the cuticle, acting as a barrier to keep moisture from escaping >> Moisturizing conditioners should not be used for several days after a perm or it will go limp >> Follow manufacturer's directions for the length of time to leave on the hair after shampooing
5. Customized Conditioners	>> Formulated to meet special needs >> When a client's hair requires a combination of moisturizing and body-building properties, you may customize the treatment, mixing a moisturizing conditioner with a body-building protein product to improve the condition of your client's hair

Ingredients for Conditioners

Most protein conditioners are derived from animal or vegetable materials, and a few come from minerals.

›› A common animal protein found in conditioners is bovine serum, a refined and sterilized cattle tissue such as blood and bone marrow.

›› The refined placentas of female cattle and sheep and collagen are also popular animal proteins found in hair conditioners.

The vegetable proteins found in conditioners are usually made from soybeans, balsam trees, olives, wheat germ and tong beans.

›› These vegetable and animal proteins are refined through a very complex method (with various combinations of chemicals into the formulation of a conditioner).

›› A conditioner need not contain protein. However, since hair is largely made up of protein, it becomes the logical choice and a major component in most conditioning products.

Additional ingredients found in conditioners include:

›› **Amines/Quats** make hair easier to comb and control static.

›› **Dimethicones** give softness to the feel of hair without weighing it down. They are a form of silicone.

›› **Fatty alcohols and acids** give hair a smooth feel when dry and make it easier to comb. Fatty alcohols are creamy in texture and help retain moisture.

Some clients may be concerned that using a conditioner will make their hair "too soft" or "weigh it down." Just remember, the right conditioner for each client should provide the needed result: great looking, healthy and well-conditioned hair.

›› Conditioners should be used sparingly and only when necessary for clients with fine, thin hair.

›› A heavier conditioner may be needed for thick or curly hair.

›› In some cases, a leave-in product may be used to help control curl and waves.

> Conditioners usually penetrate deep into the hair, so they are formulated differently from rinses.

PRODUCT INFORMATION

The understanding of specific ingredients in the products you use and what effects they have will mark you as an above-ordinary professional. Safety Data Sheets from the manufacturer are the best source of specific information about a product. Additional resources can include:

›› The Food and Drug Administration (FDA), which is an agency that regulates cosmetics in the United States

›› United States Pharmacopeia (U.S.P.), which is a book that lists and standardizes drugs

›› International Cosmetic Ingredient Dictionary and Handbook, which is published by the Personal Care Products Council, formerly known as the Cosmetic, Toiletries and Fragrance Association

COSMETIC INGREDIENTS

When you read a product label, the ingredients are listed in order of their concentration. The first ingredient on the list appears in the largest amount and so on. At present, the cosmetic industry selects from more than 13,000 different ingredients. Reading the product labels and being able to follow the manufacturer's directions are the precautions you will take when working with this expansive variety of ingredients.

DISCOVER**MORE**

A preservative is a natural or synthetic ingredient that is added to personal care products to prevent spoilage, whether from microbial growth or undesirable chemical changes. The use of preservatives is essential in most products to prevent product damage caused by micro-organisms and to protect the product from contamination by the consumer during use.

>> An ingredient that protects the product from the growth of micro-organisms is called an antimicrobial.

>> A preservative may also be added to a product to protect it against damage and degradation caused by exposure to oxygen, and in this instance, these ingredients are called antioxidants.

>> Without preservatives, cosmetic products, just like food, can become contaminated, leading to product spoilage and possibly irritation or infections.

>> Microbial contamination of products, especially those used around the eyes and on the skin, can cause significant problems.

>> Preservatives help prevent such problems.

SALON**CONNECTION**

Product Ingredients

Here are some common ingredients and their usual function:

MOISTURIZERS

Function as a moisture barrier or to attract moisture from the environment:

- Cetyl alcohol (fatty alcohol) – Keeps oil and water from separating; also a foam booster
- Dimethicone silicone – Skin conditioner and anti-foam ingredient
- Isopropyl lanolate, myristate and palmitate
- Lanolin and lanolin alcohols and oil – Used in skin and hair conditioners
- Octyldodecanol – Skin conditioner
- Oleic acid (olive oil)
- Panthenol (vitamin B-complex derivative) – Hair conditioner
- Stearic acid and stearyl alcohol

PRESERVATIVES AND ANTIOXIDANTS (including vitamins)

Prevent product deterioration:

- Trisodium and tetrasodium edetate (EDTA)
- Tocopherol (vitamin E)

ANTIMICROBIALS

Fight bacteria:

- Butyl, propyl, ethyl and methyl parabens
- DMDM hydantoin
- Methylisothiazolinone
- Phenoxyethanol (also rose ether fragrance component)
- Quaternium-15

THICKENERS AND WAXES

Used in stick products such as lipsticks:

- Candelilla, carnauba and microcrystalline waxes
- Carbomer and polyethylene thickeners

SOLVENTS	EMULSIFIERS
Used to dilute:	Break up and refine:
>> Butylene glycol and propylene glycol	>> Glyceryl monostearate (also pearlescent agent)
>> Cyclomethicone (volatile silicone)	>> Lauramide DEA (also foam booster)
>> Ethanol (alcohol)	>> Polysorbates
>> Glycerin	

COLOR ADDITIVES:	HAIR COLOR
>> Synthetic organic colors derived from coal and petroleum sources (not permitted for use around the eye):	Phenol derivatives used in combination with other chemicals in permanent hair colors:
▪ D&C Red No. 7 Calcium Lake (lakes are dyes that do not dissolve in water)	>> Aminophenols
>> Inorganic pigments – Approved for general use in cosmetics, including for the area of the eye:	
▪ Iron oxides	
▪ Mica (iridescent)	

pH ADJUSTERS	OTHERS
Stabilize or adjust acids and bases:	>> Magnesium aluminum silicate – Absorbent, anti-caking agent
>> Ammonium hydroxide in skin peels and hair waving and straightening	>> Polymers and plasticizers – Hair-stiffening agents used in hairsprays
>> Citric acid – Adjusts pH	>> Silica (silicon dioxide) – Absorbent, anti-caking, abrasive
>> Triethanolamine pH – Adjuster used mostly in transparent soap	>> Sodium lauryl sulfate – Detergent
	>> Stearic acid – Cleansing, emulsifier
	>> Talc (powdered magnesium silicate) – Absorbent, anti-caking
	>> Zinc stearate – Used in powder to improve texture, lubricates

U.S. Food and Drug Administration, Center for Food Safety and Applied Nutrition, Office of Cosmetics Fact Sheet

Now that you have a broader understanding of the physical and chemical characteristics of cosmetics, you will be better able to serve your clients and meet their needs.

LESSONS LEARNED

The six cosmetic classifications include solutions, suspensions, emulsions, ointments, soaps and powders.

Shampoos contain surfactants that remove oil from the hair and include the following types:

- All-Purpose
- pH-Balanced
- Plain
- Soapless
- Medicated
- Clarifying
- Anti-Dandruff
- Strengthening Protein Additive

- Aerosol Dry
- Non-Aerosol Powder Dry
- Liquid Dry
- Conditioning
- Neutralizing
- Color
- Shampoos for Thinning Hair

Rinses affect mostly the surface of the hair and are applied to help close the cuticle and make hair feel soft and manageable. Rinses to be familiar with include vinegar and lemon rinses, cream rinses and medicated rinses.

Conditioners fortify the damaged areas of the hair and protect the hair against further damage from chemical services or heat.

Classifications include:

- Instant Conditioners
- Normalizing Conditioners
- Body-Building Conditioners
- Moisturizing Conditioners
- Customized Conditioners

The precautions necessary when working with various classifications of chemicals and professional products and cosmetics include:

- Following manufacturer's directions
- Reading labels

HAIR THEORY
102^c.14

EXPLORE //
Have you ever had a bad hair day?

INSPIRE //

Clients know they are in excellent hands
when you demonstrate your knowledge of
the hair and scalp.

ACHIEVE //

Following this lesson on *Hair Theory*, you'll be able to:

>> State how the hair bulb is formed

>> Identify the three stages of hair growth

>> Illustrate the three major layers of the hair

>> Explain the three factors that affect the behavior of hair

>> Describe the process of how hair gains its color

FOCUS //

HAIR THEORY

Hair Bulb Formation

Hair Growth

Hair Structure and Behavior

Natural Hair Color

102ᶜ.14 | HAIR THEORY

For your clients, nothing equals the security of being able to put themselves in the hands of a caring and competent salon professional. That means you will need to know all about hair. You will need to answer questions such as: Is hair alive? How does it reproduce? Does it respond to stimulation? Applying **trichology**, the study of hair, will be the beginning of providing those answers.

The main purposes of hair are:

>> Adornment
>> Protection from heat, cold and injury

Is hair alive? Even though hair is primarily protein and protein is the basis for all living matter, **only the cells of the hair bulb are alive**. The hair fiber or strand itself is not alive.

HAIR BULB FORMATION

To understand more about hair, you need to know how the hair bulb is formed. In fetal life, the hair follicle forms from a cluster of cells in the upper layer of skin, technically referred to as the **basal layer of the epidermis**.

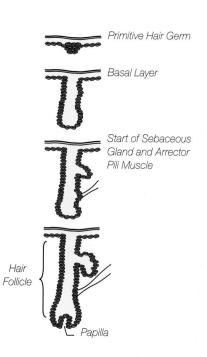

- » This cluster of cells, called the primitive hair germ, needs nourishment to grow into a fully developed hair follicle.

- » To get nourishment, the primitive hair germ works its way down into the lower (dermal) layer of the skin.

- » As the primitive hair germ works its way down, the cell cluster pulls the upper layer down with it, creating a **follicle or tube-like "pocket"** called the root sheath, out of which the hair will grow.

- » At the base of the hair follicle is a large structure called the papilla.

The shape of this follicle will determine the shape (round, oval or elliptical) of the hair shaft as it grows from the follicle.

- » Since the hair shaft actually grows out of the hair follicle, the diameter of the hair fiber will be the same as the diameter of the inside of the follicle.

- » The angle of the hair follicle determines the natural flow or wave pattern of the hair.

Primitive Hair Germ

Basal Layer

Start of Sebaceous Gland and Arrector Pili Muscle

Hair Follicle

Papilla

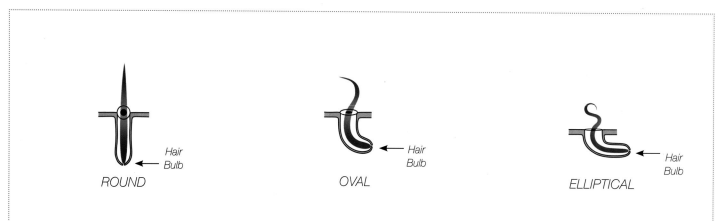

ROUND

Hair Bulb

OVAL

Hair Bulb

ELLIPTICAL

Hair Bulb

In straight hair, hair follicles are positioned perpendicular to the surface of the scalp, with a slight "tilt." The follicle in straight hair is typically round or oval.

In wavy to curly hair, hair follicles are positioned more curved to the surface of the scalp. The hair follicle that produces wavy to curly hair has a more oval shape.

In hair that is tightly curled or coily, the hair follicles grow from the scalp at a much stronger angle. The follicle is almost parallel to the surface of the scalp. Furthermore, the hair bulb itself is nearly doubled back over the follicle in a growth shape resembling a golf club. The hair follicle that produces a tightly curled or coily hair has a flattened, elliptical shape.

Two Primary Parts of the Hair

The hair root is the portion of hair that is inside the hair follicle under the skin's surface. The hair fiber, sometimes referred to as the hair shaft or strand, is the portion of the hair that extends above the skin's surface.

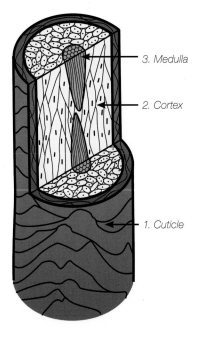

3. Medulla

2. Cortex

1. Cuticle

HAIR GROWTH

As the primitive hair germ continues its growth downward into the dermis and joins a small number of dermal cells, these cells eventually become the dermal papilla.

» The **papilla** is filled with capillaries (small blood vessels) that supply nourishment to the cells around it, called germinal matrix cells.

» The **germinal matrix** is the area of the bulb where cell division (mitosis) takes place.

» These germinal matrix cells produce the cells that ultimately keratinize (harden) and form the three major layers of the hair:

1. **Cuticle** – The outer covering of the hair shaft, made up of overlapping layers of transparent scales

2. **Cortex** – The second layer, consisting of unique protein structures (gives hair most of its pigment and strength–elasticity)

3. **Medulla** – The central core of the hair shaft, also called the pith or marrow (often absent in fine or very fine hair)

Attached to the side of the root sheath are bulges. These bulges are the beginnings of the sebaceous glands.

» The sebaceous glands, or oil glands, produce sebum (oil) and send it up through the hair follicles to the surface of the skin to prevent the hair and skin from becoming too dry.

» Sebum mixes with the body's perspiration to form the **acid mantle**.

» The acid mantle is important because it protects the cuticle, or outer covering, of the hair fiber and maintains the natural pH of hair and skin.

The **arrector pili muscle** comes from cells in the dermal layer that attach to the follicle just below the sebaceous gland.

» This is the muscle that causes the hair to stand on end when a person is scared or cold. It also aids in the secretion of sebum from the sebaceous glands.

» The other end of the arrector pili muscle attaches to the dermis (or lower layer) just beneath the basal layer of the epidermis.

Hair pulled out from the roots will grow again unless the papilla (origin of hair) is destroyed.

CELLS FORM PARTS OF THE HAIR

As cells begin their journey upward through the hair follicle, they are separated into specific types. In other words, some cells will become cuticle scales, others will make up the cortex and others will have the particular formation of medulla cells.

The journey that began deep in the skin, then grew through the outer layers now becomes the visible hair fiber (shaft or strand). Another result of this process of traveling upward is keratinization.

» **Keratinization** is a process whereby cells change their shape, dry out and form keratin protein.

» **Once keratinized, the cells that form the hair fiber or strand are no longer alive.**

DISCOVER**MORE**

Yes, what you eat does affect your hair. Here are the top 10 foods that nutritionists suggest affect healthy hair.

1. Salmon for shine
2. Greek yogurt because it is packed with protein
3. Spinach to battle brittle hair
4. Guava (tropical fruit) to prevent breakage
5. Iron-fortified cereal to prevent loss
6. Lean poultry for thickness
7. Sweet potatoes to fight dull-looking hair
8. Cinnamon for circulation
9. Eggs for growth
10. Oysters for fullness

Source: WebMD.com

AMINO ACIDS = PROTEIN = HAIR

Hair is made up primarily of protein, which is made from the linking together of amino acids. The cortex of the hair is made of chains that take the shape of a helix or coil.

» These amino acid chains coil around each other and become protofibrils.

» Protofibrils then twist around each other to become microfibrils.

» Microfibrils follow the same process and become macrofibrils that also spiral together.

» This process, when complete, forms the cortex of the hair.

» The cortex is then covered with the cuticle scales, which also contain protein.

» This twisting gives hair the ability to stretch like a spring without breaking.

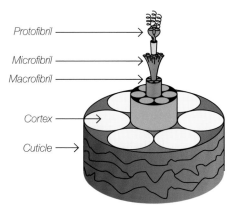

Protofibril

Microfibril

Macrofibril

Cortex

Cuticle

*Illustration of
Individual Hairstrand*

The prefix PROTO means first, the prefix MICRO means small and the prefix MACRO means large. Some examples are prototype, microscope and macrobiotics.

STAGES OF HAIR GROWTH

Genes determine the growing stages of the hair. There are three stages of hair growth:

1. **The anagen,** *or active growing stage*, during which time each hair bulb has an attached root sheath.

>> On the average 90% of a person's hair is in this stage, which can last from 2 to 6 years. Long waist-length hair is the result of long anagen stages.

>> Hair color is darker during the anagen stage.

2. **The catagen,** *a brief transitional stage,* when all cell division stops.

>> This stage lasts only a few weeks.

3. **The telogen**, *or resting stage*, when each hair bulb has no attached root sheath.

>> At this time the hair falls out.

>> On the average 10%-15% of hair is in the resting stage, which generally lasts 3-4 months.

>> Eventually, cell division is again stimulated, producing new hair, and the growth cycle starts again.

In humans, a mosaic pattern of hair growth occurs because each hair follicle has its own unique growing cycle.

>> Illness and lack of necessary vitamins and minerals can also affect hair and hair growth.

>> Anything that alters the physiological state of the body can affect the hair follicle and hair growth.

>> Disease and medication can also affect hair growth either by stimulating the onset of the telogen stage or by causing the production of abnormal, brittle hairs.

>> If a person has been ill or taking any medication, chemical services can damage hair that may be weak already.

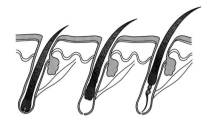

Anagen   *Catagen*   *Telogen*

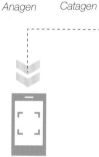

Anagen

Catagen

Telogen

Hair Facts

>> In humans, the average rate of hair growth is ½" (1.25 cm) per month.

>> Contrary to an old myth, hair does not grow after death of a human body.

>> Hair never grows on palms, soles of feet, lips or eyelids.

>> Eyebrows and eyelashes are replaced every 4-5 months.

>> Eyelashes are technically called cilia.

>> Supercilia is the technical name for the hair of the eyebrows.

>> Capilli is the technical name for the hair of the head.

HAIR STRUCTURE AND BEHAVIOR

There are three factors that affect the behavior of hair.

1. **Heredity**

   >> The genes that people inherit from their parents will determine many things about the makeup of the hair, such as its color, shape and diameter.

2. **Environment or Weather**

   >> If it's rainy or humid, hair will absorb moisture from the air.

   >> This extra moisture will alter some of the bonds that give hair its shape and, depending on the type of hair, it may become either limp or frizzy.

   >> Wind may dry out the hair and sun may damage it.

   >> Wet or dry weather conditions can cause a need for products that either take excess moisture out of the hair or put more moisture back in.

3. **Products or Appliances**

   >> Shampoos, conditioners, hair dryers, curling irons, perms, relaxers and hair color all affect the structural organization of the hair.

To better understand the differences in people's hair, you will need to take a closer look at hair's structural organization. The series of images taken of hair magnified hundreds of times show differences in the diameter of hair.

Structural Organization of Hair

Fine

Medium

Coarse

Observe the differences in the hair types shown below. Notice that the structural organization of hair as shown by diameter and amount of pigment is very different depending on ethnic origins. Keep in mind that diameter and amount of pigment may vary within each race/ethnicity as well.

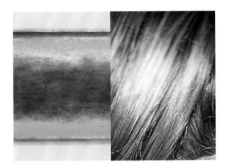

Europe

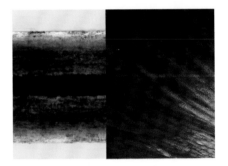

Asia, Indonesia

Africa, Caribbean, West Indies

As you've already seen, **the cuticle is the protective part of the hair shaft and is made up of a harder protein than the cortex.** If the hair is fine, treatments will affect it differently than if it's coarse.

>> Examples include how well the hair holds a set and how the hair takes a perm or relaxer.

>> It's an exaggeration to say that fine hair is "all cuticle," but that is often how it behaves.

>> In cross section, up to 40% of fine hair can be cuticle, compared with 10% or 12% in coarse hair.

>> The diameter of coarse hair is much larger than that of fine hair.

The cuticle is a hard, resistant layer of protein compared to the soft, elastic quality of the cortex.

>> If a particular hair is 90% cortex and 10% cuticle, then that hair behaves like the cortex. That means it has more elasticity and ability to be molded and reshaped.

>> But if the cuticle (which is harder or firmer and not easily stretched) makes up 40% of the hair fiber, then that hair will behave more like the cuticle and be more resistant to perms, relaxers or holding a set.

▶▶▶▶ One result of genetic coding is the diameter of the hair shaft. In the illustration below, notice the cuticle of a cross-sectional view of fine hair. Next, notice the illustration of coarse hair.

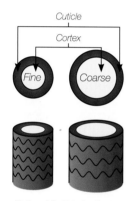

Ratio of Cuticle to Cortex

Fine Hair

Coarse Hair

SALON**CONNECTION**

Trichology

Many top salons offer trichology services that use both observation and scientific equipment to determine a regimen or course of action for a client to take for healthier hair. Some salon professionals even decide to specialize in trichology and go on to obtain certification as a trichologist.

If a salon doesn't offer trichology services, often they will connect with a lab or another salon that offers them so they can still offer recommendations for specific clients' needs.

NATURAL HAIR COLOR

One of the most fascinating aspects of hair is how it gets its color. Many people know that a pigment (coloring matter) called chlorophyll gives plants their green color. Most people don't know that a pigment called **melanin** gives skin and hair their color. In the hair, melanin is found mainly in the cortex–the hairstrand's second layer.

Here is how the natural coloring process works:

1. Melanin is produced by melanocytes, cells that exist among the dividing cells within the hair bulb.

2. Melanocytes rest near the hair bulb's nourishment center, the dermal papilla, and form bundles of a pigment protein complex called melanosomes.

3. Genes in the human body determine the amount and type of melanin produced by the melanocytes.

In simple terms, melanocytes produce melanosomes, which contain the pigment melanin.

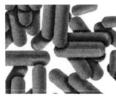 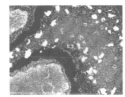 

| Melanocytes | Melanosomes | Melanin |

There are two types of melanin that create the large variety of hair colors, eumelanin and pheomelanin.

>> **Eumelanin** is brown/black in color

>> **Pheomelanin** is red/yellow in color

>> It is the amount, size and distribution of one or both of these melanins that influence the resulting hair color.

If the amount of pheomelanin is very concentrated and near the cuticle layer, the hair color will appear more red.

>> People with very dark, black hair may even have melanin in the cuticle layer, while lighter hair has melanin only in the cortex.

>> When there is a total lack of pigmentation in the hair and skin, the resulting condition is called **albinism**.

GRAY HAIR

Gray hair is caused by reduced color pigment, melanin, in the cortex layer of the hair.

Gray hair is sometimes referred to as mottled hair, indicating white spots scattered about in the hair shafts.

Gray hair grows from the papilla with the gray color; it doesn't turn gray after it has protruded above the skin.

The natural aging process in humans is the most common cause of graying hair. However, some serious illnesses or emotional conditions may cause the hair to turn gray.

A hereditary condition occurring at birth may cause some to gray prematurely. This is usually a defect in pigment formation.

Melanin in the Skin

Melanin in both the skin and hair serves as protection from the sun's damaging rays. For instance, if skin is exposed to sunlight, more melanin is created and sent to the surface to protect these sensitive cells, resulting in more color, or what is commonly called a "suntan."

>> Although skin color is passed on through the genes, races that originated closer to the equator developed a higher content of melanin in their skin to better protect it against the sun.

>> The same is true for hair. For example, white hair, which lacks melanin, is at the greatest risk for sun damage and can turn yellow from too much exposure.

>> Therefore, you should recommend products with sunscreen and encourage your clients to wear hats when they anticipate spending extended periods of time in the sun.

In the future, clients will know they are in excellent hands when you demonstrate your knowledge of the hair and scalp as you analyze and care for their hair.

LESSONS LEARNED

Hair bulb formation:

>> Develops from a cluster of cells in the basal layer of the epidermis

>> Moves downward to the dermal layer to receive nourishment

>> Forms a follicle from where the hair grows

The three stages of hair growth can be described as:

>> Anagen or active growing stage

>> Catagen or transitional stage

>> Telogen or resting stage

The three major layers of the hair include:

>> Cuticle, which is the outer covering of transparent scales

>> Cortex, which consists of protein structures that provide elasticity

>> Medulla, which is the core of the hair shaft

The three factors that affect the behavior of hair are:

>> Heredity – Genes inherited from parents

>> Environment – Air or moisture will alter some bonds

>> Products or appliances – Shampoos, curling irons, etc.

The process of how hair gains its color includes:

>> Genes determine the number of melanocytes (melanin cells) in the hair and the type of melanin (color) they produce.

>> Melanocytes produce more melanin by dividing cells within the hair bulb.

>> Melanocytes rest near the hair bulb's dermal papilla, collect together and form bundles of pigment called melanosomes.

>> Natural color is determined by the amount, size and distribution of these melanosomes.

HAIR CARE

102ᶜ.15 //

EXPLORE //
What special care does your hair require to stay healthy ?

INSPIRE //

Your confidence will grow as you identify hair and scalp problems and recommend effective treatments and courses of action for clients.

ACHIEVE //

Following this lesson on *Hair Care*, you'll be able to:

>> Identify the steps involved in doing a hair evaluation prior to a salon service

>> Describe the common hair conditions a salon professional may encounter in the salon

>> Explain common scalp conditions a salon professional may encounter in the salon

>> Offer examples of various hair-loss conditions and available treatments

FOCUS //

HAIR CARE

Hair Evaluation

Common Hair Conditions

Common Scalp Conditions

Hair Loss

102c.15 | HAIR CARE

Each person you'll work with is unique. The condition of each person's hair will differ, at least slightly, from any other you may have seen before. Sometimes those differences will be dramatic. Hair in poor condition will not hold a style or show off your design talent. Before you pick up shears or a comb, you will need to evaluate your client's hair.

HAIR EVALUATION

Hair is a fiber, and like all natural fibers, hair has different characteristics. Becoming familiar with your clients' hair prior to any service will allow you to support their individual hair needs.

1. **Determine your client's hair type and density.**

   » Knowing whether your client's hair type is fine, medium or coarse tells you what it can and cannot do on its own.

   » You will usually determine your client's hair type by touch and visual examination.

   » **The degree of coarseness or fineness in the hair fiber is referred to as texture.**

     ▪ The texture of coarse hair has the feel of wool; medium hair, the feel of cotton; and fine hair, the feel of silk.

     ▪ Other terms used to describe the feel of the hair include wiry or soft. Once you know that, you're on your way to determining the particular cleansing and conditioning products that will best meet the hair's needs.

Visual examination will give you lots of clues. You can usually see whether the hair is dry or oily but, when you suspect it's been chemically altered, confirm this with your client. Ask the client, "Is your hair currently permed or tinted? Relaxed?" These are key questions to determine which cleansing and conditioning products will work best.

A damaged or rough cuticle can cause hair to snag, look dull or be hard to manage.

» You can test for cuticle damage by running your thumb and finger along a strand of hair against the direction of growth.

» The more "drag" you feel, the more damage you can assume.

Additional visual examination would include determining hair density. **The density of the hair is judged by the number of active hair follicles per square inch on the scalp.**

» For instance, a person with a thick head of hair will have many more active hair follicles than a person with thin hair.

» Density is usually referred to as light, medium or heavy (sometimes as thin, medium or thick).

» Density of the hair influences the amount of hair that should be parted and wrapped around a perm tool, roller or curling iron. Heavy density requires smaller subsections than light hair density to allow for absorption of styling and processing lotions. In addition, placing too much hair on a perm tool or roller weakens the expected curl. Larger subsections can be used for light density hair.

2. **Determine your client's hair condition.** Once you know the type of hair fiber with which you will be working, you need to know the condition of that fiber. The condition of the hair is usually determined by two key factors:

a. **Hair porosity: The ability of the hair to absorb moisture, liquids or chemicals.** Raised cuticles influence the amount of liquid that can penetrate the hair. Healthy hair has a natural resistance to moisture due to its closed cuticle, while hair with raised cuticles is more porous.

TYPES OF POROSITY

Average Porosity *Slightly raised cuticle*	» Hair has the normal ability to absorb moisture » Hair is in good condition, suitable for most services
Resistant Porosity *Flat cuticle*	» Hair is able to absorb the least amount of moisture, usually due to the closeness of the cuticle layers » Also called "poor porosity"
Extreme Porosity *Raised cuticle*	» Hair is damaged from chemical services (overprocessing) or the environment, making it very porous » Hair with extreme porosity is not in good condition » Treatment is required prior to chemical services
Uneven Porosity *Mixed types*	» Hair has a combination of two or more different porosities

TEST FOR STRUCTURAL STRENGTH

While visual examination for elasticity is not absolutely accurate, it can tell you a great deal. Judgments can be made about what the hair needs just by looking at it and handling it. You can also perform this test for elasticity. (Note that this test is intended for straight or wavy hair.)

» Remove a strand of hair from the side of the head above the ears.

» Hold it between your thumb and forefinger and, with your thumbnail and index finger of the other hand, run the distance of hair rapidly as you would curl a ribbon with scissors. This will create a series of small curls.

» Gently pull the hair taut for 10 seconds and release.

■ If the hair completely, or almost completely, returns to the curl pattern, it is in good condition.

■ If it returns only 50% or less, it is structurally weak and needs conditioning.

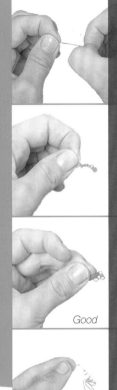

Good

Weak

b. **Hair elasticity: The ability of hair to stretch and return to its original shape without breaking.**

» Elasticity is also referred to as resiliency.

» Additional descriptive words to use when discussing elasticity with your client include pliability, buoyancy and springiness.

» Hair with normal elasticity is lively, able to spring back and usually has a shiny appearance.

» **Normal dry hair is capable of being stretched about 1/5 (20%) of its length.**

» **Wet hair is able to be stretched 40% to 50% of its length.**

3. **Once you have thoroughly evaluated the fiber, it's important to consider the climate in which you live.** Is your climate primarily dry or humid?

» Because the amount of moisture in the air governs the amount of moisture in the hair, predominant humidity makes a big difference in the way hair looks and feels and, thus, a difference in the shampoo and conditioners that can be used.

» In humid regions, where hair becomes heavy with moisture, curl retention is a challenge, and protein conditioning may be needed to balance the moisture intake.

» In dry climates, hair tends to be flyaway, so moisturizing and surface conditioning become very important to reduce static and soften the hair fiber.

The more information you can gain from the client, the easier it will be to achieve good results. You will want to give your client's hair whatever it needs to look, feel and behave beautifully, beginning with the right hair analysis and followed by proper shampooing and conditioning.

COMMON HAIR CONDITIONS

Each hairstrand has about 7-12 layers of cuticle scales. The cuticle layers protect the inside of the strand, which is called the cortex.

In healthy hair, the scales should lie flat along the cortex. The acid mantle lubricates the outermost layer of the cuticle and reduces friction. **Friction**, as in combing and brushing, is one way in which the cuticle can be damaged.

During your professional analysis of the hair fiber, a number of observations will alert you to possible problems you might encounter as you service the client's hair. Review the Common Hair Conditions chart for a close look at the condition and related info.

COMMON HAIR CONDITIONS

Condition	Also known as	Description

Broken Hair	*Also known as:* Abraded Cuticle Abraded Hair	**Cuticle becomes cracked and frayed:**
		 » Common cause of hair breakage is excessive stretching or traction.
		 » Hair subjected to excessive chemical processes, sun exposure and chlorine exposure may also exhibit breakage.
		 » Abrasion can result from brushing or manipulating the hair while performing salon services, especially when the hair is still wet.
		   ▪ Wet hair is more fragile than dry hair.
		   ▪ Treatment includes being aware of the tension when using rubber bands, hair clips, braids and wrapping hair around rollers, which can actually break the cuticle if too much tension is used.
		   ▪ In some cases cutting the hair may be a solution.

Split Ends	*Also known as:* Brittle Hair
	
	 Fragilitis Crinium (frah-**JIL**-i-tas **KRI**-nee-um)
	
	 Trichoptilosis (tri-kop-ti-**LOH**-sis)
		Start as small cracks in the cuticle that deepen into the cortex:
		 » Eventually the hair is split entirely.
		 » Often there is no cuticle left in the region of a split and, if not cut off, the ends become frayed and unsightly.
		   ▪ Split ends can be temporarily "sealed" by protein reconditioning. However, the process must be repeated frequently to keep the splits closed.
		   ▪ In severe cases, it is advisable to cut off the split ends and reinforce the hair with a protein conditioner to prevent the freshly cut ends from splitting.

Nodules	*Also known as:* Trichorrhexis Nodosa (**TRIK**-o-rek-sis no-**DO**-sa) Knotted Hair	**Characterized by the presence of lumps or swelling along the hair shaft:** » These lumps are broken or partly broken places on the hair shaft. » They can be caused by poorly performed chemical services, mechanical damage from curling irons or backcombing or by an inherited defect in the hair's keratin protein structure. » Physical knotting of the hair (known as trichonodosis); results from friction of the scalp, as in vigorous towel drying or rubbing against a pillow. ▪ Treatment includes avoiding harsh shampoos or chemicals, hot hair dryers, thermal irons and brushing the hair vigorously.

Canities (ka-**NEESH**-eez)		**Grayness or whiteness of the scalp hair:**
		 » Usually the result of natural aging
		 » Congenital canities occurs at or before birth occasionally in people with normal hair.
		 » Acquired canities refers to the loss of pigment in the hair as a person ages (graying of hair) or an onset may happen in early adult life.
		   ▪ Causes of acquired canities may be extended illness, nervous strain or heredity.
		   ▪ Oxidative haircolor products can be used to cover the gray hair.

Monilethrix (mo-**NIL**-e-thriks)	*Also known as:* Beaded Hair	**Beads or nodes formed on the hair shaft:** » Breaks in the hair occur between the beads or nodes; beaded appearance is due to periodic narrowing of the hair fiber. » People with monilethrix have sparse hair growth and short, brittle hair that breaks easily. ■ Treatment is limited; this hair condition may lessen with age.
Matting	*Also known as:* Plica Polonica (**PLY**-ca pol-**LON**-ni-ca)	**Characterized by a mass of hairstrands tangled together in a mat that cannot be separated:** » The cause of plica polonica—excessive matting—is usually excessive chemical hair lightening. » In some cases, excessive friction can be the cause, as in repeated backcombing. ■ The only remedy lies with a pair of shears.
Ringed Hair	*Also known as:* Pili Annulati (**PIL**-li an-u-**LA**-ti)	**Alternating bands of gray and dark hair:** » Ringed appearance is present from birth. » Gene passed on through one parent. » May affect any number of hair fibers. ■ There is no treatment for ringed hair.
Hypertrichosis (hi-per-tri-**KOH**-sis)	*Also known as:* Ambras Syndrome	**Abnormal coverage of hair on areas of the body where normally only lanugo or baby-fine hair appears:** » Referred to as werewolf syndrome. » Extremely rare with approximately 100 cases worldwide. ■ Laser-assisted hair removal is the most efficient method of long-term hair removal currently available.
Hirsutism (**HUR**-soot-iz-um)	*Also known as:* Superfluous Hair	**Excessive amounts of terminal hair found in women in areas of the body where men usually get hair, such as the face (lips and chin), back, abdomen and chest:** » Excess hair growth could be congenital (from birth) or acquired (such as a result of medication). ■ Removal methods range from tweezing to electrolysis, depending on the amount of hair to be removed, location and client preference.

Mechanical damage results from the incorrect use of salon tools. Some brushes can pull the hair and stretch it until it breaks, or they can wear down and loosen the cuticle cells. **If a dryer is used too close to the hair or a hot curling iron is left on too long, the hair may become brittle and the cortex could possibly melt.**

Usually, if the cortex is damaged, the cuticle has been damaged, too. However, sometimes the hair is damaged inside with only barely noticeable damage to the cuticle scales. Compare the picture of a normal cortex with the picture of the melted cortex. Other examples of heat styling damage include blistering and fracturing of the hair fiber due to improper heat-styling or use of low-quality salon appliances.

COMMON SCALP CONDITIONS

Listed below are the more common scalp disorders or diseases that you may come in contact with as a salon professional.

DISORDER OR DISEASE	MEDICAL TERM	DESCRIPTION	TREATMENT
Scales *Disorder*	Psoriasis (soh-**REYE**-ah-sis)	Thick, crusty patches of red irritated scalp resulting from an autoimmune disease of the skin	Refer client to a physician
Dandruff *Disorder*	Pityriasis (pit-i-**REYE**-ah-sis)	Chronic scalp condition with excessive flaking, which accumulates on the scalp or falls to the shoulders, as well as itchiness, tightness and irritation of the scalp	Frequent shampooing with an anti-dandruff shampoo containing either pyrithione zinc, selenium disulfide or ketoconazole
Dry Dandruff *Disorder*	Pityriasis capitis simplex (kah-**PEYE**-tis **SIM**-pleks)	Dry flakes attached to the scalp or on the hair which can appear translucent	
Greasy or Waxy Dandruff *Disorder*	Pityriasis steatoides (ste-a-**TOY**-dez)	Oily flakes combined with sebum which stick to the scalp in clusters and can appear yellowish in color	

The leading cause of dandruff is a naturally occurring microscopic fungus called **Malassezia** (mal-uh-**SEEZ**-ee-uh). The fungus feeds on the scalp's natural oils and creates byproducts that cause irritation on the scalp. The body reacts to the irritation by accelerating the amount and rate of flaking of dead skin cells.

EXTERNAL PARASITES

Be advised that the conditions listed on the chart below are contagious. Refer clients with these conditions to a physician before performing any salon services.

DISORDER OR DISEASE	MEDICAL TERM	DESCRIPTION	TREATMENT
Ringworm *Disease*	Tinea (**TIN**-ee-ah)	Red, circular patch of small blisters; caused by a vegetable parasite	Refer client to a physician
Ringworm of the Scalp *Disease*	Tinea capitis	Enlarged open hair follicles that are surrounded by clusters of red spots (papules); hair is likely to break in area infected; black spots may also be visible	Refer client to a physician
Honeycomb Ringworm *Disease*	Tinea favosa (fa-**VO**-sah) or Favus (**FAY**-vus)	Dry, yellow, encrusted areas on the scalp called scutula (**SKUT**-u-la); may have a peculiar odor; shiny pink or white scars may result	Refer client to a physician
Itch Mite *Disorder*	Scabies	Red and watery vesicles or pus-filled areas caused by an animal parasite (itch mite) burrowing under the skin	Refer client to a physician
Head Lice *Disorder*	Pediculosis capitis (pe-dik-u-**LOH**-sis)	Infestation of head lice on the scalp causing itching and eventual infection	Refer client to a physician

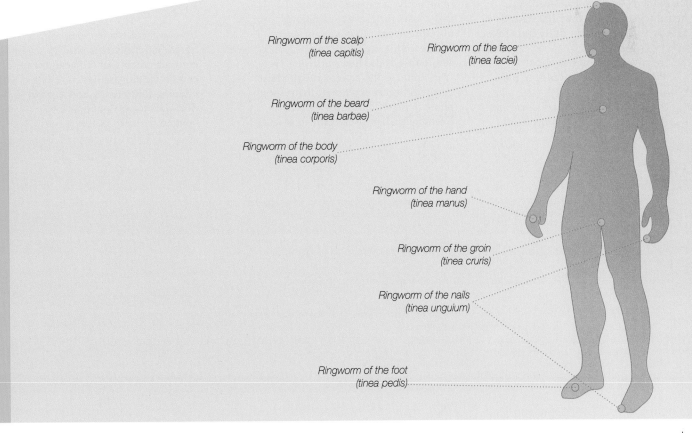

Ringworm of the scalp (tinea capitis)

Ringworm of the face (tinea faciei)

Ringworm of the beard (tinea barbae)

Ringworm of the body (tinea corporis)

Ringworm of the hand (tinea manus)

Ringworm of the groin (tinea cruris)

Ringworm of the nails (tinea unguium)

Ringworm of the foot (tinea pedis)

HAIR LOSS

As a salon professional, you are often the first person asked to respond to questions about hair loss. Knowing how to address client concerns will greatly affect your client's well-being.

NORMAL HAIR LOSS

Hair actually covers most of your body before you are born. **Lanugo** is the term assigned to this baby-fine, silky hair, which is shed shortly after birth.

>> Lanugo is replaced with vellus, which covers most of the body including the head, and is often not visible to the naked eye.

>> **Vellus** is short, fine, non-pigmented hair found more abundantly on women.

>> Around the time of puberty, vellus hair is replaced by **terminal hair**, which originates from certain predetermined follicles that produce long, thick pigmented hair, like normal scalp and eyebrow hair.

Everyone loses some hair every day. Actually between **40 and 100 strands of hair is the average daily hair loss**.

>> The average head has about 100,000 individual strands of hair.

>> There is an average of 1,000 hairs per square inch on the average head.

>> The number of hairs on the head varies by color with the following average numbers:

- Red = 90,000
- Brown = 110,000
- Black = 108,000
- Blond = 140,000

ANDROGENETIC HAIR LOSS

Alopecia, or excessive hair loss, may be caused by a fungal or bacterial infection or inflammatory disease of the scalp. This abnormal condition occurs in both men and women.

>> If the scalp appears abnormal at all, do not attempt any services. Instead suggest that your client see a dermatologist.

>> When there is no apparent scalp abnormality, hair loss may be caused by nutritional deficiency, drugs, emotional trauma and other physiological changes.

The most common form of alopecia is **androgenetic alopecia**, a combination of heredity, hormones and age that causes progressive shrinking, or miniaturization, of certain scalp follicles. This shrinking causes a shortening of the hair's growing cycle. Over time, as the active growth phase (anagen) becomes shorter, the resting phase (telogen) becomes longer. Eventually, there is no growth at all.

Progressive Miniaturization of the Hair Follicle

Recognizing Androgenetic Alopecia

In general, asking questions about family history will give a good indication of whether the hair loss is androgenetic or another type of alopecia.

>> Ask your client if any relatives, including parents or more distant relatives, have hair loss, whether thinning has been gradual over several years or sudden or patchy.

>> If the hair loss was sudden or patchy, advise your client to talk to a physician.

>> If your client is a woman, ask her about crash diets, oral contraceptives and medications for certain cardiovascular conditions, vitamin deficiencies, and thyroid disorders to rule out hair loss created by these factors.

The degree of hair loss can be evaluated by rating pattern and density:

>> Pattern refers to the shape and location of the area with hair loss.

>> Density refers to how much hair is covering the scalp in the area of hair loss.

Note: Because women experience a single pattern of hair loss, only density needs to be evaluated.

MEN WITH ANDROGENETIC ALOPECIA

Condition known as male-pattern baldness

Frequently progresses to the familiar horseshoe-shaped fringe of hair

Pattern is evaluated when reviewing loss

Common for men to "go bald"

WOMEN WITH ANDROGENETIC ALOPECIA

Condition appears as a generalized thinning of the hair over the entire crown of the head

Displays as scattered hair thinning; over time the sides may become thinner; front hairline is retained as a straight pattern or "M"-shaped

Density is evaluated when reviewing loss

Extremely rare for a woman to "go bald"

SALON**CONNECTION**

Androgenetic Alopecia ID

Here are some easy-to-follow guidelines a salon professional might use to identify possible androgenetic alopecia.

In the area where the scalp shows the most, look for a large number of miniaturized follicles that are producing shorter, thinner, fewer hairs than the long ones. Hold an index card near the scalp to help you see the miniaturized hairs. If you see a lot of miniaturized hairs, your client has androgenetic alopecia.

In addition to identifying miniaturized hairs by holding an index card close to the scalp, in the case of female clients, you may:

1. Part the hair in the middle of the scalp and look at the width of the part. A part that shows more scalp than normal indicates hair loss (a part on a normal head is very narrow).

2. Ask if the diameter of the ponytail has become smaller over the years (if applicable). A smaller diameter is one of the signs of androgenetic alopecia.

3. Ask your client if there are many hairs left on the brush after brushing once or if there are many hairs in the shower drain after shampooing. Check if your client has excessive shedding by simply running your hand through her hair. In general, anyone who has unusual, excessive shedding should see a doctor.

In the case of men, ask the client if the size of the bald spot has progressively increased over the years. In frontal balding, ask if the hairline has been progressively receding. With male clients, it is important to evaluate pattern separately from density because a man with a small pattern but a poor density may not respond to treatment as well as a man with a large area of hair loss and a fair density.

DEGREES OF MALE-PATTERN BALDNESS

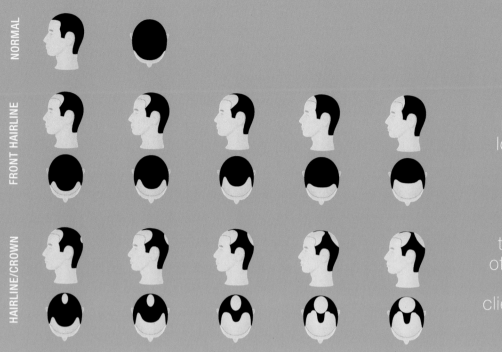

Hair loss is identified according to various measurement systems. Each system identifies the pattern and density of the hair loss. Pattern refers to the shape and location of the hair loss, while density refers to how much hair covers the scalp in the area of the hair loss. These types of illustrations are often labeled so you can record and track your client's hair loss from one visit to another.

OTHER TYPES OF HAIR LOSS

Postpartum Alopecia	» Temporary hair loss at the conclusion of pregnancy » Cause is based on hair staying longer in the anagen cycle during pregnancy » After childbirth these hairs enter the telogen phase » Many women become concerned about the sudden loss of hair, but it isn't long until the amount of hair seems balanced again
Alopecia Areata *Alopecia Areata Totalis* *Alopecia Areata Universalis*	» Autoimmune skin disease that is confined to a few areas and is often reversed in a few months, though recurrences may occur; sudden loss of hair in round or irregular patches without display of an inflamed scalp » Occurs in individuals who have no obvious skin disorder or serious disease » Alopecia areata totalis presents presents itself as the total loss of hair on the scalp » Alopecia areata universalis presents itself as the loss of hair over the entire scalp and body
Alopecia Prematura	» Refers to baldness that occurs early in life, beginning as early as late adolescence
Telogen Effluvium	» Premature shedding of hair during the resting phase » Can result from various causes such as childbirth, shock, drug intake, fever, etc. » Some women also experience sudden hair loss when they stop taking birth-control pills or if they follow a crash diet too low in protein » The hair loss is usually reversed once the condition is corrected
Traction or Traumatic Alopecia	» Hair loss due to repetitive traction (excessive stretching or pulling) on the hair as in wearing tight chignons or ponytails, tight rollers, tight cornrows or using excessive tension during brushing and combing, especially when hair is wet » Often caused by mechanical damage and sometimes by chemical damage, such as the excessive application of permanent wave solutions » This condition is usually reversed once the trauma has stopped

The National Alopecia Areata Foundation estimates that 6.5 million men, women and children suffer from alopecia areata.

DISCOVER**MORE**

Trichotillomania—sometimes referred to as "trich" or "TTM"—is a condition in which people compulsively pull hair from their bodies, and may affect up to 2%-4% of the population. People may pull from their scalp, eyebrows, eyelashes, facial hair, pubic area, or anywhere else hair grows on the body. Trichotillomania varies in severity, and ranges from unnoticeable diffused pulling to large bald areas and everything in between. There is no cure for trichotillomania, and many people with it feel intense shame and isolation. Some avoid hair, makeup, facials, and other related professional services for fear of being discovered or judged. Clients may also come to you for help concealing the effects of trichotillomania, which may include uneven hair or bald spots and missing or patchy eyelashes, eyebrows and facial hair.

As a professional, it is important for you to know what other resources are available.

The **Trichotillomania Learning Center (TLC)** provides services and hosts events for children and adults with trichotillomania, skin-picking and related disorders; their parents, families, doctors, therapists; hair and skin care providers; and the media. They also provide referral listings of skin and hair care TLC Service Providers and information on how to become one. www.trich.org

The **Canadian BFRB Support Network (CBSN)** aims to reduce the stigma, shame, and isolation information associated with trichotillomania, skin-picking and similar disorders by providing information and hosting events in Canada. www.canadianbfrb.org

Wigs for Kids provides hair replacement systems and support for children who have lost their hair for a wide range of reasons, including trichotillomania, at no cost to the children or their families. www.wigsforkids.org

—Andrea D. Kelley, MA, MSW

The Food and Drug Administration (FDA) has ruled that products claiming hair regrowth or hair loss prevention cannot be marketed without prior FDA review and approval.

HAIR-LOSS TREATMENTS

Treatment of Androgenetic Alopecia

Several products have been developed to treat androgenetic alopecia. If your client is working with a physician who has prescribed one of the treatments available to regrow hair and has requested assistance from you in applying product treatments, read and follow the manufacturer's directions.

Other hair-loss treatments that your client might consider include:

1. FDA-approved products that regrow hair or prevent hair loss.

2. Products that provide an ideal environment for possible hair regrowth or loss prevention.

3. Surgical options are available mostly for men. Hair transplants, hair plugs and scalp reductions are performed by physicians or dermatologists. Several visits are necessary to achieve gradual results that allow periods of recuperation for the patient.

4. Wigs, toupées, hair additions or hair weaving are available as non-medical options. For additional information, refer to related lessons for wigs, hairpieces and hair additions.

5. Cosmetic hair thickeners are products designed to volumize the hair. These products do not grow hair or put a halt to hair loss. They simply coat the hair, therefore giving it more body.

SALON**CONNECTION**

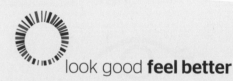

Look Good Feel Better

Look Good Feel Better is a free, non-medical, brand-neutral public service program that teaches beauty techniques to cancer patients to help them look good, improve self-esteem and manage the appearance-related side effects of cancer treatment with greater confidence.

Look Good Feel Better group programs are open to all women with cancer who are undergoing chemotherapy, radiation, or other forms of treatment. In the United States alone, more than 900,000 women have participated in the program, which now offers 15,400 group workshops nationwide in more than 2,500 locations.

Thousands of volunteer beauty professionals support Look Good Feel Better. All are trained and certified by the Personal Care Products Council Foundation, the American Cancer Society, and the Professional Beauty Association at local, statewide and national workshops. Other volunteer health care professionals and individuals also give their time to the program.

For more information and to volunteer, visit lookgoodfeelbetter.org, call the 24-hour hotline at 800-395-LOOK or contact your local American Cancer Society office.

The **Personal Care Products Council Foundation** provides the program oversight, makeup, materials and financial support to implement Look Good Feel Better's many services.

The **American Cancer Society®** administers Look Good Feel Better nationwide, manages volunteer training and serves as the primary source of information to the public.

The **Professional Beauty Association (PBA)** is the largest organization of salon professionals, with members representing salons and spas, distributors, manufacturers, and licensed professionals. PBA encourages Look Good Feel Better participation among beauty professionals, recruits its members to volunteer with the program and manages the training program.

As your career advances you will gain confidence in recognizing and managing a broad range of hair and scalp conditions. You will also feel the reward of being able to recommend effective treatments and courses of action for your clients.

Head Louse

LESSONS LEARNED

The steps involved in doing a hair evaluation prior to a salon service include determining the client's hair type and density, determining the clients hair condition and considering the effects of the climate.

Common hair conditions a salon professional may encounter in the salon include:

>> Broken hair
>> Split ends
>> Matting

>> Nodules
>> Canities
>> Ringed hair

>> Hypertrichosis
>> Hirsutism
>> Monilethrix

Common scalp conditions a salon professional may encounter in the salon include:

>> Psoriasis
>> Dandruff
>> Dry dandruff

>> Greasy or waxy dandruff
>> Ringworm
>> Ringworm of the scalp

>> Honeycomb ringworm
>> Itch mite
>> Head lice

Examples of various hair loss conditions include alopecia, androgenetic alopecia, postpartum alopecia, alopecia areata, alopecia areata totalis, alopecia areata universalis, alopecia prematura, telogen effluvium and traction alopecia.

Available hair-loss treatments include:

>> Prescribed medications

>> FDA-approved products

>> Products that provide an ideal environment for hair growth or loss prevention

>> Surgical options

>> Non-surgical options such as wigs, toupées, hair additions or hair weaving

>> Cosmetic hair thickeners that volumize hair

SHAMPOO AND SCALP MASSAGE THEORY

EXPLORE //

Why do you think many people say the shampoo and scalp massage is their favorite part of the service experience?

INSPIRE //

The shampoo experience can make or break the career of a hairstylist.

ACHIEVE //

Following this lesson on *Shampoo and Scalp Massage Theory*, you'll be able to:

>> List considerations for draping during a shampoo and scalp massage service

>> Explain the purpose of shampooing and conditioning

>> Compare the five types of massage movements used during a scalp massage

FOCUS //

SHAMPOO AND SCALP MASSAGE THEORY

Draping

Shampoo and Condition

Scalp Massage

Shampoo and Scalp Massage Service Considerations

102^c.16 |
SHAMPOO AND SCALP MASSAGE THEORY

D raping, shampooing and scalp massage are often the first services a client experiences in the salon. Making them a delightful, memorable experience can build client loyalty to you and the salon.

The safety, comfort and protection of the client's skin, hair and clothing are all part of the salon professional's responsibility and important considerations for overall client satisfaction.

Your review of shampooing and scalp massage begins with draping.

DRAPING

Draping is performed prior to hair care services, such as shampooing and scalp massage, to protect the client's skin and clothing. Prior to draping, ask the client to remove any jewelry (necklaces, earrings, hairpins or eyeglasses) and store it in a safe place. For your protection, and the protection of others in the service area, ensure that jewelry and other valuables, such as purses, do not block traffic areas, where they could cause accidents or injury.

Many regulating agencies have rules about draping, such as:

>> **Shampoo capes** used to drape the client during salon services must be **laundered in a solution capable of disinfecting the cape.**

>> **The neck of the cape cannot come in direct contact with the client's skin.**

Therefore, always place a neck strip, and/or towel, between the client's neck and the neckband of the cape.

In ancient times, many people believed that their heads were protected by gods or spirits, and that shampooing might injure these spirits. Shampooing became a ceremonial practice performed once a year in honor of a god's or goddess' birthday.

DRAPING CONSIDERATIONS

TOWEL

>> Placed around client's neck

>> Serves as protective barrier between the client's neck and plastic or waterproof cape; used for shampooing, wet hair sculpting, designing and chemical services

PLASTIC CAPE

>> Protects the client and the client's clothing from becoming wet or damaged during shampooing, wet hair sculpting, designing and chemical services

NECK STRIP

>> Replaces towel following shampoo service if hair sculpting service follows

>> Allows hair to fall naturally because it is less bulky than a towel

>> Prevents loose hairs from embedding into client's clothing during dry hair sculpting

CLOTH CAPE

>> Used for designing and sculpting services on dry hair

>> Lighter-weight and therefore more comfortable

>> Allows dry hair to slide to floor easily

SHAMPOO AND CONDITION

Proper maintenance of the hair and scalp begins with what most of us are already familiar with: shampooing and conditioning. **The purpose of shampooing is to cleanse the scalp and hair by removing dirt, oils and product buildup. The purpose of conditioning is to fortify the damaged areas of the hair and protect it against further damage from chemical services or heat.**

>> **The hair should be shampooed as often as necessary with a shampoo specifically designed for the type and condition of hair.**

>> **If the hair is not cleansed properly, oil and dirt can accumulate and lead to scalp disorders.**

>> **Conditioners provide a temporary remedy for existing hair problems.**

>> **If a client has any infectious diseases or scalp disorders, refer them to a physician; do not proceed with the service.**

The shampoo service is performed prior to most hair services, except certain hair color or chemical services. For example, shampooing is not performed prior to chemical relaxing services since shampoo could cause increased irritation, a burning sensation or actual burning if it interacts with the chemical product that is applied to the hair.

Most hair colors are applied to dry hair, so for these services, shampooing is also skipped, unless a client's hair is extremely oily or dirty. And some hair color products might specify application to towel-dried hair following a shampoo service. Always read the manufacturer's directions to be certain.

Understanding the pH (potential hydrogen) level of shampoos and conditioners will help you select the right product for each client's hair type and condition. For instance, a shampoo with a high pH level can make hair dry and brittle, so for already brittle hair, a pH-balanced (4.5 to 5.5) shampoo is recommended. Shampoo and conditioner products are introduced in the lessons *pH* and *Hair Care Product Knowledge*.

WATER

Water (H_2O) is classified as soft or hard. Knowing which type of water you're working with will help you choose the proper shampoo.

>> **Soft water is generally preferred for shampooing.**

>> **Soft water is rainwater or water that has been chemically treated.**

>> **Hard water contains minerals and does not allow the shampoo to lather freely.**

>> **Hard water can be softened by a chemical process.**

Test water temperature prior to applying.

Always remember to **monitor the water temperature before applying the water stream to your client's scalp,** and during the rinsing portion of the service.

>> Hold the shampoo hose and position a finger in the water stream.

>> Make sure the water pressure is moderate and comfortable for your client.

　▪　 Excess water pressure is a primary cause of water-spill accidents.

Sometimes water may be present on the floor in the shampoo area. **Always wipe up water spills to prevent accidents and wet floors in the school or salon.**

BRUSHING AND COMBING

Prior to the shampoo service, the client's hair should be brushed to remove tangles.

» **Brushing also increases blood circulation to the scalp while removing dust, dirt and product buildup.**

» Combing with a large-tooth comb, or plastic brush with wide spacing, is generally performed after a shampoo service to remove tangles from wet hair.

Under all circumstances, brush the hair from the ends first, then work toward the scalp. Brushing the hair from the ends first allows you to detangle the hair without adding stress or tangles. Once the hair is free of tangles, you can brush thoroughly from the scalp to the ends.

Brushes made from natural bristles are recommended; their overlaying bristles clean hair better than nylon bristles. **Brushing hair prior to a chemical service and/or if cuts or abrasions are evident is not recommended.** When brushing hair, consider the following factors:

» Does the client's hair have extreme product buildup that makes parting the hair prior to brushing difficult?

» Is the hair long or short?

» Is the hair naturally straight or curly?

Brush tangles from the hair.

Remove tangles in a methodical manner.

REMOVING TANGLES FROM WET HAIR

After the shampoo service, tangles should be removed in a specific, methodical manner:

>> Start at the lowest point of the tangled area (in this photo, the nape section).

>> Release a section of hair with a large-tooth comb while lifting the weight of the tangled hair.

>> Begin at the ends of the hair and work toward the scalp, combing down through the hair.

   ▪ Holding the hair at the base minimizes discomfort while detangling; remember that chemically treated hair tends to tangle.

>> Continue combing this section until all tangles are removed; to remove stubborn tangles, use short, gentle strokes.

>> Part off another section immediately above the first section.

>> Remove tangles in the same manner as before, starting at the ends.

>> Comb through the two untangled sections and blend the hair together.

>> Continue this procedure throughout the crown, sides and, finally, the top.

While it is important to know proper draping and shampooing, understanding the theory behind scalp massage and its relaxing and stimulating effects can benefit you and enhance your client's shampoo experience.

Product use combined with massage improves the condition of the scalp.

SCALP MASSAGE

Massage is a scientific method of manipulating the body by rubbing, pinching, tapping, kneading or stroking with the hands, fingers or an instrument. Dating back to antiquity, massage is used for health, beauty and medical reasons. Many believe that massage improves blood circulation, relieves headaches, reduces fat, diminishes fatigue and induces sleep. Today massage is not only a service in itself but is included in other services such as shampooing, manicures and facials. This section will focus on scalp massage offered alone or during a shampoo service.

Scalp massage involves movements performed on the scalp to relax the muscles and increase blood circulation.

>> Scalp treatments combine the benefit of massage with products designed to improve the condition of the scalp.

>> The relaxation experienced during scalp massage is a benefit that helps build client loyalty.

Although using essential oils, lotions or creams in scalp treatments can provide specific benefits, these products may leave residue on the hair. Plus the stimulation from the massage may cause scalp sensitivity.

For these reasons, avoid performing a scalp treatment immediately prior to a chemical service. Be guided by the condition of the client's hair and scalp as well as manufacturer's directions.

It is important to:

>> **Establish a soothing or stimulating rhythm when performing the massage movements**

>> **Maintain contact with the client throughout the massage for a relaxing experience**

>> **Use firm, controlled movements to maximize the benefit and gain your client's confidence**

>> **Keep your nails at a moderate length to avoid scratching the scalp**

Just as products vary, so will the movements you use during the scalp massage. Customizing your own sequence of movements might help generate client satisfaction and loyalty. Listed here are the basic massage movements and the effects they cause.

As you review, consider these important points:

>> Effleurage, petrissage and tapotement are the three primary scalp movements, with petrissage being the most important.

>> Petrissage stimulates the sebaceous glands, which produce a natural oil, sebum, that is often lacking in dry hair and scalp.

THE 5 BASIC MOVEMENTS OF MASSAGE

MOVEMENT	DESCRIPTION	EFFECT
1. **Effleurage** (**EF**-loo-rahzh)	» Light, gliding strokes, or circular motions made with the palms of the hands or pads of the fingertips » Often used to begin and/or end a treatment » Also used on the face, neck and arms	Relaxing, soothing
2. **Petrissage** (**PEH**-treh-sahzh)	» Light or heavy kneading and rolling of the muscles » Performed by kneading muscles between the thumb and fingers or by pressing the palm of the hand firmly over the muscles, then grasping and squeezing with the heel of the hand and fingers » Generally performed from the front of the head to the back » Also used on the face, arms, shoulders and upper back	Deep stimulation of muscles, nerves and skin glands; promotes the circulation of blood and lymph
3. **Tapotement** (tah-**POHT**-mant) *Also known as percussion or hacking*	» Light tapping or slapping movement applied with the (sometimes partly flexed) fingers » Also used on arms, back and shoulders	Stimulates nerves, promotes muscle contraction; increases blood circulation
4. **Friction** (**FRIK**-shun)	» Circular movement with no gliding used on the scalp, or with a facial when less pressure is desired » Applied with fingertips or palms	Stimulates nerves; increases blood circulation
5. **Vibration** (vi-**BRAY**-shun)	» Shaking movement » Arms shake as fingertips or palms touch the client	Highly stimulating

DISCOVER**MORE**

The term aromatherapy describes the combination of our sense of smell and the use of plant extracts and their healing abilities. "Aroma" refers to the natural fragrance of plants, and "therapy" means "cure." Aromatherapy is incorporated into many salon services including scalp treatments.

Essential oils and scalp products containing vitamins and plant extracts address many health and wellness concerns. Therapeutic effects include invigorating the scalp, encouraging renewed hair growth, relieving flaking associated with dryness or dandruff, increasing blood circulation and calming and soothing the mind and body.

Aromatherapy expert Dr. Blossom Kochhar has shared a list of essential oils she uses in her scalp recipes. Note that essential oils should be blended with a base oil, such as sweet almond oil or grapeseed oil, rather than used directly on the skin. When blending oils, follow the chart shown here.

Recommended Use

Essential Oil	Base Oil
20-60 drops	3.5 fl oz (100 ml)
7-25 drops	1 fl oz (25 ml)
3-5 drops	1 tsp (5 ml)

Premixed scalp therapy oils, whether purchased from a manufacturer or hand-mixed, can be applied directly to the scalp prior to scalp massage. Essential oils, which can also be mixed with shampoo, can then be applied to the scalp prior to the scalp treatment, or incorporated into a shampoo service.

Hair or Scalp Condition	Recommended Oils
Normal hair and scalp	Rosemary Chamomile
Oily hair and scalp	Patchouli Cedarwood Clary sage
Dry hair and scalp	Ylang-ylang Sandalwood Lavender
Oily dandruff	Lemon Rosemary Cedarwood Thyme
Alopecia (hair loss)	Sandalwood Bay Lavender Clary sage Rosemary

SHAMPOO AND SCALP MASSAGE SERVICE CONSIDERATIONS

Draping, shampooing and conditioning preparation and procedures vary based on the timing allowed for the service and each client's needs. For example, you might use a booster chair when shampooing a young child or, in some cases, elderly or disabled clients might lean forward into the shampoo bowl, rather than lean back, for medical or comfort purposes. Clients in wheelchairs might need to remain in wheelchairs rather than transfer to the shampoo chair.

Your understanding of basic draping, shampooing and scalp massage techniques will help strengthen the foundation of your skill level. Remember how powerful your touch can be. As you move through the service, ask how your client is doing. Be aware of your client's needs, making adjustments and recommendations for hair condition, water temperature and massage movements.

Check the Neck

Ask your client if they are comfortable after they have reclined into the shampoo bowl. Observe the position of their neck to ensure it is not hyperextended or at a severe angle. Along with being uncomfortable, in rare cases this position was found to be responsible for serious damage to blood vessels in the back of the neck. The term "Beauty Salon Stroke Syndrome" refers to these rare cases. If needed, adding a neck rest pad or a few folded towels in the neck rest area of the shampoo bowl can make the client more comfortable and help them avoid hyperextending their neck.

SALON**CONNECTION**

Shampoo Comfort

There are several types of shampoo bowls and chairs. Some bowls allow you to stand behind the client, which helps reduce back fatigue. Other chairs have hydraulic controls that allow you to adjust the height or recline.

LESSONS LEARNED

While draping during a shampoo and scalp massage service, consider:

>> Using a towel to protect the neck from touching the plastic or waterproof cape

>> Protecting the client and the client's clothing from becoming wet or damaged

>> Replacing the towel with a neck strip if a hair sculpting service will follow

>> Using a cloth cape for designing and sculpting services on dry hair

The purpose of shampooing is to cleanse the scalp and hair by removing dirt, oils and product buildup. The purpose of conditioning is to fortify the damaged areas of the hair and protect it against further damage from chemical services or heat.

The five types of massage movements are:

1. Effleurage – Light, gliding strokes, or circular motions, for a relaxing, soothing effect

2. Petrissage – Light or heavy kneading and rolling of the muscles to achieve deep stimulation of the muscles, nerves and skin glands, and promote the circulation of blood and lymph

3. Tapotement – Light tapping or slapping movement to stimulate nerves, promote muscle contraction and increase blood circulation

4. Friction – Circular movement with no gliding to stimulate nerves and increase blood circulation

5. Vibration – Shaking movement with a highly stimulating effect

What nonverbal signs do you think clients display as they receive shampoo or scalp massage services?

SHAMPOO AND CONDITION
GUEST EXPERIENCE | 102^c.17

This lesson focuses on the consultation for shampooing; a review of the products, tools, supplies and equipment needed for shampooing; conditioning and scalp massage; and the infection control and safety guidelines for a healthy service experience in the salon.

INSPIRE //

Consulting with the client, plus working safely, will result in a satisfied client.

ACHIEVE //

Following this lesson on *Shampoo and Condition Guest Experience*, you'll be able to:

>> Identify the information found in the client record related to shampooing and scalp massage

>> Summarize the service essentials related to the shampoo and condition client visit

>> Explain how knowing the products, tools, supplies and equipment related to shampoo and condition services benefits your client and the salon

>> Provide examples of infection control and safety guidelines for shampoo, condition and scalp massage services

FOCUS //

SHAMPOO AND CONDITION GUEST EXPERIENCE

Guest Relations

Shampoo and Condition Products

Shampoo and Condition Tools and Supplies

Shampoo and Condition Equipment

Shampoo and Condition Infection Control and Safety

GUEST RELATIONS

Prior to the client consultation, check the information in the salon's client record. The purpose of a client record is to better meet the needs of the client.

>> Client records might be stored in a computer system and managed with software

   ▪ If so, preview client information, note any changes during a client's visit and update the electronic record after the visit

>> Client records might be updated from a mobile handheld device at your workstation and electronically transferred to a central server

>> Client records might be printed, updated with each visit and then returned to a file storage area

>> Client records might entail a questionnaire or profile for the client to complete

A typical client record should include:

>> Name, address and contact numbers

>> Date of last skin patch test (predisposition)

>> Hair and scalp condition, including, if applicable, any contraindications

>> Any relevant medication

>> Date of last service

>> Products used, formula, timings and if heat was used

>> Technique and application method

>> Price of the service

>> Retail products purchased

>> Comments by the stylist and client

No matter what your situation is—if your client is new, regular or a referral—make sure their status is indicated in their record. If the client is a regular, access their record and update as necessary. Double-check the client's name and address. If the client is new to the salon, or if their information is incomplete, update the information. If the salon has a receptionist, they often record and confirm most of this information when a client makes an appointment or arrives at the salon.

There are four important considerations for client records:

>> Make sure information is secure

>> Ensure information is accurate

>> Make sure, if using handwritten notes, that the notes are legible

>> Keep the information relevant to the service

During the consultation, be aware and take account of:

>> Verbal and nonverbal communication, your own and your client's

>> Your client's expectations and whether they can be achieved

>> Previous services and their results

>> Type of service and product requested and their cost

>> Hair type and condition

CONTRAINDICATIONS

During your analysis of the hair and scalp, you will be alerted to possible problems. In some cases, hairstyling services cannot be carried out, and clients should be referred to a medical professional. These cases are referred to as contraindications. The following are example contraindications:

>> Infectious skin and scalp disorders

■ If your client has an infectious disorder, always refer them to a physician

>> Cuts, abrasions and injuries

■ No treatment should be carried out if there are open cuts

■ If there are injuries that have healed, they may still be tender, so use gentle massage to avoid discomfort (the same applies to areas of scar tissue)

>> Allergies

■ Always check if your client has allergies or has had adverse reactions to previous products or services; if a client has allergies, check the ingredients in the products you intend to use and, if necessary, recommend alternatives

Always use caution before conducting a massage. Avoid scalp massage for clients who have had head, neck or jaw surgeries. Be careful not to use excessive pressure in the area directly behind the earlobe, which can be sensitive. If a client is pregnant, use very gentle pressure. If any concerns arise, don't perform the massage until the client has consulted with a doctor.

SHAMPOO AND CONDITION SERVICE ESSENTIALS (4 Cs)

All hair services require that you communicate with your client to ensure predictable results that meet your expectations and those of your client. This important communication is often referred to as the four Service Essentials, or the 4 Cs, because it is composed of four key elements: Connect, Consult, Create and Complete. Following the steps of the 4 Cs will help ensure that all important areas of the service are addressed while working with the client before, during and after the service.

Look for facial expressions or body language the client might display to let you know that things aren't going well. Signs of discomfort might include:

>> Furrows across their forehead
>> Eyebrows turning downward
>> Clenched teeth
>> Fingers wrapped tightly around the arm of the chair

CONNECT

>> Meet and greet the client with a firm handshake and a pleasant tone of voice.

>> Communicate to build rapport and develop a relationship with the client.

CONSULT

>> To uncover the client's wants and needs, ask questions such as:

   ▪ "How frequently do you shampoo your hair?"

   ▪ "What products do you use to shampoo or condition your hair?"

>> Visualize the possibilities that will enhance the client's end result or well-being.

>> Analyze your client's hair and scalp and check for any contraindications.

>> Assess the facts and thoroughly think through your recommendations.

>> Introduce the shampoo and conditioner you will use by describing the products as you use them and the benefits the client will receive from their use.

>> Organize and summarize your plan with the client.

>> Gain feedback and approval of your plan from your client before proceeding with the service.

CREATE

>> Protect the client by draping them with a towel and a cape.

>> Make sure the client is comfortable during the service by asking them about the:

   ▪ Water pressure

   ▪ Water temperature

   ▪ Pressure being used with the massage movements

>> Show and tell the client what you're doing, the products you are using and why.

>> Focus on delivering the shampooing and conditioning service to the best of your ability.

>> Be economical with products.

>> Teach your client how to care for their hair at home.

COMPLETE

>> Ask questions and look for verbal and nonverbal cues to determine your client's level of satisfaction.

>> Escort client to the retail area (if not moving on with additional services) and show products you used.

>> Recommend products to maintain the appearance and condition of your client's hair and invite your client to make a purchase.

>> Suggest a future appointment time for your client's next visit.

>> Offer sincere appreciation to your client for this visit and end with a warm goodbye.

>> Discard single-use items, disinfect tools and multi-use supplies and arrange workstation in proper order.

>> Complete client record for future visits, including any contraindications and recommended products.

After-Care and Advice

After-care and advice should include:

>> Correct brushing and combing – Start at the ends and work up to the root area to remove tangles and prevent damage

   ▪ Use a wide-tooth comb on wet hair

>> Product recommendation – Recommend suitable products, and provide information on how to use the products and how often

In addition to the 4 Cs, you will want to consider shampoo and condition products, tools and supplies, equipment, and infection control and safety guidelines which will be used together to provide a safe and healthy service experience for your guest.

SHAMPOO AND CONDITION PRODUCTS

Many shampoos are designed for specific hair types and conditions. Shampoos are designed for dry, oily, normal, color-treated and gray hair, to name but a few. Selecting the proper shampoo, rinse, conditioner or scalp massage product will allow you to achieve the desired results.

PRODUCTS SHAMPOOS	FUNCTION
All-Purpose	Cleanses the hair without correcting any special condition
pH-Balanced	Cleanses all hair types; recommended to cleanse lightened, color-treated or dry, brittle hair
Plain	Removes oil; contains a high alkaline base; not recommended for chemically treated or damaged hair
Soapless	Cleanses hair with either soft or hard water
Medicated	Treats scalp and hair problems and disorders; prescribed by the client's doctor
Clarifying	Removes residue such as product buildup
Anti-Dandruff	Controls dandruff and scalp conditions; requires massaging the scalp vigorously and rinse thoroughly
Strengthening Protein Additive	Cleanses and conditions; deposits protein fragments along the hair shaft
Aerosol Dry	Absorbs oil at the roots; used by clients wanting to expand the time between shampoos and add texture
Non-Aerosol Powder Dry	Cleanses the hair of clients whose health prohibits them from receiving a wet shampoo service; absorbs oil and distributes oil as the product is brushed through the scalp and hair
Liquid Dry	Cleanses the scalp and hair for clients who are unable to receive a normal shampoo; very drying to the hair; effective in cleaning wigs and hairpieces
Conditioning	Improves the tensile strength and porosity of the hair
Neutralizing	Restores the hair to its 4.5-5.5 pH by neutralizing any remaining alkaline values; used generally in conjunction with a chemical relaxing service
Color	Enhances color-treated hair and tones non-color-treated hair temporarily
Thinning Hair	Cleanses the hair without weighing it down; provides a healthy environment for the maximum amount of hair growth

PRODUCTS RINSES	FUNCTION
Vinegar; Lemon (Acid)	Keep the cuticle compact, remove soap scum, return the hair to its pH balance and counteract the alkalinity present after a chemical service
Cream	Softens, adds shine to and smooths the hair while making it tangle-free for ease in combing
Anti-Dandruff	Controls dandruff and scalp conditions
Acid-Balanced	Closes the cuticle after a color service to prevent the color from fading
Acid	Removes soap scum
Color	Adds temporary color to the hair, which lasts from shampoo to shampoo; for more information on color rinses, refer to nonoxidative colors

PRODUCTS CONDITIONERS	FUNCTION
Instant	Coats the hair shaft and restores moisture to the hair
Normalizing	Closes the cuticle after alkaline chemical services
Body-Building	Displaces excess moisture, providing more body to the hair; made from protein
Moisturizing	Adds moisture to dry, brittle hair
Customized	Moisturizes and builds body

PRODUCTS SCALP TREATMENTS	FUNCTION
Essential Oil	Provides invigorating, stimulating or soothing scents; allows fluid movement on the scalp
Scalp Toner	Adds a refreshing, stimulating feeling to the scalp; may have mild antiseptic properties and cleansing ability
Moisturizing Agent	Replenishes or restores moisture to dry scalp; formulated as creams, oils or lotions

SHAMPOO AND CONDITION TOOLS AND SUPPLIES

Follow area regulatory agency guidelines for the proper infection control practices for tools and supplies. The reminder here is to discard or disinfect.

TOOLS/SUPPLIES	FUNCTION
Towel	Protects the client's skin and clothing; also used to dry the hair
Plastic Client Cape	Protects the client and his/her clothing during wet and/or chemical hair services
Cloth Client Cape	Protects the client and his/her clothing during dry hair sculpting or designing
Neck Strip	Protects the client's skin
Natural-Bristle Hair Brush	Increases blood circulation to the scalp; removes dirt, debris and product buildup from the hair prior to the shampoo service
All-Purpose Comb	Detangles and distributes the hair after the shampoo service
Plastic Cap	Covers hair to allow deeper penetration of conditioning treatment

SHAMPOO AND CONDITION EQUIPMENT

Paying careful attention to the equipment in the salon will make you and your clients safer, and also help the equipment last longer.

EQUIPMENT	FUNCTION
Shampoo Chair	Allows client to sit or lie down during the shampoo service
Shampoo Bowl	Holds and drains water and product during a shampoo service
Shampoo/Conditioner Dispensary (Cabinet)	Displays shampoos and conditioners
Towel Shelves or Cabinet	Stores towels
Accelerator or Steamer	Helps speed the penetration of conditioner or massage product

SHAMPOO AND CONDITION INFECTION CONTROL AND SAFETY

Infection control and safety guidelines are essential while performing draping, shampoo and condition services. They help protect the health and well-being of you and your client. It's important that you 1) let your area's regulatory agency be your guide, and 2) read and follow manufacturer's directions.

PERSONAL CARE

Wash your hands prior to the shampoo service.

Keep your fingernails well groomed to avoid scratching your clients.

Minimize fatigue by maintaining good posture and position during the service. Distribute your weight equally on both feet to allow yourself to use your body fully during the massage.

Ensure any necessary equipment is easily available.

Ensure your hands are protected against long-term damage such as dermatitis (inflammation of the skin) by drying them thoroughly with a single-use towel after shampooing, and applying moisturizer.

CLIENT CARE PRIOR TO SERVICE

Drape the client for appropriate service.

Do not brush the hair prior to a chemical service. If cuts or abrasions are evident, a chemical service should not be performed.

Protect the client's skin and clothing with a towel and plastic or waterproof cape.

Check and question the client for contraindications, allergies, medical advice or instructions. If in doubt, seek advice from a relevant professional.

Avoid giving a scalp massage when scalp abrasions, or a serious scalp disorder, are present.

Avoid giving a scalp massage immediately prior to the application of a chemical service, such as perming, relaxing, lightening or coloring.

Avoid giving a scalp massage when the client has a history of high blood pressure or a heart condition; ask client to consult with physician before proceeding, since scalp massage may increase the circulation of the blood.

CLIENT CARE DURING SERVICE

Keep the back of the cape on the outside of the chair during the shampoo service to prevent the water from running down the client's back and dampening their clothes.

Check that the client is correctly seated and comfortable throughout the service.

Detangle the hair, from ends to roots, prior to shampooing the hair.

Always test the temperature of the water prior to applying the water stream to your client's scalp.

Continue to monitor the water temperature during rinsing by positioning a finger in the water stream.

Ensure that the amount of water pressure is moderate to strong and not so forceful that it is uncomfortable for the client. Excess water pressure is a primary cause of water-spill accidents.

If shampoo gets into the client's eye, rinse immediately with tepid water. An eyewash cup* is recommended. If irritation persists, recommend that the client see a physician.

Detangle the hair thoroughly after the shampoo service.

Decrease pressure during massage if client expresses sensitivity.

Make sure the client's head is always supported or cradled.

If the client is wearing makeup, avoid touching the client's face with your hands, which could remove their makeup while you are shampooing or massaging.

When performing massage movements, do not break contact and use slow, rhythmic motions.

Check the nape area, which is sometimes a difficult area from which to remove all shampoo or massage product.

*An eyewash cup–a cup that is held over the eye–is used to flush the eye with water.

SALON CARE

Promote a professional image by ensuring your shampoo area is clean and tidy throughout the service.

Check that your area contains the resources, such as clean towels and products, necessary to complete the service.

Ensure that water, products and supplies are used economically.

Keep in mind the location of the Safety Data Sheets (SDS) for quick referencing in case of accidents.

Wipe up any water-spill areas immediately.

Update the client record, noting the results of any tests (if applicable) or contraindications.

Complete the service within the timeframe recommended by your salon.

CARE OF PRODUCTS, TOOLS, SUPPLIES, EQUIPMENT

Read and follow manufacturer's directions for all products, tool, supplies and equipment.

Discard contaminated and single-use supplies (neck strip, cotton, etc.).

Disinfect shampoo bowl as required by your area's regulatory agency.

Disinfect tools as required by your area's regulatory agency such as removing hair; cleaning, then disinfecting, the hairbrush; and cleaning, then disinfecting the large, wide-tooth detangling comb.

Launder towels as required by your area's regulatory agency.

Wipe down the shampoo chair to ensure that the client is not asked to sit in a chair that is wet or has hair in it.

Ensure that there are sufficient resources, such as clean towels and product, for the next service. It may be necessary to report low stock levels to the relevant person.

If you use an accelerator or steamer to aid the penetration of conditioner, ensure that the equipment, plugs and cables are in good condition and the water level is sufficient. Never use with wet hands, and remember to turn it off after use. Always check that the client is comfortable during the process.

DERMATITIS

Due to frequent contact with water and chemicals, a hairstylist has a higher than normal risk of contracting dermatitis. After shampooing, rinse and dry your hands thoroughly; then use a barrier cream or moisturizer. Always wear single-use non-latex gloves when using chemicals. Extreme cases can result in the skin cracking and bleeding, plus it can recur at any time, so prevention is critical.

Contact dermatitis is inflammation of the skin that occurs due to:

Contact with products that irritate the skin

An allergy

Constant shampooing

Not rinsing and drying the skin after each service

Not moisturizing regularly

The symptoms are:

Dryness

Itching

Redness

Soreness

DISCOVER**MORE**

Expectations for the global shampoo market are projected to reach a value of 25.73 billion dollars by 2019. The major drivers of the shampoo market include product innovation, the emerging men's grooming market, increasing pollution, increasing concern of consumers about their appearance and increasing demand for natural or organic shampoos. Best sellers, top down, are:

» Anti-dandruff shampoo
» Cosmetic shampoo
» Dry shampoo
» Herbal shampoo

SALON**CONNECTION**

Relaxing Salon Experience

Shampooing is an opportunity for you to provide the client with a relaxing salon experience, free from the stresses of the day. Some salons use soft lighting and play relaxing music in an area dedicated to shampooing, conditioning and scalp massage services. Others combine the power of aromatherapy with shampoo service by placing drops of a pleasing essential oil on the towels being used. When performed well, the shampoo experience can feel as good as a body massage. The goal is a satisfied, happy client. If the client is happy with the shampoo portion of the service, they will likely be satisfied with the service to follow.

Demonstrating attention to detail and client comfort marks a true professional. As you gain more experience with client relations and are better able to ensure their safety, you will develop an ease and competence that earns you trust and loyalty from each client.

LESSONS LEARNED

The client record should include:

- Name, address and contact numbers

- Date of last skin patch test (predisposition)

- Hair and scalp condition including, if applicable, any contraindications

- Any relevant medication

- Date of last service

- Products used, formula, timings and if heat was used

- Technique and application method

- Price of the service

- Retail products purchased

- Comments by the stylist and client

Using the four Service Essentials (4 Cs) to connect, consult, create and complete helps ensure that all important areas of the client service experience are addressed while working with the client.

Selecting the proper shampoo, rinse, conditioner or scalp massage product—along with related tools and supplies—will allow you to achieve the desired results. And paying careful attention to the equipment in the salon will make you and your clients safer, and also help the equipment last longer, which benefits the salon.

To work safely and reduce health risks when performing shampooing, conditioning and scalp massage services, follow the infection control and safety guidelines published by your area's regulatory agency, and read and follow manufacturer's directions.

102^c.18

SHAMPOO AND CONDITION WORKSHOP

EXPLORE //

Why does it feel so good to have someone else shampoo your hair?

INSPIRE //

Some clients choose their designer based on their shampoo skills alone!

ACHIEVE //

Following this *Shampoo and Condition Workshop*, you'll be able to:

>> Identify the steps in performing a shampoo and condition

>> Demonstrate a shampoo and condition

FOCUS //

SHAMPOO AND CONDITION WORKSHOP

Shampoo and Condition Service Overview

Shampoo and Condition Procedure

Shampoo and Condition Rubric

SHAMPOO AND CONDITION WORKSHOP

Draping, shampooing and conditioning preparation and procedures vary based on the timing allowed for the service and each client's needs. Shampooing for salon services using chemicals can be found in separate lessons.

SHAMPOO AND CONDITION SERVICE OVERVIEW

- >> Ask client to remove jewelry and glasses and secure in a safe place
- >> Clip client's hair out of the way (if applicable)
- >> Turn client's collar under (if applicable)
- >> Drape client
- >> Position cape over shampoo chair
- >> Examine client's hair and scalp
- >> Brush hair
- >> Test temperature and pressure of water
- >> Wet hair
- >> Apply shampoo
- >> Perform scalp massage movements throughout entire scalp
- >> Remove excess shampoo
- >> Rinse entire scalp area until water runs clear
- >> Repeat shampoo and rinse procedures if necessary
- >> Apply conditioner
- >> Rinse conditioner while protecting face
- >> Towel-dry client's hair
- >> Detangle hair
- >> Dry hair or move to next scheduled service
- >> Clean and disinfect shampoo area

PERFORMANCE GUIDE

SHAMPOO AND CONDITION PROCEDURE

10 mins
Suggested
Salon Speed

It is assumed in this procedure that you are moving directly from draping to shampooing. If there is a time lapse between draping and shampooing, it will be necessary for you to wash your hands again prior to shampooing.

View the video, review this Performance Guide, then perform this workshop. Complete the self-check as you progress through the workshop.

PREPARATION ✔

Assemble the following materials prior to draping, shampooing and conditioning your client:
>> Towels
>> Plastic cape
>> Neck strip
>> Booster chair (if applicable)
>> Shampoo, rinse or conditioning products

Wash your hands.

DRAPE

1. Ask client to remove jewelry and glasses and secure in a safe place.
2. Clip client's hair out of the way (if applicable).
3. Turn client's collar under (if applicable).

4. **Drape client:**
>> Place towel lengthwise over client's shoulders, and cross in front
>> Position plastic cape over towel and secure.
>> Fold towel outward over neckband of cape for protection

5. **Examine client's hair and scalp thoroughly:**
   >> Check for cuts or abrasions
   >> Check for dry scalp

   Note: Choose the shampoo according to the scalp analysis.

6. **Position cape on outside of shampoo chair.**

7. **Remove tangles by starting to brush from hair ends.**

SHAMPOO

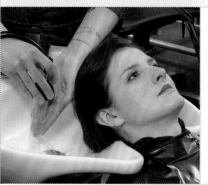

8. **Test pressure and temperature of water:**
   >> Ensure water is warm and comfortable for client

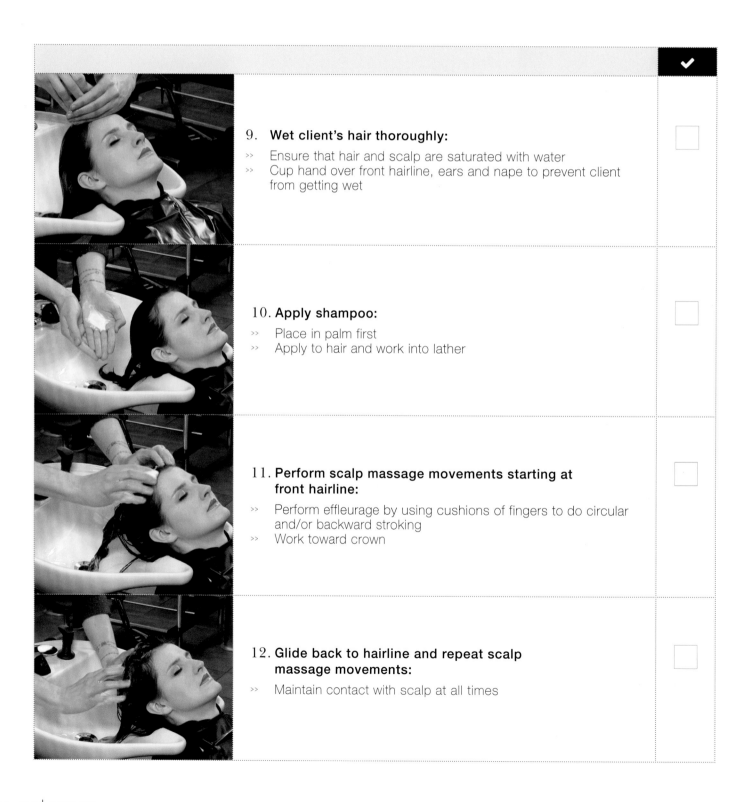

9. **Wet client's hair thoroughly:**
   >> Ensure that hair and scalp are saturated with water
   >> Cup hand over front hairline, ears and nape to prevent client from getting wet

10. **Apply shampoo:**
    >> Place in palm first
    >> Apply to hair and work into lather

11. **Perform scalp massage movements starting at front hairline:**
    >> Perform effleurage by using cushions of fingers to do circular and/or backward stroking
    >> Work toward crown

12. **Glide back to hairline and repeat scalp massage movements:**
    >> Maintain contact with scalp at all times

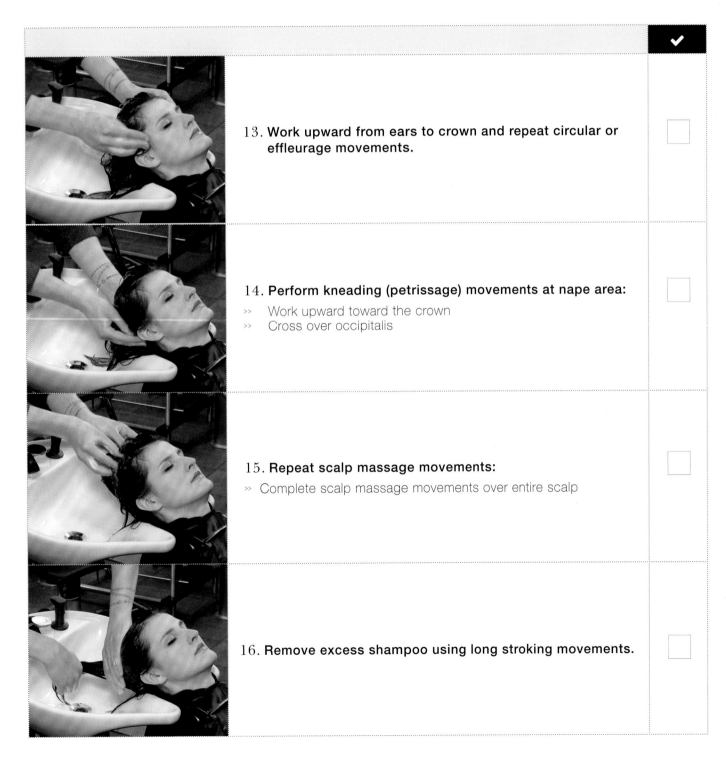

13. **Work upward from ears to crown and repeat circular or effleurage movements.**	☐
14. **Perform kneading (petrissage) movements at nape area:** » Work upward toward the crown » Cross over occipitalis	☐
15. **Repeat scalp massage movements:** » Complete scalp massage movements over entire scalp	☐
16. **Remove excess shampoo using long stroking movements.**	☐

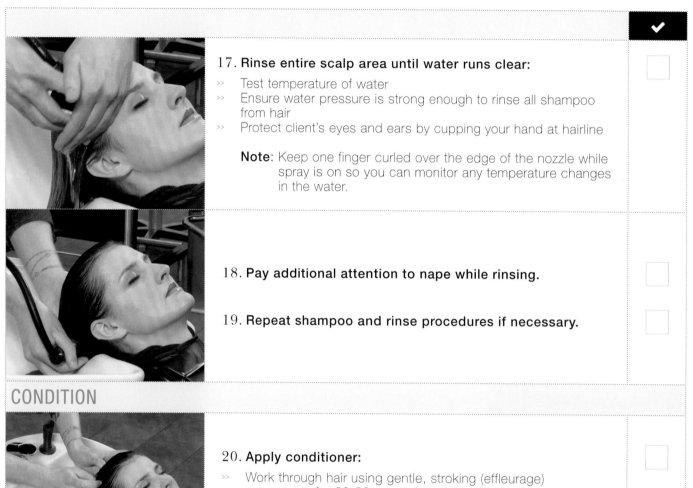

✔

17. **Rinse entire scalp area until water runs clear:**

>> Test temperature of water
>> Ensure water pressure is strong enough to rinse all shampoo from hair
>> Protect client's eyes and ears by cupping your hand at hairline

Note: Keep one finger curled over the edge of the nozzle while spray is on so you can monitor any temperature changes in the water.

18. **Pay additional attention to nape while rinsing.**

19. **Repeat shampoo and rinse procedures if necessary.**

CONDITION

20. **Apply conditioner:**

>> Work through hair using gentle, stroking (effleurage) movements for 30-60 seconds
>> Follow manufacturer's instructions for conditioning treatments that may need to be left on hair for a longer period of time and may require a plastic cap and heat

21. **Rinse conditioner while protecting face:**

>> Lift hair and allow water to run down length of strands
>> Squeeze excess water from hair ends

22. **Towel-dry client's hair with fresh towel:**
    >> Wipe away any moisture from client's face

☐

23. **Detangle hair:**
    >> Begin at nape
    >> Comb outward from ends of hair and work toward scalp

☐

24. **Dry hair or move to next service scheduled for client.**

☐

COMPLETION

25. **Clean shampoo service area before continuing with client:**
    >> Place soiled towel(s) in appropriate covered receptacle
    >> Discard single-use supplies
    >> Disinfect tools and multi-use supplies
    >> Disinfect workstation and arrange in proper order

☐

10 mins
Suggested Salon Speed

My Speed
_____
_____

INSTRUCTIONS:
Record your time in comparison with the suggested salon speed. Then, list here how you could improve your performance.

_____

_____

_____

LONG HAIR CONSIDERATIONS

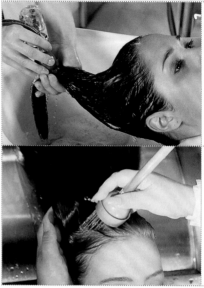

Lift longer lengths upward while rinsing to remove hair from shampoo suds that have accumulated in bowl.

Allow hair to fall naturally to help prevent tangles if using shampoo bowl with an extended basin designed for long hair.

VARIATION – STANDING AT THE SIDE

A variation of the shampoo workshop is available online.

Remember that shampooing and conditioning procedures basically remain the same, whether you are standing at the back or at the side of your client. However, your body position will change, and you may choose to include slightly varied scalp movements.

Alert!

Never use firm massage movements when shampoo is to be followed by any kind of chemical service. In these instances, massage during shampoo should be very brief and very light.

Optional Neck and Shoulder Massage

Before detangling the hair after the shampoo procedure, you may wish to perform this additional massage treatment:

>> Place fingers over muscles near shoulder joints.

>> Begin a combination of effleurage and petrissage movements at bottom of neck.

>> Move fingers up outside of neck, back down toward spine, and back up and out to shoulder muscle joints.

>> Repeat.

SHAMPOO AND CONDITION RUBRIC

Allotted Time: 10 Minutes

Student Name: _____ ID Number: _____

Instructor: _____ Date: _____ Start Time: _____ End Time: _____

Each scoring item is marked with either a "Yes" or "No." Each "Yes" counts for one point. Total number of points attainable is 35.

CRITERIA	YES	NO	INSTRUCTOR ASSESSMENT
PREPARATION: *Did student...*			
1. Set up workstation with properly labeled supplies?	☐	☐	
2. Wash their hands?	☐	☐	
Connect: *Did student...*			
3. Meet and greet client with a firm handshake and pleasant tone of voice?	☐	☐	
4. Communicate to build rapport and develop a relationship with client?	☐	☐	
5. Refer to client by name throughout service?	☐	☐	
Consult: *Did student...*			
6. Ask questions to discover client's wants and needs?	☐	☐	
7. Analyze client's hair and scalp and check for any contraindications?	☐	☐	
8. Introduce recommended shampoo and conditioner and their benefits?	☐	☐	
9. Gain feedback and consent from client before proceeding?	☐	☐	
PROCEDURE: *Did student...*			
10. Ask client to remove jewelry and glasses and secure in a safe place?	☐	☐	
11. Properly drape client?	☐	☐	
12. Ensure client protection and comfort by maintaining cape on outside of chair at all times?	☐	☐	
Create: *Did student...*			
13. Examine client's hair and scalp?	☐	☐	
14. Remove tangles by starting to brush from hair ends?	☐	☐	
15. Test temperature and pressure of water?	☐	☐	
16. Ensure water is warm and comfortable for client throughout service?	☐	☐	
17. Wet client's hair?	☐	☐	
18. Apply shampoo?	☐	☐	
19. Perform and complete scalp massage movements?	☐	☐	
20. Rinse shampoo until water runs clear?	☐	☐	
21. Apply conditioner?	☐	☐	
22. Rinse conditioner while protecting face?	☐	☐	
23. Towel-dry and detangle client's hair?	☐	☐	
24. Practice infection control procedures and safety guidelines throughout service?	☐	☐	
COMPLETION *(Complete):* *Did student...*			
25. Ask questions and look for verbal and nonverbal cues to determine client's level of satisfaction?	☐	☐	
26. Make professional product recommendations?	☐	☐	
27. Ask client to make a future appointment?	☐	☐	
28. End guest's visit with a warm and personal goodbye?	☐	☐	
29. Place soiled towels in a covered receptacle?	☐	☐	
30. Discard single-use supplies?	☐	☐	
31. Disinfect tools and multi-use supplies, disinfect workstation and arrange in proper order?	☐	☐	
32. Clean/mop water spillage from floor?	☐	☐	
33. Complete the service within scheduled time?	☐	☐	
34. Complete client record?	☐	☐	
35. Wash their hands following service?	☐	☐	

COMMENTS: _____ TOTAL POINTS = _____ ÷ 35 = _____ %

SCALP MASSAGE
WORKSHOP
102ᶜ.19

EXPLORE //

Which massage movement will you use to set your scalp massage apart from others?

INSPIRE //

Relaxing your client's scalp muscles prompts them to return for future salon visits.

ACHIEVE //

Following this *Scalp Massage Workshop*, you'll be able to:

>> Identify the steps used in performing a scalp massage

>> Demonstrate a scalp massage

FOCUS //

SCALP MASSAGE WORKSHOP

Scalp Massage Service Overview

Scalp Massage Procedure

Scalp Massage Rubric

SCALP MASSAGE WORKSHOP

Basic scalp massage treatments involve massage movements designed to relax your client's muscles and increase blood circulation. Treatments can vary according to the products and machines used. For instance, a dry scalp treatment may include a moisturizing scalp cream along with a scalp steamer or warm towels to help product penetration.

SCALP MASSAGE SERVICE OVERVIEW

- >> Drape client for a wet hair service
- >> Detangle hair
- >> Apply scalp product
- >> Perform effleurage massage movements
- >> Perform petrissage massage movements
- >> Perform effleurage massage movements
- >> Perform tapotement
- >> Rotate scalp, squeeze gently and release

- >> Conclude scalp massage
- >> Shampoo client's hair
- >> Rinse hair
- >> Dry hair or move to next service
- >> Clean and disinfect service area

■ PERFORMANCE GUIDE

SCALP MASSAGE PROCEDURE

Be sure to follow manufacturer's directions when using scalp treatment products. View the video, review
this Performance Guide, then perform this workshop. Complete the self-check as you progress through
the workshop.

15
mins
Suggested
Salon Speed

PREPARATION	✔
Assemble the following materials prior to providing a scalp massage service: >> Moisturizing agent, scalp toner or essential oils >> Towel >> Client cape >> Neck strip	☐
Wash your hands.	☐

PROCEDURE

1. Ask client to remove jewelry and glasses and secure in a safe place. ☐
2. Clip client's hair out of the way (if applicable). ☐
3. Turn client's collar under (if applicable). ☐
4. Drape client for a wet hair service. ☐
5. Detangle hair from ends to scalp. ☐

6. Apply scalp product according to treatment being performed and according to manufacturer's directions: ☐
   >> Ensure even coverage

7. **Perform effleurage scalp massage movements:**

>> Stand behind client
>> Begin stroking movements at front hairline (frontalis)
>> Glide at approximately 1" (2.5 cm) intervals to nape area
>> Work from side to side and repeat until all areas are covered

8. **Perform petrissage massage movements:**

>> Massage with kneading action in a circular motion
>> Keep fingers and thumbs spread out and firmly pressed to scalp as you massage
>> Release your hands from scalp only as you move to another part of scalp
>> Start at front hairline and finish in nape

9. **Perform effleurage massage movements:**

>> Use lighter, circular movements
>> Move from front hairline to area above ears at crest (parietal)
>> Slowly return to top and repeat massage movements
>> Work from crown to nape
>> Cover entire head

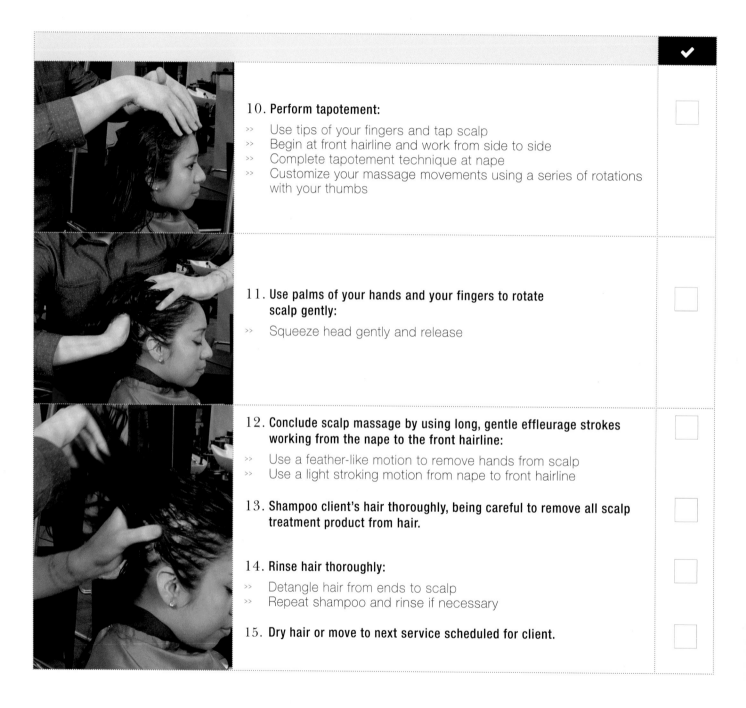

	✔
10. Perform tapotement: >> Use tips of your fingers and tap scalp >> Begin at front hairline and work from side to side >> Complete tapotement technique at nape >> Customize your massage movements using a series of rotations with your thumbs	☐
11. Use palms of your hands and your fingers to rotate scalp gently: >> Squeeze head gently and release	☐
12. Conclude scalp massage by using long, gentle effleurage strokes working from the nape to the front hairline: >> Use a feather-like motion to remove hands from scalp >> Use a light stroking motion from nape to front hairline	☐
13. Shampoo client's hair thoroughly, being careful to remove all scalp treatment product from hair.	☐
14. Rinse hair thoroughly: >> Detangle hair from ends to scalp >> Repeat shampoo and rinse if necessary	☐
15. Dry hair or move to next service scheduled for client.	☐

COMPLETION

16. Clean service area:

>> Place soiled towel(s) in appropriate covered receptacle
>> Discard single-use supplies
>> Disinfect tools and multi-use supplies
>> Disinfect workstation and arrange in proper order
>> Ensure there is no water left standing in shampoo service area

15 mins
Suggested Salon Speed

My Speed
_____
_____
_____

INSTRUCTIONS:

Record your time in comparison with the suggested salon speed. Then, list here how you could improve your performance.

_____

_____

_____

_____

_____

_____

_____

SCALP MASSAGE RUBRIC

Allotted Time: 15 Minutes

Student Name:_____ ID Number: _____

Instructor: _____ Date: _____ Start Time: _____ End Time: _____

Each scoring item is marked with either a "Yes" or "No." Each "Yes" counts for one point. Total number of points attainable is 33.

CRITERIA	YES	NO	INSTRUCTOR ASSESSMENT
PREPARATION: *Did student...*			
1. Set up workstation with properly labeled supplies?	☐	☐	
2. Wash their hands?	☐	☐	
Connect: *Did student...*			
3. Meet and greet client with a welcoming smile and pleasant tone of voice?	☐	☐	
4. Communicate to build rapport and develop a relationship with client?	☐	☐	
5. Refer to client by name throughout service?	☐	☐	
Consult: *Did student...*			
6. Ask questions to discover client's wants and needs?	☐	☐	
7. Analyze client's hair and scalp and check for any contraindications?	☐	☐	
8. Introduce recommended shampoo and conditioner and their benefits?	☐	☐	
9. Gain feedback and consent from client before proceeding?	☐	☐	
PROCEDURE: *Did student...*			
10. Ask client to remove jewelry and glasses and secure in a safe place?	☐	☐	
11. Properly drape client?	☐	☐	
12. Ensure client protection and comfort by maintaining cape on outside of chair at all times?	☐	☐	
13. Detangle the hair from ends to scalp?	☐	☐	
Create: *Did student...*			
14. Apply scalp product to entire head according to treatment being performed?	☐	☐	
15. Perform effleurage massage movements throughout the entire head?	☐	☐	
16. Perform petrissage massage movements throughout the entire head?	☐	☐	
17. Perform tapotement massage movements throughout the entire head?	☐	☐	
18. Rotate scalp, squeeze gently and release?	☐	☐	
19. Conclude scalp massage using long, gentle effleurage strokes?	☐	☐	
20. Shampoo and rinse client's hair, repeat if necessary?	☐	☐	
21. Dry hair or move to next service?	☐	☐	
22. Practice infection control procedures and safety guidelines throughout service?	☐	☐	
COMPLETION (Complete): *Did student...*			
23. Ask questions and look for verbal and nonverbal cues to determine client's level of satisfaction?	☐	☐	
24. Make professional product recommendations?	☐	☐	
25. Ask client to make a future appointment?	☐	☐	
26. End guest's visit with a warm and personal goodbye?	☐	☐	
27. Place soiled towels in a covered receptacle?	☐	☐	
28. Discard single-use supplies?	☐	☐	
29. Disinfect tools and multi-use supplies, disinfect workstation and arrange in proper order?	☐	☐	
30. Clean/mop water spillage from floor?	☐	☐	
31. Complete the service within scheduled time?	☐	☐	
32. Complete client record?	☐	☐	
33. Wash their hands following service?	☐	☐	

COMMENTS: _____ TOTAL POINTS = _____ ÷ 33 = _____ %

Abraded Hair   *192*
Technical term for broken hair, or excessive stretching or traction of the hair.

AC Current   *109*
Alternating current; electrons flow first in one direction and then in the other.

Acid   *152, 154*
Water-based solution measuring more positive hydrogen ions than negative hydroxide ions; measures less than 7 on the pH scale.

Acid Mantle   *162, 179, 192*
A layer of oil and sweat found in the sebaceous glands; keeps the skin smooth, prevents dirt and grime from entering the outer layer of the epidermis and also prevents the skin from drying or chapping; protects the cuticle or outer covering of the hair fiber and maintains the acid balance of hair and skin.

Acid Rinse   *168, 223*
Used to remove soap scum.

Acid-Balanced Rinse   *223*
Used to close the cuticle after a color service to prevent the color from fading.

Active Immunity   *14*
Is the result when exposure to a disease organism triggers the immune system to produce antibodies to that disease.

Active Stage   *8*
The stage at which bacteria (germs) grow and reproduce rapidly.

Aerosol Dry Shampoo   *165, 222*
Absorbs oil at the roots; used by clients wanting to extend the time between shampoos and add texture.

AIDS – Acquired Immunodeficiency Syndrome   *10*
A disorder caused by HIV (Human Immunodeficiency Virus); HIV interferes with the body's natural immune system, causing it to break down.

Albinism   *185*
Congenital failure of the skin to produce melanin pigment.

Alkaline   *152, 154*
Water-based solution measuring more negative hydroxide ions than positive hydrogen ions; measures higher than 7 on the pH scale.

All-Purpose Shampoo   *164, 222*
Used to cleanse the hair without correcting any special condition.

Alopecia   *196*
Excessive hair loss.

Alopecia Areata   *198*
Sudden loss of hair in round or irregular patches without display of an inflamed scalp.

Alopecia Prematura   *198*
Refers to baldness that occurs early in life, beginning as early as late adolescence.

Amines   *170*
Ingredients found in conditioners; makes hair easier to comb and control static.

Amp   *106, 107*
A unit of electric strength.

Anabolism   *50*
The process of building up larger molecules from smaller ones during metabolism.

Anagen   *182*
The active or growing stage of hair, during which time each hair bulb has an attached root sheath.

Anaphoresis   *125*
Negative pole of galvanic current that produces an alkaline reaction.

Anatomy   *49*
The study of the organs and systems of the body.

Androgenetic Alopecia   *196, 197*
Hair loss caused by a combination of heredity, hormones and age that causes progressive shrinking or miniaturization of certain scalp follicles.

Anode   *125*
A positively charged electrode; usually red in color or displays a large "P" or a positive sign (+).

Anti-Dandruff Rinse   *223*
Controls dandruff and scalp conditions.

Anti-Dandruff Shampoo   *164, 222*
Used to control dandruff and other scalp conditions.

Antiseptic   *20*
Liquid or foam-based sanitizer products applied to the skin to reduce microbes; sometimes referred to as waterless sanitizers.

Aponeurosis   *71*
A tendon that connects the frontalis and the occipitalis muscles in the epicranium.

Aromatherapy   *212*
The combination of our sense of smell and the use of plant extracts and their healing abilities.

Arrector Pili Muscle   *179*
Comes from cells in the dermis that attach to the follicle just below the sebaceous gland. This is the muscle that causes the hair to stand on end when a person is scared or cold.

Asymptomatic Carrier   *13*
A person or thing that can carry disease-producing bacteria without symptoms.

Atom *141*
The smallest complete unit of
an element.

Autonomic Nervous System *101*
Responsible for all involuntary
body functions.

Bacilli *7*
The most common form of bacterial
cells; bar or rod-shaped cells that can
produce a variety of diseases including
tetanus, bacterial influenza, typhoid
fever, tuberculosis and diphtheria.

Bacteria *6*
One-celled micro-organisms;
sometimes called germs or microbes.

Bactericidal *22*
Disinfectant designed to kill bacteria.

Bacteriology *6*
The study of bacteria.

Basal Layer *178*
A cluster of cells in the upper layer of
the epidermis.

Battery *109*
A source of electrical current with
a positive and negative terminal;
produces direct current only.

Belly *70*
The term applied to the midsection of
the muscle, between the two attached
sections.

Blood *84*
The sticky, salty fluid that circulates
through the body bringing nourishment
and oxygen to all body parts and
carrying toxins and waste products to
the liver and kidneys to be eliminated.
  ◼ Red and white blood cells *86*
  ◼ Blood platelets *86*
  ◼ Plasma *86*
  ◼ Blood vessels – Arteries,
    veins, capillaries *86*

Bloodborne Pathogens *12*
Disease-causing bacteria or viruses
that are carried through the blood or
body fluids

Bloodborne Pathogens Standards *24*
Regulations requiring the use of an
EPA-registered hospital disinfectant
when tools or multi-use supplies come
into contact with blood or body fluids.

Body-Building Conditioner *169, 223*
Used to displace excess moisture,
providing more body to the hair;
made from protein.

Bone *58*
Composed of $^2/_3$ mineral matter and
$^1/_3$ organic matter and produces red and
white blood cells and stores calcium.

Brain *95*
Organ that controls all three
subsystems of the nervous system;
referred to as the command center;
weighs between 44 and 48 ounces.

Canities *193*
Refers to the grayness or whiteness of
the hair.

Capilli *182*
The technical term for the hair on
the head.

Cardiac Muscle *69*
The muscle of the heart itself; the only
muscle of its type in the human body.

**Cardiovascular or
Blood-Vascular System** *83*
Responsible for the circulation of
blood, includes the heart, arteries,
veins and capillaries.

Catabolism *50*
The process of breaking down larger
molecules or substances into smaller
ones during metabolism.

Catagen *182*
A brief transitional stage of hair
growth, when all cell division stops.

Cataphoresis *125*
Positive pole of galvanic current that
produces an acidic reaction.

Cathode *125*
A negatively charged electrode;
usually black in color or displays a
large "N" or a negative sign (-).

Cell Membrane *50*
The outer surface of the cell, which
encloses the protoplasm.

Cells *50*
The basic units of living matter (life).

Central Nervous System *95, 103*
Also called the cerebrospinal nervous
system; composed of the brain
and spinal cord; responsible for all
voluntary body action.

Chemical Bond *143*
Bond involving the sharing of
electrons of two or more atoms.

Chemical Change *138*
A change in a substance that creates
a new substance with chemical
characteristics different from those of
the original substance.

Chemistry *137*
The scientific study of matter and the
physical and chemical changes of matter.

Circuit *110*
Flow of electrons along a path called
a conductor.

Circuit Breaker *115*
Reusable safety device that breaks the
flow of current when an overload occurs.

Circulatory or Vascular System *52, 83*
Controls the circulation of blood and
lymph through the body.
  ◼ Arteries and veins of the face,
    head and neck *88*
  ◼ Arteries of the hand and arm *90*
  ◼ Arteries and veins of the
    lower leg and foot *90*

Clarifying Shampoo *164, 222*
Used to remove residue such as
product build-up.

Cleaning *19, 20*
The process of scrubbing to remove
dirt and debris to aid in preventing the
growth of microbes; it is the first level
of infection control; cleaning methods
clean and reduce microbes on the
surface but do not kill germs; also
known as sanitation.

Closed Circuit 110
A path of electron flow from the source to operate an appliance.

Cocci 7
Spherical bacterial cells that appear singularly or in groups.

Color 131
The visual perception of the reflection of light; if white light (sunlight or light from a light bulb) passes through a prism, the wavelengths are separated and become visible to the eye as color.

Color Rinse 223
Used to add temporary color to the hair, which lasts from shampoo to shampoo.

Color Shampoo 165, 222
Used to enhance color-treated hair and tone noncolor-treated hair temporarily; available in a variety of colors.

Combination Equipment 121
Generates heat and produces a flow of air (for example, hood dryers, blow dryers and blow combs).

Communicable Disease 6, 12
Contagious infection that can be transmitted from one person to another via contact.

Compound 142
Molecule formed when two or more different atoms combine chemically.

Concentrated Solution 160
Solution that contains a large quantity of the solute in comparison to the quantity of solvent.

Conditioning Shampoo 165, 222
Used to improve the tensile strength and porosity of the hair.

Conductor 106
A material that allows electricity to flow through it easily.

Connective Tissue 51
Supports, protects and holds the body together.

Contagious Infection 6, 12
Transmitted from one person to another, usually through touch or through the air; also known as communicable disease.

Contaminated 5, 12
Covered with dirt, oil and/or microbes.

Contraindications 218
Possible problems that are determined during an analysis of the hair and scalp, which indicate services cannot be carried out and the client should be referred to a medical professional.

Cortex 179
The inside the second layer of the hair fiber (gives hair most of its pigment and strength [elasticity]).

Cranium 59
Consists of eight bones that form the top, sides and back of the head; encloses and protects the brain and primary sensory organs.

Cream Rinse 168, 223
Used to soften, add shine and smoothness to the hair while making the hair tangle-free for ease in combing.

Customized Conditioner 169, 223
Used to moisturize and build body.

Cuticle 179
The outer covering of the hair shaft.

Cytoplasm 50
The production department of the cell where most of the cell's activities take place.

Dandruff 194
Pityriasis; overabundance of epithelial cells that have accumulated on the scalp or fallen to the shoulders.
- Dry dandruff 194
- Greasy, waxy dandruff 86

DC Current 109
Direct current; electrons move at an even rate and flow in one direction.

Density 190
The number of active hair follicles per square inch on the scalp.

Desincrustation 125
A treatment in which sebum is broken down or blackheads are liquefied, as in deep-pore cleansing.

Digestive System 101
Breaks food down into simpler chemical compounds that can be easily absorbed by cells or, if not absorbed, eliminated from the body in waste products.
- Enzymes 101
- Salivary glands 101
- Pharynx 101
- Esophagus 101
- Peristalsis 101
- Hydrochloric acid 101
- Polypeptide molecules 101
- Small intestine 101
- Large intestine 101
- Villi 101

Dilute Solution 160
Solution that contains a small quantity of the solute in comparison to the quantity of solvent.

Dimethicone 170
Ingredient found in conditioners; gives softness to the feel of hair without weighing it down.

Diplococci 7
Bacterial cells that grow in pairs and are the cause of certain infections, including pneumonia.

Direct Transmission 12
Spread of infectious disease when an infected person touches or exchanges body fluids with someone else.

Disease 19
Sickness; illness; unhealthy condition.

Disinfectants 22
Chemical products used to destroy or kill bacteria and some viruses (except bacterial spores).

Disinfection 19, 22
The act of destroying or killing a broad spectrum of microbes on a nonporous surface. Disinfection is the second level of infection control.

Disulfide Bond 145
Most important side bond containing sulfur; formed when two sulfur-type side chains join together; directly affected by chemical services.

Draping 205
Performed prior to hair care services, such as shampooing and scalp massage, to protect the client's skin and clothing.

Efficacy 24
The ability to produce results or effectiveness of products used for infection control.

Efficacy Label 24
Informs product user of what the product is effective in fighting against.

Effleurage 211
Light, gliding massage strokes or circular motions made with the palms of the hands or pads of the fingertips; often used to begin and/or end a treatment; used on the face, neck and arms.

Elasticity 191
Ability of hair to stretch and return to its original shape without breaking.

Electric Current 106
The flow of electrons that moves along a path called a conductor.

Electric Muscle Stimulation (EMS) 126
Alternating current with a mechanical effect that stimulates the nerve and muscle tissue; also known as faradic current.

Electricity 106
A form of energy that produces light, heat, magnetic and chemical changes.

Electrochemical Effect 122
Electric current traveling through a waterbased solution to produce relaxing or stimulating effects.

Electrode 124
Safe contact point through which current can pass to the client.

Electrons 141
Negatively charged particles that orbit around the nucleus of an atom.

Electrotherapy 123
The use of a specific electrical current or piece of equipment for corrective and therapeutic benefits on the skin.

Elements of Matter 138
Basic substances that cannot be broken down into simpler substances.

Emulsion 160
Two or more nonmixable substances united with the help of a binder.

Endocrine System 103
Carefully balanced mechanism that directly affects hair growth, skin conditions and energy levels.

EPA (Environmental Protection Agency) 24
Approves the efficacy of products used for infection control.

EPA-Registered Disinfectant 24
Chemical products assigned by the EPA as being effective on nonporous surfaces to control the spread of disease; efficacy against *Salmonella choleraesuis* and *Staphylococcus aureus*; also known as broad spectrum disinfectant.

EPA-Registered Hospital Disinfectant 24
Chemical products assigned by the EPA as being effective to work in a hospital setting; effective against *Pseudomonas aeruginosa*; required for incidents involving exposure to blood and body fluids.

Epicranium 71
Consists of all of the structures above the cranium, including muscle, skin and aponeurosis.

Epicranius or Occipitofrontalis 71
Broad muscle covering the scalp or epicranium.

Epithelial Tissue 51
Covers and protects body surfaces and internal organs.

Essential Oils 212
A natural oil of a plant that provides invigorating, stimulating or soothing scents; always blended with a carrier oil, such as almond or grape seed oil.

Eumelanin 185
Type of melanin that produces brown/black hair color.

Excretory System 102
Eliminates solid, liquid and gaseous waste products from the body.
  Skin 102
  Liver 102
  Kidneys 102
  Nephrons 102
  Ureter 102

External Parasites 11
Plants or animals that live on or obtain their nutrients from another organism.

Facial Nerve 98
Emerges from the brain at the lower part of the ear and is the primary motor nerve of the face; also known as the seventh cranial nerve.

Fatty Alcohol 170
Ingredient found in conditioners; gives hair a smooth feel when dry and makes it easier to comb; creamy in texture and helps retain moisture.

Fifth Cranial Nerve 97
The largest of the cranial nerves; also known as the trifacial or trigeminal nerve.

First Aid 41
Techniques used to assist individuals in emergency situations.

Flagella 8
Also called cilia (SIL-ee-a); hair-like projections that propel bacterial movement.

Flat Bones 58
Plate-shaped and located in the skull, scapula and sternum.

Follicle 178
Cluster of cells in the upper layer of the skin; the cell cluster pulls the upper layer down with it, creating a tubelike pocket called the root sheath, out of which the hair will grow.

Fragilitas Crinium 192
Technical term for split ends: small cracks in the cuticle of the hair that deepen into the cortex.

Friction 211
Circular or wringing movement with no gliding used on the scalp or with a facial when less pressure is desired; applied with the fingertips or palms; a way in which the hair cuticle can be damaged by combing and brushing.

Frontalis 245
Muscle that extends from the forehead to the top of the skull; it raises eyebrows or draws the scalp forward.

Fungicidal   *22*
Disinfectant designed to kill fungus.

Fuse   *114*
A safety device that contains a fine metal wire that allows current to flow through it.

Galvanic Current   *125*
A direct current (DC) that has a electrochemical effect and is the oldest form of electrotherapy in the salon.

Gas   *137*
Form of matter having definite weight but indefinite volume and shape.

General Infection   *13*
Also called systemic infection; occurs when the circulatory system carries bacteria and their toxins to all parts of the body.

Generator   *109*
Power source most often used in a salon; produces alternating current; uses mechanical energy to produce a flow of electrons.

Germinal Matrix   *179*
Area of the hair bulb where cell division (mitosis) takes place.

Germinal Matrix Cells   *179*
Produce the cells that ultimately keratinize (harden) and form the three major layers of the hair.

Glands   *102*
Organs in the body by which certain substances are separated from the blood and changed into some secretion for use in the body, such as oil (sebaceous gland).

Good Samaritan Laws   *41*
Give legal protection to people who provide emergency care to ill or injured persons.

Gray Hair   *185*
Sometimes referred to as mottled hair, indicating white spots scattered about the hair shaft, caused by reduced color pigment in the cortex layer of the hair.

Gross Anatomy   *49*
The study of the structures of the body that can be seen with the naked eye.

Hair   *143*
Form of protein called keratin.

Hair Fiber   *178*
Sometimes referred to as the hair shaft or strand; the portion of the hair that extends above the skin's surface.

Hair Root   *178*
Portion of hair that is inside the hair follicle under the skin's surface.

Hard Water   *207*
Water that contains minerals and does not allow the shampoo to lather freely.

Head Lice   *12, 195*
Parasitic insects transmitted directly from one person to another, or by contact with articles that have come in contact with an infested person (such as combs and brushes, etc.).

Heart   *84*
A cone-shaped, muscular organ located in the chest cavity, normally about the size of a closed fist.
   Right and left atrium   *84*
   Right and left ventricle   *84*
   Heart rate   *85*

Hemoglobin   *86*
A protein in the red blood cells that attracts oxygen molecules through the process known as oxygenation.

Hepatitis B Virus (HBV)   *10*
Bloodborne pathogen that causes a highly infectious disease, which infects the liver.

Heredity   *183*
Genes that people inherit from their parents.

Hertz   *108*
A rating providing the number of cycles per second that a generator alternates the current from the source; also known as frequency.

High-Frequency Current   *127*
Alternating current that can be adjusted to different voltages to produce heat; also known as Tesla or the "violet ray."

Hirsutism   *193*
Condition where women grow hair in areas of the body that men typically grow hair, such as the face, chest and back.

Histology   *49*
The study of the structures of the body too small to be seen except through a microscope; also called microscopic anatomy.

Human Immunodeficiency Virus (HIV)   *10*
Virus that interferes with the body's natural immune system and causes it to break down; can lead to Acquired Immunodeficiency Syndrome (AIDS).

Human Papillomavirus (HPV)   *10*
Common viral infection that can lead to health problems such as genital warts, plantar warts, cervical changes and cervical cancer.

Hydrogen Bond   *145*
Side bond that works on the principle that unlike charges attract; can easily be broken by heat or water; makes up about 35% of hair's strength.

Hydrophilic   *162*
Refers to the water-loving part of a molecule.

Hypertrichosis   *193*
Superfluous hair; the abnormal coverage of hair on areas of the body where normally only lanugo hair appears.

Immunity   *14*
The ability of the body to destroy infectious agents that enter the body.

Inactive Stage   *8*
Stage during which bacteria become inactive or dormant.

Indirect Transmission   *12*
Infectious disease that can spread through the air or by contact with a contaminated (dirty) object.

Infection   *12*
Occurs when disease-causing (pathogenic) bacteria or viruses enter the body and multiply to the point of interfering with the body's normal state.

Infection Control 19
The efforts taken to prevent the spread of communicable disease and kill certain or all microbes.

Infrared Lamp 133
A lamp that provides a soothing heat that penetrates into the tissues of the body; softens the skin to allow penetration of product and increased bloodflow.

Infrared Light 132
Produces heat; over half of sunlight is composed of invisible rays beyond red.

Inorganic Chemistry 137
Studies all matter that is not alive, has never been alive and does not contain carbon, such as rocks, water and minerals.

Insertion 70
The portion of the muscle joined to movable attachments: bones, movable muscles or skin.

Instant Conditioner 169, 223
Used to coat the hair shaft and restore moisture to the hair.

Insulator 106, 107
Material that does not allow the flow of electric current.

Integumentary System 52
The skin and its layers.

Inverter 109
Special instrument that changes direct current to alternating current.

Involuntary or Non-Striated 69
Muscles that respond automatically to control various body functions including the functions of internal organs.

Iontophoresis 125
A process that uses galvanic current to infuse (acidic) water-based products for deeper penetration into the skin.

Irregular Bones 58
Found in the wrist, ankle or spinal column (the back).

Keratin 143, 180
A protein that accounts for 97% of the makeup of hair.

Keratinization 180
The process in which cells change their shape, dry out and form keratin protein; once keratinized, the cells that form the hairstrand are no longer alive.

Kilowatt 106, 108
Equals 1,000 watts of electrical energy; measurement of how fast energy is used.

Lanugo 196
The term for baby-fine, silky hair, which covers most of the body and is shed shortly after birth and replaced with vellus hair.

Light Therapy 130
The production of beneficial effects on the body through treatments using light rays or waves.

Lipophilic 162
Refers to the oil-loving part of a molecule.

Liquid 137
Form of matter having definite weight and volume, but no definite shape.

Liquid Tissue 51
Carries food, waste products and hormones.

Liquid-Dry Shampoo 165, 222
Used to cleanse the scalp and hair for clients who are unable to receive a normal shampoo; effective in cleaning wigs and hairpieces.

Load 106
The technical name for any electrically powered appliance.

Local Infection 13
Located in a small, confined area; often indicated by a pus-filled boil, pimple or inflamed area.

Logarithmic 154
Each step or number increases by multiples of 10.

Long Bones 58
Found in the arms and legs.

Lymph 91
Colorless liquid produced as a byproduct in the process through which plasma passes nourishment to capillaries and cells.

Lymph Nodes 91
Glands that filter out toxic substances, like bacteria.

Lymph Vascular System 83
Responsible for the circulation of lymph through lymph glands, nodes and vessels.

Magnetic Effect 122
A push-pull effect causing motors to turn; also known as mechanical effects.

Malassezia 194
The leading cause of dandruff; naturally occurring microscopic fungus.

Massage 210
Scientific method of manipulating the body by rubbing, pinching, tapping, kneading or stroking with the hands, fingers or an instrument.
▪ Scalp massage 210

Matter 137
Refers to anything that occupies space and has weight.

Mechanical Equipment 121
Any equipment with a motor (for example, clippers and massagers).

Medicated Shampoo 164, 222
Prescribed by the client's doctor to treat scalp and hair problems and disorders such as minor dandruff conditions; may affect color-treated hair.

Medulla 179
Central core of the hair shaft, also called the pith (often absent in fine or very fine hair).

Melanin 185
A pigment that gives skin and hair their color.

Melanocytes 185
Cells that exist among the dividing cells within the hair bulb.

Melanosomes 185
Bundles of a pigment protein complex that rest near the hair bulb's nourishment center, the dermal papilla.

Metabolism 50
The chemical process in which cells receive nutrients (food) for cell growth and reproduction.

Microbiology   *3*
The study of small living organisms called microbes, such as bacteria.

Microcurrent   *127*
An alternating current with a mechanical effect, that produce muscle contractions; also known as sinusoidal current.

Mitosis   *50*
A process of cell division when a cell divides into two identical new cells.

Moisturizing Agent   *223*
Replenishes or restores moisture to dry scalp; formulated as creams, oils or lotions.

Moisturizing Conditioner   *169, 223*
Used to add moisture to dry, brittle hair.

Molecule   *142*
Two or more atoms joined together by a chemical bond.

Monilethrix   *193*
Beads or nodes formed on the hair shaft.

Motor Nerves   *96*
Also called efferent nerves; carry messages from the brain to the muscles.

Mottled Hair   *185*
Hair with white spots scattered about in the hair shafts.

Muscles   *69*
Fibrous tissues that contract, when stimulated by messages carried by the nervous system, to produce movement.

Muscular System   *69, 71*
Supports the skeleton, produces body movements, contours the body, involved in the functions of other body systems, includes:
- Scalp and face muscles   *72*
- Ear muscles   *72*
- Eye and nose muscles   *73*
- Mouth muscles   *74*
- Mastication muscles   *74*
- Neck and back muscles   *76*
- Shoulder, chest, arm and hand muscles   *77*
- Hand muscles   *78*
- Leg and foot muscles   *78*

Muscular Tissue   *51*
Contracts, when stimulated, to produce motion.

Myology   *69*
The study of the structure, function and diseases of the muscles.

Natural Immunity   *14*
A partially inherited, natural resistance to disease.

Nerve Cell   *96*
Neuron; cells with long and short threadlike fibers called axons; responsible for sending messages in the form of nerve impulses.
- Axons   *96*
- Dendrites   *96*

Nerve Tissue   *51*
Carries messages to and from the brain and coordinates body functions.

Nervous System   *95*
Coordinates and controls the overall operation of the human body.

Neuroscience   *95*
The study of the nervous system.

Neutral   *152, 154*
Indicates equal number of positive hydrogen ions and negative hydroxide ions; measures 7 on the pH scale.

Neutralizing Shampoo   *165, 222*
Restores the hair to its 4.5-5.5 pH by neutralizing any remaining alkaline values; used generally in conjunction with a chemical relaxing service.

Neutron   *141*
Particle with no electric charge found in the nucleus of an atom.

Non-Aerosol Powder Dry Shampoo   *165, 222*
Cleanses the hair of clients whose health prohibits them from receiving a wet shampoo service; absorbs oil and distributes oil as the product is brushed through the scalp and hair.

Nonpathogenic Bacteria   *6*
Non-disease-producing bacteria; they are harmless and can be very beneficial.

Normalizing Conditioner   *169, 223*
Used to close the cuticle after alkaline chemical services.

Nucleus   *50, 141*
The control center of cell activities; the dense core of an atom that contains protons and sometimes neutrons.

Ohm   *106, 108*
A unit of electric resistance.

Ointment   *160*
Mixtures of organic substances and a medicinal agent, usually found in a semi-solid form.

Open Circuit   *110*
A broken path of electron flow.

Organic Chemistry   *137*
Deals with all matter that is now living or was alive at one time, with carbon present, such as plants and animals.

Organs   *52*
Separate body structures that perform specific functions; composed of two or more different tissues.

Origin   *70*
Nonmoving (fixed) portion of the muscle attached to bones or other fixed muscles.

OSHA (Occupational Safety and Health Administration)   *22, 24*
The regulating agency under the Department of Labor that enforces safety and health standards in the workplace.

Osteology   *58*
The study of bones.

Overload   *111*
The passage of more current than the line can carry.

Papilla   *179*
Filled with capillaries (small blood vessels) that supply nourishment to the cells around it, called germinal matrix cells.

Parallel Wiring   *110*
Wiring system with the ability to power several loads all at once or at different times.

Passive Immunity — 14
Developed through the injection of antigens, which stimulate the body's immune response.

Pathogenic Bacteria — 6
Disease-producing bacteria; they are harmful because they cause infection and disease; some produce toxins.

Pediculosis Capitis — 11, 195
Medical term for head lice; infestation of head lice on the scalp causing itching and eventual infection.

Peptide Bond — 143
A chemical bond formed by two amino acid molecules where amino end attaches to acid end; also known as an end bond.

Pericardium — 84
A membrane that encases the heart and contracts and relaxes to force blood to move through the circulatory system.

Peripheral Nervous System — 96
Composed of sensory and motor nerves that extend from the brain and spinal cord to other parts of the body.
    ▪ Face, head and neck nerves — 97
    ▪ Arm and hand nerves — 99
    ▪ Lower leg and foot nerves — 99

Petrissage — 211
Light or heavy kneading and rolling of the muscles; performed by kneading muscles between the thumb and fingers or by pressing the palm of the hand firmly over the muscles.

pH (Potential Hydrogen) — 151
A numerical measurement that indicates the acidity or alkalinity of a water-based substance.

pH Balanced — 155
A product with a pH from 4.5-5.5 (average pH range of hair, skin and nails).

pH Meter — 155
Determines the pH value of a solution.

pH Scale — 154
A logarithmic scale that ranges from 0-14; substances with a pH less than 7 are acidic; substances with a pH more than 7 are alkaline; substances with a pH of 7 are neutral.

Ph-Balanced Shampoo — 164, 222
Cleanses all hair types; recommended to cleanse lightened, color-treated or dry, brittle hair.

Pheomelanin — 185
Type of melanin that produces red hair color.

Phoresis — 125
The process of forcing an acid (+) or alkali (-) into the skin by applying current to the chemical; also referred to as bleaching of the skin.

Physical Change — 138
A change in the physical characteristics of a substance without creating a new substance.

Physiology — 49
The study of the functions that bodily organs and systems perform.

Pityriasis — 194
Medical term for dandruff; over-abundance of epithelial cells (small, white scales) that have accumulated on the scalp or fallen to the shoulders.

Pityriasis Capitis Simplex — 194
The medical term for dry dandruff; dry epithelial cells attached to the scalp or on the hair; itchy; caused by poor circulation, poor diet, uncleanliness or emotional disturbance.

Pityriasis Steatoides — 194
Medical term for greasy or waxy dandruff; epithelial cells combine with sebum (oil) and stick to the scalp in clusters; itchy.

Plain Shampoo — 164, 222
Used to cleanse normal hair but not recommended for chemically treated or damaged hair.

Plica Polonica — 192
Excessive matting of hair, characterized by a mass of hair strands tangled together in a mat that cannot be separated.

Porosity — 190
Refers to the ability of the hair to absorb moisture, liquids or chemicals.

Postpartum Alopecia — 198
The temporary hair loss at the conclusion of pregnancy.

Powders — 160
Equal mixtures of inorganic and organic substances that do not dissolve in water and that have been sifted and mixed until free of coarse, gritty particles.

Prism — 131
A three-sided glass object that produces individual wavelengths when white light passes through it.

Protein — 143, 181
Formed by amino acids; hair is a form of protein called keratin.

Proton — 141
Positively charged particle in the nucleus of an atom.

Protoplasm — 50
Gel-like substance found in cells containing water, salt and nutrients obtained from food.

Pseudomonacidal — 22
Disinfectant designed to kill pseudomonas.

Psoriasis — 194
Thick, crusty patches of red irritated scalp resulting from an autoimmune disease of the skin; refer client to a physician.

Pulmonary Circulation — 87
The system that allows blood to travel through the pulmonary artery to the lungs where it is oxygenated (combined with oxygen).

Receptors — 96
Nerve cells located in the papillary layer of the dermis.

Rectifier — 109
Special instrument that changes alternating current to direct current.

Reflex Action — 96
Action caused by interaction of sensory and motor nerves.

Reproductive System — 103
Responsible for the process by which a living organism procreates.

Resistance   108
The measure of how difficult it is to push electrons through a conductor.

Respiratory System   102
Responsible for the intake of oxygen and the exhalation of carbon dioxide.
- Lungs   102
- Diaphragm   102

Ringed Hair   193
Alternating bands of gray and dark hair.

Ringworm   195
Red, circular patch of small blisters; caused by a vegetable parasite; refer client to a physician
- Ringworm of the scalp   195
- Honeycomb ringworm   195

Rinse   167
Helps close the cuticle of hair and makes hair feel soft and manageable.

Salt Bond   145
Side bond that helps organize protein chains; can easily be weakened by water leaving hair more pliable.

Saturated Solution   160
Solution that cannot take or dissolve any more solute than it already holds.

Scabies   195
Medical term for itch mite; red and watery vesicles or pus-filled areas caused by an animal parasite.

Scalp Toner   223
Adds a refreshing, stimulating feeling to the scalp; may have mild antiseptic properties and cleansing ability.

SDS (Safety Data Sheet)   23, 43
An information sheet designed to provide the key data on a specific product regarding ingredients, associated hazards, combustion levels, and storage requirements; formerly known as Material Safety Data Sheet (MSDS).

Sebaceous Glands   179
Oil glands; partially controlled by the nervous system; sac-like glands that are attached to hair follicles; result in oily skin when an overabundance of sebum is produced by the glands.

Sensory Nerves   96
Also called afferent nerves; carry messages to the brain and spinal cord; determine the sense of touch, sight, smell, hearing and taste.

Series Wiring   110
Travels from one load to the next forcing the user to have all loads running at the same time.

Short Circuit   113
Occurs anytime a foreign conductor comes into contact with a wire carrying current to the load (appliance).

Side Bond   145
Bond formed when amino acids are lined up side by side.

Skeletal System   58
The physical foundation of the body, composed of 206 bones of different shapes and sizes, each attached to others at movable or immovable joints.
- Bones of the cranium   59
- Bones of the facial skeleton   60
- Neck bones   61
- Back, chest and shoulder bones   62
- Arm, wrist and hand bones   63
- Leg, ankle and foot bones   64

Soap   160
Mixtures of fats and oils converted to fatty acids by heat and then purified.

Soapless Shampoo   164, 222
Used to cleanse hair with either soft or hard water.

Soft Water   207
Rain water or water with very small amounts of minerals.

Solid   137
Form of matter having definite weight, volume and shape.

Solute   160
Any substance that dissolves into a liquid to form a solution.

Solution   160
Mixtures of two or more kinds of molecules, evenly dispersed.

Solvent   160
Any substance that is able to dissolve another substance.

Spinal Cord   95
Composed of long nerve fibers; originates in the base of the brain and extends to the base of the spine; holds 31 pairs of spinal nerves that branch out to muscles, internal organs and skin.

Spirilla   7
Spiraled, coiled, corkscrew-shaped bacterial cells that cause highly contagious diseases such as syphilis, sexually transmitted disease (STD), cholera and lyme disease.

Staphylococci   7
Pus-forming bacterial cells that form grape-like bunches or clusters and are present in abscesses, pustules and boils.

Sterilization   19, 30
The third and most effective level of infection control; sterilization procedures kill or destroy all microbes.

Strengthening Protein Additive Shampoo   164, 222
Cleanses and conditions; deposits protein fragments along the hair shaft.

Streptococci   7
Pus-forming bacterial cells that form in long chains and can cause septisemia (sometimes called poisoning), strep throat, rheumatic fever and other serious infections.

Supercilia   182
Hair of the eyebrows.

Surfactant   162
Used to remove oil from hair; also called surface active agent.

Suspension   160
Mixtures of two or more kinds of molecules that will separate if left standing.

Systemic Circulation   87
The process of blood traveling from the heart throughout the body and back to the heart.

Systems   52
Group of body structures and/or organs that together perform one or more vital functions for the body.

Tapotement 211
Also called percussion or hacking; light tapping or slapping movement applied with the fingers or partly flexed fingers.

Telogen 182
The resting stage of hair growth when each bulb has no attached root sheath, at which time hair falls out; eventually, cell division is again stimulated, producing new hair, and the growth cycle starts again.

Telogen Effluvium 198
Premature shedding of hair in the resting phase (telogen) resulting from various causes such as childbirth, shock, drug intake, fever, etc.

Texture 189
The degree of coarseness or fineness in the hair fiber.

Thermal Equipment 121
Used to generate heat (for example, curling irons, heat lamps, color machines, manicure heaters, facial steamers, and scalp steamers).

Thinning Hair Shampoo 165, 222
Used to cleanse the hair without weighing it down.

Thorax 62
The bony cage composed of the spine, vertebrae, sternum and the ribs; also known as the chest.

Tinea 195
Medical term for ringworm; red, circular patch of small blisters; caused by a vegetable parasite.

Tinea Capitis 195
Medical term for ringworm of the scalp; enlarged open hair follicles that are surrounded by clusters of red spots (papules); hair is likely to break in infected area.

Tissues 51
Groups of cells of the same kind performing a specific function in the body.

Traction or Traumatic Alopecia 198
Hair loss due to repetitive traction on the hair by pulling or twisting.

Trichology 177
The technical term for the study of hair.

Trichoptilosis 192
Fragilitis crinium or brittle hair; technical name for split ends.

Trichorrhexis Nodosa 192
Knotted hair, characterized by the presence of lumps or swelling along the hair shaft.

Trifacial (Trigeminal) Nerve 97
The largest of the cranial nerves, responsible for transmitting facial sensations to the brain and for controlling the muscle movements of chewing (mastication).

Tuberculocidal 22
Disinfectant designed to kill tuberculosis microbes.

UL Rating 109
Underwriter's Laboratory designation; means the appliance has been certified to operate safely under the conditions the instructions specify.

Ultraviolet Light 134
Invisible rays beyond violet; has positive and negative effects on the skin, small doses can tan the skin and produce vitamin D; can be more damaging than infrared rays; also known as actinic rays.

Universal Precautions 13
The practice of using infection control procedures for all clients, regardless of their health history.

Vagus 96, 103
Tenth cranial nerve; helps regulate heartbeat.

Varicose Veins 86
Bulges that form if veins stretch and lose their elasticity.

Vellus 196
Hair that covers most of the body, including the head; often not visible to the naked eye.

Vibration 211
Shaking massage movement; your arms shake as you touch the client with your fingertips or palms.

Vinegar and Lemon Rinse 168, 223
Used to keep the cuticle compact, remove soap scum, return the hair to its pH balance.

Virucidal 22
Disinfectant designed to kill viruses.

Virus 10
Sub-microscopic particles that cause familiar diseases like the common cold and other respiratory and gastrointestinal infections, chicken pox, mumps, measles, smallpox, yellow fever, rabies, HIV (AIDS), hepatitis and polio.

Visible Light 131
The portion of the electromagnetic spectrum humans can see.

Volt 106, 107
A unit of electric pressure.

Voluntary or Striated Muscles 69
Muscles that respond to commands regulated by will.

Watt 106, 108
A measure of how much electrical energy (power) is being used per second.

PIVOT POINT

>> **ACKNOWLEDGMENTS**

Pivot Point Fundamentals is designed to provide education to undergraduate students to help prepare them for licensure and an entry-level position in the cosmetology field. An undertaking of this magnitude requires the expertise and cooperation of many people who are experts in their field. Pivot Point takes pride in our internal team of educators who develop cosmetology, esthetics and nails education, along with our print and digital experts, designers, editors, illustrators and video producers. Pivot Point would like to express our many thanks to these talented individuals who have devoted themselves to the business of beauty, lifelong learning and especially for help raising the bar for future professionals in our industry.

EDUCATION DEVELOPMENT | **Janet Fisher** // **Sabine Held-Perez** // **Vasiliki A. Stavrakis**

Markel Artwell
Eileen Dubelbeis
Brian Fallon
Melissa Holmes
Lisa Luppino
Paul Suttles
Amy Gallagher
Lisa Kersting
Jamie Nabielec
Vic Piccolotto
Ericka Thelin
Jane Wegner

EDITORIAL | **Maureen Spurr** // **Wm. Bullion** // **Deidre Glover**

Liz Bagby
Jack Bernin
Lori Chapman

DESIGN & PRODUCTION | **Jennifer Eckstein** // **Rick Russell** // **Danya Shaikh**

Joanna Jakubowicz
Denise Podlin
Annette Baase
Agnieszka Hansen
Kristine Palmer
Tiffany Wu

PROJECT MANAGEMENT | **Jenny Allen** // **Ken Wegrzyn**

DIGITAL DEVELOPMENT | John Bernin
Javed Fouch
Anna Fehr
Matt McCarthy
Marcia Noriega
Corey Passage
Herb Potzus

Pivot Point also wishes to take this opportunity to acknowledge the many contributors and product concept testers who helped make this program possible.

INDUSTRY CONTRIBUTORS

Linda Burmeister
Esthetics

Jeanne Braa Foster
Dr. Dean Foster
Eyes on Cancer

Mandy Gross
Nails

Andrea D. Kelly, MA, MSW
University of Delaware

Rosanne Kinley
*Infection Control
National Interstate Council*

Lynn Maestro
Cirépil by Perron Rigot, Paris

Andrzej Matracki
*World and European
Men's Champion*

MODERN SALON

Rachel Molepske
*Look Good Feel Better, PBA
CUT IT OUT, PBA*

Peggy Moon
Liaison to Regulatory and Testing

Robert Richards
Fashion Illustrations

Clif St. Germain, Ph.D
Educational Consultant

Andis Company

International Dermal Institute

HairUWear Inc.

Lock & Loaded Men's Grooming

PRODUCT CONCEPT TESTING

Central Carolina
Community College
Millington, North Carolina

Gateway Community Colleges
Phoenix, Arizona

MC College
Edmonton, Alberta

Metro Beauty Academy
Allentown, Pennsylvania

Rowan Cabarrus
Community College
Kannapolis, North Carolina

Sunstate Academy of
Cosmetology and Massage
Ft. Myers, Florida

Summit Salon Academy
Kokomo, Indiana

TONI&GUY Hairdressing Academy
*Costa Mesa, California
Plano, Texas*

Xenon Academy
*Omaha, NE
Grand Island, NE*

LEADERSHIP TEAM

Robert Passage
Chairman and CEO

Robert J. Sieh
*Senior Vice President,
Finance and Operations*

Judy Rambert
Vice President, Education

Kevin Cameron
*Senior Vice President,
Education and Marketing*

R.W. Miller
*Vice President, Domestic Sales
and Field Education*

Jan Laan
*Vice President, International
Business Development*

Katy O'Mahony
Director, Human Resources

In addition, we give special thanks to the North American Regulating agencies whose careful work protects us as well as our clients, enhancing the high quality of our work. These agencies include Occupational Health and Safety Agency (OSHA) and the U.S. Environmental Protection Agency (EPA). *Pivot Point Fundamentals*™ promotes use of their policies and procedures.

Pivot Point International would like to express our SPECIAL THANKS to the inspired visual artisans of Creative Commons, without whose talents this book of beauty would not be possible.

#MOOD